INSATIABLE GOVERNMENT

BOOKS BY GARET GARRETT:

Where the Money Grows, 1911
The Blue Wound, 1921
The Driver, 1922
The Cinder Buggy, 1923
Satan's Bushel, 1924
Ouroboros, Or the Mechanical Extension
    of Mankind, 1926
Harangue, 1927
The American Omen, 1928
Other People's Money, 1931 (pamphlet)
A Bubble that Broke the World, 1932
A Time is Born, 1944
A Wild Wheel, 1952
The People's Pottage, 1953, consisting of:
    "The Revolution Was" (1944)
    "Ex America" (1951)
    "Rise of Empire" (1952)
The American Story, 1955
Salvos Against the New Deal, 2002
Defend America First, 2003

Insatiable Government

BY GARET GARRETT

INTRODUCTION BY

BRUCE RAMSEY

CAXTON PRESS

2008

Introduction and editing ©2008 by the Caxton Press

Editorials reprinted with permission of the
Saturday Evening Post Society
©1923, 1931, 1932, 1933, 1934, 1935,1936, 1938,
1939, 1940, 1941, (renewed) SEPS Inc.
and The Conference Board © 1946, 1947, 1949, 1950

Cover image, "The Boss," by Thomas Nast, was
provided courtesy Harper's Weekly, LLC.

ISBN 978-0-87004-463-2

Library of Congress Cataloging-in-Publication Data

Garrett, Garet, 1878-1954.
  Insatiable government / by Garet Garrett ; introduction by Bruce
Ramsey.
    p. cm.
  Includes index.
  ISBN 978-0-87004-463-2 (pbk.)
  1. Finance, Public--United States--History--1933- 2. Government
spending policy--United States--History. 3. United States--Politics
and government--1901-1953. 4. United States--Social policy. 5.
United States--Economic policy. I. Title.
  HJ257.G37 2008
  320.97309'041--dc22
                                                    2007052909

Printed in the United States of America
CAXTON PRESS
176417

CONTENTS

INTRODUCTION ix

CHAPTER 1: CREDO

THE LAW OF STRENGTH (1924) 1

CHAPTER 2: THE VISIBLE HAND

INSATIABLE GOVERNMENT (1932) 5

THEN IT RAINED (1936) 22

AT HIS EASE (1938) 25

THE YES PRINCIPLE (1941) 28

CHAPTER 3: A FINISHED WORLD

TO STABILIZE INDUSTRY (1933) 33

THE WEALTH QUESTION (1935) 44

THE PROMISE OF SECURITY (1936) 63

STATUS FOR LABOR (1940) 68

STATUS FOR THE POOR (1947) 71

CHAPTER 4: ON THE LAND

A KEPT INDUSTRY (1932) 75

A KIND OF PROGRESSION (1935) .84

NEVER A PRAYER (1939) 95

CHAPTER 5: REPUDIATION

'AT ALL HAZARDS' (1934) 103

THE PARAMOUNT MONEY (1940) 114

CHAPTER 6: ENTANGLEMENTS

SENTIMENTAL IMPERIALISTS (1931) 121

GIVE, FORGIVE AND LEND (1923) 132

'ALL OF EUROPE MAY CRASH' (1932) 145

A FORMERLY CAPITALIST PEOPLE (1947) 159

CHAPTER 7: WAR

WAR HAS LOST ITS POCKET (1940) 163

TERRIFIC TAXATION (1941) 179

THE LAW OF CONTROLS (1950) .182

CHAPTER 8: A NEW PROPRIETOR

PEACE ON THE RAILS (1939) 189

Contents

AN ACT OF SEIZURE (1946) 205

PENSIONS FOR CAPITAL (1950) 210

CHAPTER 9: ORIGINS

THE DAWN OF STEEL (1923) 213

LAISSEZ FAIRE (1949) 223

INDEX 243

Introduction

By Bruce Ramsey

Toward what sort of social system is America moving? "If you say it is toward socialism," Garet Garrett wrote in 1950, "you leave out the possibility that it may turn into something else." Also, he wrote, "You. . . may fail to see clearly what it already has in common with every other kind of totalitarian government we know anything about, namely insatiability."

Insatiable government. Thomas Jefferson had famously said government's appetites were unlimited, and tended always to devour the people's freedom. The other founders thought so, and had attempted to put government in a cage. With the Constitution they did, and as long as people agreed on that cage it held, most of the time. But in the 20th century the thinking of the people changed. Crises happened, government demanded to be let out, and the people let it out.

Not only here. By the 1930s, government was exalted everywhere. The state-expanding political doctrines of the communists, socialists, national socialists, fascists and social democrats had different particulars. Some created states far more vicious than the American one, but underneath was a certain commonality. "All alike," Garrett wrote, "are resolved to control the people's way of living according to a plan, and all alike creating a dependent society."

Garrett was a journalist of what is now called the Old Right, a defender of what he called "limited, constitutional government in the republican form." He had been born under a government like that, in 1878. He died in 1954, in the age of the managed economy and the welfare state. In his lifetime had come the progressives, the New Deal and two world wars. Government had expanded insatiably.

Garrett's bedrock idea was the self-reliant individual. In a letter to his libertarian friend Rose Wilder Lane, the ghost-writer of her mother's *Little House on the Prairie* books, Garrett wrote of his vain effort to talk his neighbors out of their support for the Townsend Plan, a Depression-era scheme of guaranteed incomes. "When they were gone I realized that I had not touched them," he wrote. "They wanted manna and water out of the rock. I wanted people to stay hard and fit and self-responsible."

Socialists and progressives tend to ascribe responsibility to "society," or some structure of it. It is how they think. To Garrett, responsibility was individual. When the socialists said private enterprise had failed to house the poor, Garrett wrote, "It is the business of people to house themselves. And if and as they do it for themselves, they have free private enterprise without knowing it. They had it for more than one hundred years without ever thinking to give it a name."

Garet Garrett would have been forgotten but for *The People's Pottage* (1953), a collection of three essays that assault the fundamental trends in American government in the first half of the 20th century. *Pottage* fortifies rightist book-shelves like a bottle of absinthe. Most of what it says—about the New Deal being a revolution, and other things—had been said by others, but not *that way*. *Pottage* is written in rhetorical acid, and that is why it endures. It is why I read it, why I kept it, and why I developed an interest in Garrett.

Pottage was the distillation of his journalistic career. He had been a prominent financial reporter in New York, writing for the *Sun*, the *Wall Street Journal*, and the *Evening Post*. By 1913 he was doing economic commentary as the first editor of the *New York Times Annalist*. At the onset of World War I he was on the editorial board of the *New York Times*, and during

U.S. participation in the war he was managing editor of the nationalistic *Tribune*. From 1922 to 1942 he wrote for the *Saturday Evening Post*, where he defended the interests of the self-reliant American. From there he attacked the New Deal, and in the year and a half before Pearl Harbor he became the Post's "isolationist" voice against Franklin Roosevelt's moves to take sides in the European war.

The Caxton Printers, which had published *The People's Pottage*, were agreeable to a revival of Garrett half a century later. It published two Garrett collections I assembled: *Salvos Against the New Deal* (2002) and *Defend America First* (2003). These recalled the two big battles of Garrett's career, over the New Deal and the pre-Pearl Harbor involvement in the war. Caxton followed them in 2004 with a reissue of *The People's Pottage* under the name *Ex America*. Its new endnotes, index and introduction—and also hard covers—distinguished it from two bootleg printings that had been mopping up readers' dollars in the absence of an authorized edition.

I had also assembled a third collection of Garrett's work: this one. It was more difficult to categorize—and to sell. In 2005 I published a small edition of it myself, and went on to work on a biography of Garrett. In 2007, when Scott Gipson, vice president and publisher at Caxton, agreed to take on my biography, he also expressed interest in bringing out a proper edition of *Insatiable Government*.

This is that edition. It is in no way the leftovers. Its theme is broader than *Salvos* and *Defend*, so that I could choose among a much wider field of work.

I chose pieces written over 28 years, beginning and ending with excerpts from Garrett's fiction. The penultimate piece, "The Dawn of Steel," is taken from *The Cinder Buggy* (1923), a novel of the 19th century steel men who challenged the established interests of iron. It shows Garrett's organic conception of capitalism, which had little to do with the mathematical equations of the economists. To Garrett, the essence of capitalism was struggle—to adapt to change and to create it.

I begin the book with "The Law of Strength," a speech from *Satan's Bushel* (1924), Garrett's allegorical novel about the economy of wheat. In the excerpt, a busted farmer advises a group of husbandmen of the Darwinian rules under which they live. It is a philosophy that Garrett absorbed when he was growing up. Much of rest of the book is the chronicling of how his country departed from it.

Garrett had been raised on a farm and in his mature years owned another one. For the *Saturday Evening Post* he followed the struggles of farmers and the schemes of agricultural commissars for almost 20 years. Three of his articles are excerpted here. They show how the dependency of the American farmer began. It was not the bumper-sticker history Americans learn today—that in the Depression the farmers suffered and the government came to their aid. One of the three pieces is pre-New Deal.

The agitation for a federal rescue of farmers began after World War I, when food prices came down. Garrett was against federal rescue. Commenting on the farm-support bill that was vetoed by Calvin Coolidge, Garrett wrote in the *Saturday Evening Post* of April 2, 1927, "If the government guarantees you a profit, it is obliged also to limit your profit, limit your production and limit your freedom of action." The government never guaranteed the individual farmer a profit, but it tried even before the New Deal to obtain him one, and in the New Deal it did limit his production and freedom of action.

To Garrett, the farm program was the New Deal in microcosm. As economic policy it fought against reality and against itself; as political policy it consistently expanded governmental power. Its political result was to turn the American farmer into a dependent of the state.

"Suddenly," he wrote in the *Saturday Evening Post* of Dec.

29, 1934, "it is impossible that farmers should be trusted to conduct agriculture. As free and unrestrained individuals they ruin it and ruin themselves collectively. Where formerly there were six million farmers lying awake at night, each with his own problems, now for each kind of farmer... there is a bureau to stay awake for him, to do his thinking, to make his decisions..."

In support of the self-reliant individual are created the institutions of capitalism and constitutional government. In defense of that, Garrett was a nationalist. America had created a unique culture, and it was the government's job to protect that.

Garrett was for a free market at home, but at the border he was open to restrictions. He opposed government-administered trade because that would subordinate commerce to war. But a tariff on private transactions might protect the country from being squeezed by foreigners. He thought the Jones Act, the law that reserves trade between two U.S. ports to U.S. ships, was necessary to protect America from the British merchant marine, and to create a market for the Liberty ships built to feed Britain during World War I. He thought the immigration restrictions of 1924 were necessary because free immigration had diluted America's distinct political values—which may be a roundabout way of saying we had let in too many European socialists.

Garrett's nationalism is expressed in several articles here. The first is "Sentimental Imperialists," which is unlike any other in the book. In 1931 the *Saturday Evening Post* sent Garrett to the Philippines, then an American colony. He arrived with the view that the islands were American property, won fair and square from Spain. He immediately saw they were not really American. In the piece printed here, he pictures a place that is culturally too different to be absorbed into the American republic. In Garrett's view, America did not owe the Filipinos independence; he wasn't one for arguing that Americans *owed* foreigners anything. In "Sentimental Imperialists," he creeps toward the view, never quite saying it, that Americans should give the Filipinos independence for America's sake.

The target of Garrett's nationalism was usually the apologists for Europe. For a decade their focus was on relieving Germany, Britain and France of their war debts. His first nonfiction article for the *Saturday Evening Post,* Nov. 15, 1922, was about those debts. His second, from early 1923, is reprinted here. It contains a flat statement that America could stand alone with no foreign trade at all. That is not what Garrett wanted to do. He was replying to the argument that America should cancel Europe's debts and lend it more money because America needed Europe's trade. He was not opposed to trade; he was opposed to being taken for a sucker.

In 1923 the country to be saved was Germany. In the next piece, written after the foreign payments crisis of 1931, the rescue was of Germany, Britain and France. This is the event that turned the Crash of 1929 into the Great Depression. The stock market collapse and bank failures had prepared the ground. The Smoot-Hawley tariff had contributed (though, Garrett thought, not much). But what wrecked it all was the collapse of the international debt structure and the scramble by borrowers for liquidity and gold.

This book is not mainly about international economics. It is about a political point of view. I include Garrett's piece on the 1931 crisis because of its argument that Americans were setting themselves up once again to be sacrificed for Europe. That view comes up again in the final piece, in which Garrett argues against the Marshall Plan. One can understand his disdain toward paying for the rebuilding of Europe after World War II after one reads of Europe's unwillingness to keep its sovereign promises after World War I. That story, wrote Garrett in the *Saturday Evening Post* of Sept. 29, 1934, showed that "we had turned into the worst lenders the world ever knew." Americans avoided defaults a decade later by becoming the biggest philanthropists the world ever knew.

The argument of America's duty to save other countries would be heard in 1940 and 1941, and it is heard today. We must rescue other countries because they are important to us economically, or because they are allies; always because they need it and because we can. Garrett rejected these arguments. He did not accept that America had duties outside our hemisphere, and he questioned the motives of those who said we did. Above all, he worried of commitments that would swell the size and authority of the federal government, tearing off the constitutional and cultural wrappings that had kept it small. Behind every argument for "helping" foreign nations he saw a threat to wreck the domestic constitutional order.

Garrett's first response to the Depression was that people should stick it out. The slump of the 1930-32 wasn't the first American depression; we had had a short, tough one in 1921 and a long one in the mid-1890s. Always Americans had got through without a federal dole. In the 1930s we had the wealth to do it again—more than ever before—if we still had the will.

In the *Saturday Evening Post* of March 14, 1931, he wrote:

> *Have you seen a bread line? Say it is one in New York City, at St. Vincent's Hospital, at six in the evening, weather cold. There may be 200 men in line. If in that whole line there are three or four without overcoats, they will be noticeable for that reason. They may be hungry, but they are comfortably clothed. Do you remember what a bread line was like twenty or thirty years ago? If not, ask someone who can to tell you. It was terrible. Men in rags, shivering with cold. And they were uncounted. We do a new thing to count the unemployed.*

That is not what people would say today—and it was not what most people were saying then. "To Stabilize Industry," written before Roosevelt took office and presented here, is Garrett's argument for the older, individualist view.

Depressions end. The economic tide always turns. In the *Saturday Evening Post* of Oct. 8, 1932, Garrett argued that the economy had reached that point:

> *Never in its history has the American banking system been so liquid... The amount of credit involved in Stock Exchange speculation is almost nothing... All that incredible quantity of overvalued merchandise has been liquidated; the shelves of merchants are light with goods. . .*
>
> *All this has happened. None of it can happen twice.*

It was true. By the fall of 1932 the recovery had begun worldwide, and also on the New York Stock Exchange. But there was one more crisis: the bank runs of early 1933. It happened only in the United States; its cause was word leaking out from Democratic Party leaders that president-elect Roosevelt intended to take the country off the gold standard.

The story of Roosevelt's abandonment of gold, and his betrayal of the Democrats' champion of gold, Sen. Carter Glass of Virginia, is told in "At All Hazards." It is forgotten today; ending the gold standard is taken as a thing that had to be done. Garrett argues otherwise, and even if one would disagree with him, there is also the shameful matter of *how* it was done.

America met the Depression with a vast expansion of government. In some ways it was a mutation, and this view is implicit in "Then It Rained." But only in some ways. Government had grown in the progressive era, again in World War I and again under Hoover, a man who Coolidge had dismissed as "the wonder boy." This book's title essay, "Insatiable Government," is a measure of where the country was in the summer before the New Deal. As in "To Stabilize Industry," this essay shows that the ideas of the New Dealers were already in the air.

When the New Deal came, Garrett attacked Roosevelt's policies, but not the man. It was not because he didn't hate Roosevelt; he did. But he was a gentleman. He occasionally quoted one of Roosevelt's speeches or books, and always respectfully called him "the President." Garrett was not a member of the White House press corps, but once attended a press conference and wrote about it. I have included that brief account here under the title "At His Ease." It captures Garrett's deference to, but also dislike of the president opponents called "*that man*," who, in the eyes of many Americans, was acting as a dictator. This is not the genial FDR commemorated today. But look back at the political cartoons of the 1930s, at the columns of Walter Lippmann, H.L. Mencken and others, and at the 1940 campaign buttons offered for sale on eBay. There are many references to dictatorship.

Another personification of power was Jesse Jones, the kingpin of the Reconstruction Finance Corp. In his day the *Saturday Evening Post* called Jones the second most powerful man in the United States. In "The Yes Principle," Garrett pictures him asking Congress for more power.

In hindsight, the American republic righted itself somewhat after Roosevelt was gone. The president was constitutionally limited to two terms. Congress did take some of its power back. But the power of the state as a whole was hardly reduced.

Politically Garrett saw the New Deal as a revolution; in *The People's Pottage* he described it in the words one might use for a communist takeover. Economically he saw it as a reversion to pre-capitalist ideas, particularly in its preference to stability over change. The hard-core New Dealers believed the germ of innovation within capitalism was spent. It seems strange today that anyone would assume that, but they did. Readers of Ayn Rand's *Atlas Shrugged* (1957) will recall that the government declares all economic relations frozen. That comes from the New Deal. Roosevelt's program never went that far, but much of what his government did came out of a yearning for stability, an itch to tie down and domesticate what Keynes called the "animal spirits."

The New Deal also promised the working American a "more abundant life." This was to be brought about not by an aggressive program of saving and investing, but by taxing the corn of the successful and eating it now. The idea was offensive to Garrett's Newtonian mind. In "The Wealth Question," he argues that the result of redistributing wealth would be the wearing-out of the tools that created it. In "The Promise of Security," he asks how the government can create real security if it doesn't produce anything. In "Status for Labor," he decries the government's division of Americans into two castes, "exempt" and "nonexempt," only one of them allowed freely to negotiate the sale of their labor. In "Status for the Poor" he discusses the consequences of public housing.

Much of the New Deal—the labor law, Social Security and a managed paper currency—has been absorbed into the American system. We have learned to live with it. Garrett's writing is a reminder that we didn't have to accept those things, and that there were other things that we have discarded: the idea of raising taxes during a depression, the idea of raising prices by restricting output, and the relentless, mean-spirited cultural warfare, conducted by the president and his friends, against business and individualist values generally. (For a taste of that, look up FDR's State of the Union address for 1936.) Garrett lamented the part of the New Deal that stuck, but he neglected to be thankful for the part that washed away.

After the New Deal came World War II, and a struggle

between a president who wanted to get in and a people who wanted to stay out. Historians, who tend to see greatness in power, side mostly with Roosevelt. Garrett did not.

His political arguments against joining the war are in *Defend America First*. *Insatiable Government* includes three pieces on the economy of war. The first, "War Has Lost Its Pocket," published in 1940, is my favorite of his *Saturday Evening Post* essays. In it he argues that no longer can there be an economic motive for war. Wilson had said economic rivalries were the cause of World War I. Garrett argued against that idea in the *Saturday Evening Post* in 1928, and he restates his argument in the piece here. Garrett also recalls his 1915 interview with Germany's economic kaiser, Walter Rathenau. The interview had been off the record, but Rathenau had since died, 25 years had passed, and Garrett was finally able to make a story of it. "War Has Lost Its Pocket" is also notable in being more optimistic about foreign trade and a global economy.

Though Garrett was opposed to picking a fight with Hitler, he was for a strong defense. Conscription troubled him, but he supported it as necessary. (His argument is in *Defend America First*.) In "Terrific Taxation," printed here, he proclaims that painfully high taxes are necessary as well. But for all his patriotism, Garrett was labeled as isolationist and anti-New Deal, and shortly after the attack on Pearl Harbor he and the *Saturday Evening Post*'s editor both lost their jobs.

Garrett did not have a steady outlet for his writing during the war. But in the five years after the war he edited the National Industrial Conference Board's magazine, *American Affairs*, from which I take several of his later writings. In "The Law of Controls," he argues that total war requires economic controls, taking the opposite view of most libertarians. In a war of national survival, Garrett argued, a citizen cannot be allowed to bid in the market against his own government, or to stand in line ahead of the army for, say, a load of steel. But controls were necessary only in a war of survival. At war's end they had to come off.

War opens the door to other things. As Robert Higgs wrote in *Crisis and Leviathan* (1987), the argument was, "If A is all right, then X is certainly all right, where A was military conscription and X was any governmental suppression of individual rights whatsoever, especially any denial of private property rights." In World War I, Wilson's government had seized the railroads, and though it gave them back, it was with constraints on labor relations that the owners were obliged to accept. In "Peace on the Rails," Garrett shows how those constraints operated two decades later—a picture of a quasi-nationalized industry. In "An Act of Seizure," Garrett follows Truman's temporary nationalization of the coal mines after World War II, which also forced upon owners permanent changes in labor relations. In "Pensions for Capital" Garrett reaches the question: If government undertakes to protect an industry in the name of national defense or creating employment, does it become responsible for the industry not to fail? Put another way: If the welfare state offers pensions for the worker, will it be led to offer pensions for capital?

I have never seen the phrase "pensions for capital" outside of Garrett. It is a striking phrase, and one example of why he is worth reading a half-century after he died.

The final essay, "Laissez Faire," is on the history and essence of capitalism. It was not the first such piece for Garrett, who had spent a lifetime writing about various aspects of the economic system. On May 10, 1934, when industry labored under the weight of Depression and the early New Deal, the *Saturday Evening Post* published "The Balance Sheet of Capitalism." Here Garrett had written of capitalism:

> *Never was it imposed on life as a system, or at all. It grew out of life, not all at once but gradually, and is therefore one of the great natural designs. When it was found and identified by such men as Adam Smith, who wrote its*

bible, and Karl Marx, who wrote its obituary too soon, it was already working.

The doctrine of laissez faire, he wrote, was at first a political idea:

> *The men who moved it were thinking not of economic liberty primarily, if at all; certainly they were not thinking of economic equality. They were thinking of political liberty and political equality.*

"Laissez Faire" builds upon this observation, linking the freedom of enterprise with the freedom of religion. After his pained endorsements of conscription, taxes and wartime controls, here again is Garrett the libertarian, making an argument that might make some conservatives uncomfortable today.

"Laissez Faire" is unedited. Most of the other pieces, like those in *Salvos Against the New Deal*, are edited or excerpted. Most of them come from long articles, in which Garrett was his most garrulous. He also tended to back into a subject, painting the preliminaries in broad strokes before putting a point on it. The modern reader is not used to that, and will have patience for only so much of it. To limit it, I have truncated the first section of "The Wealth Question," and have also trimmed "Insatiable Government" from the top. There are other cuts, always done to focus on the essential line of Garrett's argument.

As a writer, Garrett had the power to reach to an idea and clarify it in two sentences. In *Satan's Bushel*, he wrote: "What ruins the gambler is not ill luck. It is counting on the future to pay for the past." In *The Cinder Buggy*, viewing the steel magnates who became so rich they were constricted by their fortunes, he wrote: "If you had all the wealth in the world, you could not sell it. There would be no one to buy it." And in this volume, in an essay written more than 70 years ago, he reaches right to the issue of the Social Security trust fund: "There is one little difficulty to be cleared up... How can the Government earn money by investing money in its own promissory notes?"

A man who writes like that has to be saved.

Garet Garrett, 1951

Chapter One
CREDO

Garet Garrett's credo was self-reliance. No passage expresses this clearer than this excerpt from Satan's Bushel, a fable of the farmer, the speculator and the wheat. The passage begins with an advocate of agricultural co-ops who argues that farmers need to act in solidarity in order to beat the forces of the market.

The Law of Strength

From *Satan's Bushel,* 1924

The speaker was reaching his climax. It was this: "The farmer sells and the farmer buys. What does he sell? A primal substance, the food that sustains the world. What does he buy? Machinery, wagons, building materials, hardware, cloth, sugar, sometimes a piano or a phonograph—such things. When he sells the primal substance what does he say to the buyer? He says, 'How much will you give me?' But when he buys what does he say? He says: 'How much will you take?' Think it over. In every case it is like that: 'How much will you give me?' for what he sells; 'How much will you take?' for what he buys."

At this an assenting, brooding murmur went through the crowd. Until then it had listened in a stolid manner. Now the speaker, who was the organizer of a statewide cooperative marketing association, began to solicit signatures, passing the printed blanks around.

A voice was lifted up, calling, "Weaver!"

The old man did not stir. Other voices took up his name, calling: "Ab! Weaver! Absalom Weaver! What about it?"

As they kept insisting, the old man arose.

"Sign," he said. "Go on and sign. It will be educating. Each generation must learn for itself and when it has learned it is ready to die."

With that he sat down. It was not enough. They continued to call on him. He arose again and said:

"Luke, eighteenth chapter, twenty-second verse: 'Sell all that thou hast and follow me.' That is the sublime thought for cooperative marketing. I commend it to you. It works. But it works in heaven. Don't let anybody tell you it will pay on earth."

And a second time he sat down. They said: "Preach us a sermon." And when it was irresistible he got up and walked to the place under the three lanterns. He did not stand on the box.

He had not yet begun to speak, but was peering about in the grass, stooping here and there to pluck a bit of vegetation. He walked as far as the fence for a bramble leaf. Returning he snapped a twig from the elm above his head and faced them.

"This natural elm," he began, with an admiring look at the tree, "was once a tiny thing. A sheep might have eaten it at one bite. Every living thing around it was hostile and injurious. And it survived. It grew. It took its profit. It became tall and powerful beyond the reach of enemies. What preserved it—cooperative marketing? What gave it power—a law from Congress? What gave it fullness—the Golden Rule? On what strength was it founded—a fraternal spirit? You know better. Your instincts tell you no. It saved itself. It found its own greatness. How? By fighting. Did you know that plants fight? If only you could see the deadly, ceaseless warfare among plants, this lovely landscape would terrify you. It would make you think man's struggles tame. I will show you some glimpses of it.

"I hold up this leaf from the elm. The reason it is flat and thin is that the peaceable work of its life is to gather nourishment for the tree from the air. Therefore it must have as much surface as possible to touch the air with. But it has another work to do. A grisly work. A natural work all the same. It must fight. For that use it is pointed at the end as you see and has teeth around the edge—these.

"The first thing the elm plant does is to grow straight up out of the ground with a spear thrust, its leaves rolled tightly together. Its enemies do not notice it. Then suddenly each leaf spreads itself out and with its teeth attacks other plants; it overturns them, holds them out of the sunlight, drowns them.

"And this is the tree! Do you wonder why the elm plant does not overrun the earth? Because other plants fight back, each in its own way.

"I show you a blade of grass. It has no teeth. How can it fight? Perhaps it lives by love and sweetness. It does not. It grows very fast by stealth, taking up so little room that nothing else minds, until all at once it is tall and strong enough to throw out blades in every direction and fall upon other plants. It smothers them to death.

"Then the bramble. I care not for the bramble. Not because it fights. For another reason. Here is the weapon. Besides the spear point and the teeth the bramble leaf you see is in five parts, like one's hand. It is a hand in fact, and one very hard to cast off. When it cannot overthrow and kill an enemy as the elm does, it climbs up his back to light and air, and in fact prefers that opportunity, gaining its profit not in natural combat but in shrewd advantage, like the middleman.

"Another plant I would like to show you. There is one nearby. Unfortunately it would be inconvenient to exhibit him in these circumstances. His familiar name is the honeysuckle. He is sleek, suave, brilliantly arrayed, and you would not sus-

3

pect his nature, which is like that of the preying speculator. Once you are in his toils it is hopeless. If you have not drowned or smothered him at first, he will get you. The way of this plant is to twist itself round and round another and strangle it.

"This awful strife is universal in plant life. There are no exemptions. Among animals it is not so fierce. They can run from one another. Plants must fight it out where they stand. They must live or die on the spot. Among plants of one kind there is rivalry. The weak fall out and die; the better survive. That is the principle of natural selection. But all plants of one kind fight against plants of all other kinds. That is the law of their strength. None is helped but who first helps himself. A race of plants that had wasted its time waiting for Congress to give it light and air, or for a state bureau with hired agents to organize it by the Golden Rule, or had been persuaded that its interests were in common with those of the consumer, would have disappeared from the earth.

"The farmer is like a plant. He cannot run. He is rooted. He shall live or die on the spot. But there is no plant like a farmer. There are nobles, ruffians, drudges, drones, harlots, speculators, bankers, thieves and scalawags, all these among plants, but no idiots, saying 'How much will you give?' and 'What will you take?' Until you fight as the elm fights, think as the elm thinks, you will never be powerful and cannot be wise."

Chapter Two
THE VISIBLE HAND

Big government did not begin in the New Deal. Here is proof, from the last year of Herbert Hoover, at the bottom of the Depression.

Insatiable Government

From "Insatiable Government," the *Saturday Evening Post,* June 25, 1932

In the minutes of the Chicago City Council, May twelfth last, is the perfect example of how commonly we regard public credit. From bad taxation, reckless borrowing and reckless spending, the city of Chicago had so far prejudiced its own credit that for months it had been unable to meet its municipal payrolls either out of revenues or by discounting its notes at the bank. Therefore, it knew what could happen to the public credit of a city. But with the public credit of a nation it was different. On that day the City Council adopted two resolutions: One called upon Congress to reduce the Federal Government's expenditures one-fifth; the other called upon Congress to vote a Government bond issue for as many billions as might be necessary and spend the money "to make possible the American citizen's inalienable right to earn an honest living for himself and his family."

As if the taxpayer were willing, for the sake of some immediate relief, to increase the load of those who come next. And of course he is. Hence the passion for public borrowing.

Not only are all these ideas of refuge and solution in public credit to some degree plausible; very often they are of good and wistful intention. This is notably so in the present. There is a crisis in the economics of human welfare. The intention is to overcome it. If truly it could be overcome by the use of public credit, no objection on the ground of precedent or political theory would long prevail. Public credit belongs to the people as a whole and they may do anything with it they like. Therefore, as to these ideas—any and all of them—there are only two questions:

First, will they work? Nobody can answer that. Nobody knows what lies in the future. Sometime the tide, of itself, will rise again. We take that for granted. Therefore these unprecedented uses of the public credit now being made, and proposed to be made, are to meet a crisis that must soon pass. President Hoover says: "I have no taste for any such emergency powers in the Government. But we are fighting the economic consequences of overliquidation and unjustified fear as to the future of the United States. The battle to set our economic machine in motion in this emergency takes new forms and requires new tactics from time to time. We used such emergency powers to win the war; we can use them to fight the depression."

But the risk is real. If the natural level of economic recovery were long delayed, then all these measures would very soon fail in the total ruin of public credit.

Yet suppose differently. Suppose they did work, the tide rising to save and redeem them, and that we should be able to perform the terrific gymnastic feat of getting back our equilibrium. What then?

Well, in that case we should have established certain things in the way anything is established—by the fact of its having once been done before, such as these:

That when the industrial rhythm breaks and there is an crisis in employment, it becomes a function of government to provide people with work; thus responsibility for unemployment comes at rest not upon industry, where we had thought it belonged, but upon government—the state—and must be charged to the public credit.

That when from bad banking, wild speculation, senseless credit inflation, or no matter from what cause, the private banking structure seems about to fall, it becomes a function of government to support it with public credit, not particularly to save the banks, but to save depositors. Thus responsibility for the solvency of banking as a whole passes to the government.

That when railroads, in a crisis, are unable to meet their interest charges, it becomes a function of government to save them with loans of public credit, as through the Reconstruction Finance Corporation, not for the sake of any railroad as such, but because if the railroads go bankrupt the savings banks, the insurance companies and many thousands of investors who hold railroad bonds will be hurt.

That when liquidation of commodities and securities has gone too far it becomes the business of government to stop it, using public credit by such means as it may think fit.

That when prices are too low—prices taken all together—it becomes a function of government to manipulate them back to where they belong. This it will do by inflating money and credit.

And it follows by necessity that certain functions of government are assumed, as, for example, the wisdom to know when a crisis is such a crisis, to know when liquidation has gone far enough, when prices are too low, when they are high enough again, how many bank failures constitute a crisis in banking, how many railroad failures constitute a crisis in railroad credit, and so on.

Whether this would be all for the best, or otherwise, is not yet the point. There cannot even be a discussion of it until we see clearly where we are going. It may be that industry cannot accept responsibility for unemployment; if so, perhaps the government must. It may be that in a crisis finance cannot any longer be responsible for its own solvency, nor business for its own continuity. It may be that we are done with the anarchy of prices which we have so long justified by supposing a law of supply and demand.

But if these things are true, and if now in any crisis such responsibilities must pass to the government, we have gone far unawares toward an experimental state we know nothing of by experience, almost nothing of by theory. That is to say, we have not consciously intended it. We have not considered what kind of state that would be, much less to decide if we want it. It is clear, however, that in passing these responsibilities to government we should be exchanging freedom for something else as yet unnamed.

Hilaire Belloc,[1] in his book, *The Servile State*, defined that something else as economic status. Security according to the economic status of persons, classes and groups, in place of freedom.

And we shall have done another thing. If only such ideas as these now current do prevail, and if they work, we shall have enormously increased the power of self-extension which is already inherent in government.

There are many aspects of government. The one least considered is what may be called the biological aspect, in which government is like an organism with such an instinct for growth and self-expression that if let alone it is bound to destroy human freedom—not that it might wish to do so but that it could not in nature do less. No government ever wants less government—that is, less of itself. No government ever surrenders power, even its emergency powers—not really. It may mean to surrender them, but on the first new occasion it will take them all back. One of the American Government's wartime powers was the War Finance Corporation. The present Reconstruction Finance Corporation is a revival of that power in time of peace. And so it goes.

Observe that in time of prosperity government is bound to extend itself because revenues are plenty and there is always a purblind demand for special benefits to be conferred by public credit.

If now it is established that in time of depression government must extend itself even faster, prodigiously, in order to meet the responsibilities which we are so willing to pass to it by default, then the growth of government will be uninterruptible, without time or season, and the last problem of all is how people shall defend themselves against it.

Already the cost of government is absorbing, roughly, one-quarter of the total national income. One day's work in every four belongs to government. We speak here of all government—national, state, city and local—from Washington above down to the counties, townships, boroughs and districts, all exercising the tax power.

As the total national income falls, the proportion of it absorbed by government will rise. It must rise because government is the one thing that cannot be liquidated or deflated in time of economic depression. To the contrary, as we have seen, it must extend itself to meet new responsibilities. Therefore, taxes must be increased, first in order to provide as much public revenue as before, and then further increased to provide more revenue than before. Thus, in bad times like these, the proportion of the total national income absorbed by government will rise in a special manner. Nevertheless, the rise, irrespective of the state of the times, is continuous. The cost of government rises faster than the national income when the national income is rising. It rises even faster when the national income is falling.

The increase in the past few years has been such that if it should continue at the same rate, the cost of government fifty years hence would absorb the whole national income. Then we should all be working for government, either directly as state employees or indirectly to support the employees of the state.

Already of those above ten years of age gainfully employed in the whole country, male and female, about one in ten is directly employed in government service.

The per capita cost of all government has increased as follows:

In 1880 it was............................	$13.56
In 1903 it was............................	$19.39
In 1913 it was............................	$30.24
In 1923 it was............................	$88.94
In 1929 it was............................	$107.37
In 1932 it will be, approximately	$124.00

The first thought will be that the war did it—the war itself and the after costs of the war in such things as veterans' relief, pensions and national defense. But these are Federal expenditures, and they have much less to do with the rise in the cost of all government than you would suppose. By the figures of the National Industrial Conference Board, the per-capita costs of government separately stated, are:

	1913	1929
Federal...............	$7.17	$32.36
State....................	$3.97	$16.38
Local...................	$19.10	$58.64

Half the total cost of all government is the cost of city and local government, and that per-capita cost in 1929 was three times what it was in 1913.

Taxes have risen to a point at which they begin to devour people's possessions, and the taxpayer is wild for relief. What relief does the taxpayer imagine? This—that the cost of government shall be reduced.

How shall the cost of government be reduced? By economy, by the elimination of graft and needless waste, by a consolidation of government's competitive parts, by a reform of its structure to limit the number of local and civic units because duplication is costly. In brief, government shall find ways to do what it does for less money. Not less government, you see; the same amount of government for less money.

And all this intelligent uproar is in a sense superficial and probably delusive. It is superficial wherein it aims only to abate a very acute pain in the taxpayer's pocket, and if anyone supposes that reducing the cost of government by economy and greater efficiency will limit government itself, it is elusive at the crucial point. More than that, reducing the cost of government by measure tends to serve the most potent forces now acting to extend government.

Why? The explanation is simple. The more efficient government is, the less it costs per measure, all the faster it may be extended without producing that very acute pain in the taxpayer's pocket. This pain is the terror of government because it arrests its growth.

And now you will see a selective struggle taking place within government itself. The impulse is to select the more extensible forms.

The structure of government is by strata, beginning with innumerable small local units, such as boroughs, townships, school districts, improvement districts, and so on, each one exercising the tax power; rising thence to counties, cities and states. At the top is the Federal Government. In the whole country there are approximately 500,000 separate units of government. This is the estimate of the tax commissioner of the state of New York, writing an essay in *Community Service* magazine on the preposterous duplication of parts, offices and powers in government.

"Take the case of New York," he says. "That state has sixty-two counties and sixty cities... In addition there are 932 towns, 507 villages, and, at the last count, 9,600 school districts... Just try to render efficient service... amid the diffused identities and inevitable jealousies of, roughly, 11,000 independent administrative officers or boards!"

This extreme of home rule is not good for government. The tax power, in so many hands, is much less effective than it might be. So now there is a movement—a movement within government, independent of the taxpayer—to rationalize the structure from the bottom up, each next higher stratum with an impulse to absorb the powers of the one below, or, where they cannot be absorbed, to divide them reasonably. And at the top the Federal Government, with no authority over the sovereign states, would very much like to come to an understanding about taxation, because more and more Federal and state taxes collide at the same source, as with the income tax, which now some states are using in competition with the Federal Government. Such competition is embarrassing and unscientific from the common point of view of government seeking revenue. It is well known that a cow milked by a few expert hands in a regular manner will give more milk than the same cow milked in a haphazard manner by the neighborhood.

Certainly if the structure of government were rationalized, we could easily have as much government as before for less money. But there is the specious point again. Not less government; only as much government as before for less money. The cost of government by measure is one thing; the quantity of government, at any cost, is another.

Tax rates have been rising by necessity because the national income has been shrinking. It takes a higher rate of taxation to produce a given amount of revenue. At the same time, new taxes have been invented. There is yet everywhere a deficit in the public revenue because the shrinkage in everything taxable was so sudden and violent.

Now suppose that under stress of abnormal public revenue the structure of government is somewhat rationalized and that by such means as economy and efficiency the cost of government by measure is much reduced. Suppose it. Then what will happen when the national income rises to normal again?

There will be an enormous increase of public revenue, as there was after the war from the carry-over of the wartime taxes. All the public treasuries will be rich. And there is bound to be, again as it was after the war, a terrific extension of government.

The rise in the cost of government is not from increase of graft and corruption, for these evils in a relative sense are diminishing; nor is it from an increase of waste, for of this the ratio has probably been fairly constant. What it means is extension of government—not bad government only but good and bad together.

Let it be asked: What are the political and social forces now acting to absorb the national income for purposes of government—acting, that is, to increase taxation? First by habit one thinks of those for which we have traditional images: The machine, the boss, the pork barrel, the spoils system, the politician everywhere in his popular character, acquiring merit and power by spending public money; doing things for his people with the money of other people, taking care at the same time to do enough for himself with everybody's money. The spender of public money will never want followers.

"Of course," said the Secretary of the Treasury[2] recently, in a speech before the New York City Bar Association, "the people are in a large measure themselves to blame. They have not only tolerated but given encouragement to an ever-expanding cost of government. The spenders were the ones elected to office and bond issues voted with cheerful alacrity."

One who remembers a Southern senator shouting out loud that he would steal for his people a hog every time a Yankee got a ham may be indignant, but the feeling is not personal. The senator was only human. These predatory, parasitic, more or less shameless forces are inseparable from government. They do increase the cost of popular government. Nevertheless, they are limited. That is to say, corrupt government tends to limit and defeat itself. Moreover, these forces are thoughtless. They have no theory among them. They do not want to redistribute wealth; they want only to prey upon it.

Now, much more potent are the forces acting upon a definite political doctrine. Such are the extreme liberals, the Socialists, the radicals, themselves perfectly honest, all haters of graft and corruption in government, yet who are for increasing popular taxes on any pretense of public benefit because that is one way of redistributing wealth downward, according to their doctrine.

What are popular taxes? The Secretary of the Treasury, in the speech just referred to, tells what they are: "the income and inheritance taxes, because they are so levied as to reach comparatively few people." The income tax is popular because fewer than 2 percent of the people pay income taxes. Why should not everyone pay an income tax? The principal reason, from the point of view of government, is that a universal income tax would be a powerful restraint upon the expansion of government.[3]

And now observe how it is that on one side, the government—even a conservative government—and on the other side, all the forces moving to effect a redistribution of wealth downward by political theory, are bound for different reasons to favor popular taxes. The government favors them naturally—"the most feathers for the least squawk." And those radical forces, who may have nothing else in common with this government, favor them on the ground of doctrine.

Observe another strange bedfellowship. When the railroads throw themselves on the hands of the government and demand public credit to save them from bankruptcy, these radical forces do not protest, or, if they do, it is in an academic sense only; and the reason for this is that they believe in the public ownership of railroads, and see, perhaps more clearly than the others, that such use of public credit tends to bring the experiment of state ownership to pass. For the same reason they protest lightly or not at all against the use of public credit to save the private banking structure, for that will tend to bring about state control of credit. They are for anything that tends directly or indirectly to get the government into business, for that leads to state ownership of the means of production. If taxation meanwhile has to be heavily increased, so much the better, so long as the increase is, as it certainly will be, in the field of popular taxes, for thereby wealth is redistributed downward and capitalist society, in which they disbelieve, is on its way to trouble.

A third formation of forces moving in a parallel manner to absorb the national income by extension of government is made up of practical reformers, idealists, good-government people, with or without any political theory. What they have in common is a certain reaction to the sight of human misery, squalor, discomfort, disadvantage or what they believe to be curable wretchedness.

They preach a gospel of the responsibility of the state to administer happiness, not because the state should, not because they themselves would prefer the kind of state that does, but simply that the state can. Thus, government responsibility for old-age security, child life, tonsils, widows, backward mentalities, employment insurance, better maternity, public nursing, recreation, adult play, plumbing, housing, right nurture, infant feeding, vocational guidance, the use of leisure, everything of the good life for everybody, as a responsibility of the state, to procure it, provide it, superintend it.

Everyone knows that impulse. How many times, on looking at slum dwellings or some other distasteful human spectacle, have you yourself said, "There ought to be a law," and so forth? Well, but "a law" means in every case to interfere by power of government, backed by the public credit.

Demands upon the public credit for social service are most difficult to resist. There is the emotional appeal, and to this is added the practical suggestion that, after all, it will pay, or that it will be cheaper in the end.

Two children in every nine are so far handicapped physically or mentally as to need special treatment and training. Who so mean that he will not himself be taxed, who so mindful of wealth that he will not favor increasing the popular taxes, in aid of these defective children?

Moreover, as the report of the White House Conference on Child Health and Protection said: "It is unquestionably better policy to spend more money today in helping the handicapped child to help himself than it is to spend many times as much tomorrow in supporting him at public expense."

At the recent national conference of the American Association for Old Age Security, Representative Connery,[4] who is moving an old-age pension bill in Congress, said: "Evidence was introduced before the House Committee to show that the cost of old-age pensions would be much less to the states and municipalities than is the present cost of the workhouse institutions. It is my hope that the Congress, which has seen fit to provide $2 billion to protect the banking interests of the United States, will see the necessity of passing this legislation to protect the old people."

Fourteen states now have old-age pension laws, and 100 other old-age security measures are pending in forty state legislatures. The Assistant Commissioner of the Department of Social Welfare reported on the first year of old-age pensions in the state of New York, saying the protest against them came mainly from people in the rural districts where the pensioners were visible to those who were struggling to pay the taxes out of which old-age pensions are provided; and the delegate representing the corresponding work in California complained that the operation of the old-age pension law in that state was hampered by the two conditions that to be eligible one must be a citizen and of good character.

Whether old-age pensions would be cheaper than poorhouses is a question which, even if it is permissible, cannot be determined as a matter of fact. The same sprit that moves old-age pensions has been improving the poorhouses. Trenton, for example, has made the word taboo. Its poorhouse is a municipal colony, governed by the idea, says the magazine of the New Jersey League of Municipalities, that as a refuge for the unfortunate it differs from people's homes "only in its larger facilities and the greater number of its inhabitants. Every resource to soften its institutional features has been used, including motion-picture shows, concerts, an extensive library, pool tables, newspapers, magazines." It is really a better place to live than many of the private homes taxed to support it.

The cost of social service, exclusive of education, now is representing one-fifth or more of the total expense of cities. In enlightened states it runs even higher. For Massachusetts the cost of it is nearly two-fifths of all state outlay.

The effects and works of social service are very flattering to our sense of benignity; we are doing well by the less fortunate. Yet this unction is by most of us undeserved; it comes after the fact, with some sourness in it. Very little social service is really spontaneous, straight from the taxpayer's heart. The promotion of it for many is an avocation, for increasing numbers it is a profession, and for a very great number of more or less trained men and women it is employment and livelihood.

"But where do many of these governmental elaborations come from?" asks the secretary of the Des Moines Bureau of

17

Municipal Research. "Many originate with educational, recreational and sociological enthusiasts... These enthusiasts usually start by stating that such and such neighboring city has a certain public service or improvement; therefore, we ought to have it. And so these ideas spread like wildfire from community to community. But when one expresses a timid doubt regarding the necessity for such and such a project because of the expense, these boosters argue, 'The public demands it,' when, as a matter of fact, they themselves originated the scheme. . . Further tax-boosting influences emanate from the 'per capita' or 'model' standards. Certain national groups, particularly in the field of education, recreation, health or sociology, have set up per-capita targets toward which they assert every city in a certain population range should aim. Then these enthusiasts return home from their national gatherings, and if they find that their city spends less for such service, they make it their business to see that it soon attains such a standard."

There is another reason why the taxpayer himself is not entitled to that unctuous feeling in the presence of social service. Now the oldest object of his animosity—namely, the political boss—has annexed the idea. Formerly the benefactions of the boss were intimate and personal, but to these he now adds the more diffuse benefactions of social service, and his base is wider. Such a boss as this now commands the support—first, of all the beneficiaries of social service; secondly, of all who promote and live by social service; thirdly, of those whose doctrine is to take and give; and he has still his machine as it was before. He is fairly secure.

"Cities have assumed new obligations," writes Lent Upson, director of the Detroit Bureau of Governmental Research. "Increased wealth, with its higher standard of living, creates a demand for public services not known a generation ago."

18

In twenty years, 135 new activities were added to the responsibilities of government in Detroit, such as high-school evening classes, children's clinic, child-welfare nurses, transportation of the crippled, classes for mental defectives, training library personnel, testing gas, testing materials, health-education nurses, camps for tubercular children, public-health education, medical college, college evening classes, college summer classes, employment bureau, symphony concerts, cancer clinic, cancer nurses, human antiserum nurses, cooperative high school and the use of radio in schools.

Results, typical: Taxes in the same twenty years have increased from $14 to $53 per capita; public debt has increased from $15 to $175 per capita. A great deal of that admirable work was not paid for; the people could not afford to pay for it. They borrowed the money, and now the problem of Detroit is what to do about its debt. Bankers are loath to lend it any more money because investors are reluctant to buy any more of its bonds. Creditors are hard, yes; only, suppose there had been no creditors to borrow from. Out of the city's own resources, unaided by creditors, the people of Detroit could not have enjoyed these benefits of social service.

What should or should not be is a question that belongs to argument. Here is the intent only to show how unlike and differently motivated forces, economic, social and political, are tending together not only to swallow up the national income in government but also to produce a result which some intend and some do not.

The loss of public credit, the complete ruin of it, would be the least of the consequences.

In a recent report on the "new poor," made by the Welfare Council of New York City, there is a reference to "the mental infection of dependency." This was upon the investigation of unemployment relief. But taking refuge in public credit will cause that same infection to attack business, banking, industry, agriculture, the entire body of private enterprise.

Increasingly, as it may seem, irresistibly, we are using public credit to create an indigent caste, indigence becoming more and more comfortable until for many it may seem a goal; then a very great dependent caste referred to as people in the "lower income ranges," who, without being indigent at all, are yet dependent upon public credit for security, for modern housing, for care in illness, protection in health, economic insurance, amusement and guidance; then a social-service caste to mind the indigent and oversee the dependent. In all of these ways we are exchanging freedom for something else—for security, for status, for refuge from the terrors of individual responsibility. The last may go very deep.

Émile Faguet, a Frenchman, in a book entitled *The Dread of Responsibility*, wrote: "We like to surrender ourselves to the state while allowing it to impose even heavy tasks upon us. The basis of this paradoxical inclination is the lack of personal will, and this lack of personal will itself comes from the horror of responsibility... We imagine today that everything is done by the aggregate without the will to act of any of the individuals composing the aggregate."

He was writing about French people, and he supposed this weakness in them was from having lived so long under a crown that did everything for them. But what of American individualism? Was it a myth? That you will be hearing. Has the modern circumstance overwhelmed it? The city, of course, is an important factor. The modern city is a new form of life, really, and one that we have no science for; in that form individual helplessness is a rising social liability.

Whatever else may go by conjecture, this will be evident in itself—namely, that a rise in the cost of government, suddenly in one generation, from a traditional basis to a point at which it begins to absorb one-quarter of the total national income, is a political and social omen of great significance. It will be evident in the same way that taxation has reached a point where it represents an active redistribution of wealth by hand and power of government. No particular kind of state is sacred, nor is any particular doctrine of wealth, but it is all the more dangerous to be going this road with no theory of either the kind of state it leads to or what shall be the status of private wealth within it.

Until about 1910, excepting only the period of the Civil War, the cost of the Federal Government was met almost entirely by customs duties and the tobacco and liquor taxes; and until about 1910 the cost of state and local government was met by the property tax, supplemented somewhat by corporation taxes, license fees and death duties.

"Since 1910," says the Secretary of the Treasury, "the picture has materially changed... The Federal Government adopted a full-fledged income tax in 1913, and estate tax in 1916... Beginning with Wisconsin, in 1911, state after state adopted an income tax, though at very moderate rates, until today there are twenty-two with this form of taxation. The states have also invaded the field of consumption taxes formerly used almost exclusively by the Federal Government. Today every state imposes a gasoline tax, and thirteen make use of taxes on tobacco or cigarettes. . ."

And he cites, for example, one state where the state income tax, which has just been doubled, plus the new and higher Federal income tax, will amount to more than one-fifth of a personal income above $12,000 a year, rising to more than three-fifths of a personal income above $100,000 a year. In the same state the levy upon corporation income, state and federal taxes together, will be one-fifth or more. This is the income tax alone! And thus the national income is absorbed.

Obviously we cannot continue in this direction without consequences either disastrous in fact or revolutionary in principle. A total ruin of the public credit would be a disaster in fact. We might then wipe the slate and begin all over. Any alternative would be revolutionary in principle, such, for example, as for the state to appropriate all wealth and administer it directly.

With a national income of not more than $60 billion this year, we are obliged to buy more government than we bought with a national income of nearly $90 billion in 1929; moreover, in this depression we are obliged to buy a good deal of it on the deferred-payment plan. That is what it means to sell bonds. All of it has sometime to be paid out of taxes; and even those who may not pay these future taxes directly will pay them indirectly in the cost of the houses they rent, the food they eat, the clothes they wear, the gas they burn in their motor cars—in every item of the cost of getting born, growing up, growing old, even dying. It is imperative to reduce the cost of government by measure—that is, to make the tax dollar buy more than before. But that will be only like pruning the tree, for lustier growth hereafter, unless we settle what public credit is for in principle and limit in a drastic manner the ferocious growth of government.

And all that was when only a handful paid federal income tax! By 1940, after seven years of the New Deal, in which the government repeatedly raised taxes with more than 15 percent of people out of work, the IRS was processing nearly 15 million returns. By 1945, after five years of undeclared and declared war, it was 50 million returns. By 2007 it was 139 million returns.

Then It Rained

From "New Government," the *Saturday Evening Post,* February 1, 1936

Washington is the only city in the world entirely devoted to government. Everybody lives on government. Such an expansion as did take place, suddenly, was like the bringing in unexpectedly of a string of new gushers in an oil town.

Before the New Deal, Washington had been feeling the depression. When the Republican Administration departed, in March, 1933, Washington, like nearly every other city, had the appearance of being overbuilt. The principal hotels and most of the new apartment houses were either in bankruptcy or staring at it. Private houses could be had for the taxes and upkeep. Many mansions were boarded up. Shops were closing, leaving whitened plate-glass windows behind them. Your taxi fare was less than the tip in New York and the driver was so grateful that you were ashamed. Elsewhere people might still be hopeful, not knowing the worst; but here, with all the sources drying up, it was not going to rain for four more years. Was not the incoming Administration pledged to lay the ax against government and cut it down one-quarter?

Then it rained. Miraculous rain from an invisible cloud in a new world. First the hotels filled up and overflowed. Next all the apartments and private houses were taken and they were not enough. Rents began to rise. The closed shops reopened. New ones appeared. Walking on errands of government ceased, because everyone was so earnestly making haste in the new world. The leisurely, old-fashioned left turn, wide around on the red light, had to be abandoned and one-way streets had to be ordained by the police, owing to the increase in motor traffic. Taxicabs multiplied prodigiously.

Gaiety took back its place in the life—eating, drinking and dancing, with all the most expensive places crowded; and touching all of this a kind of guilty embarrassment, as of people taking pleasure in unreconciled circumstances. Not that so many of them were new to government and had arrived without apprenticeship. That was not it. Many of them, especially the younger ones, came to government very earnestly disbelieving in wealth and with ideas of how to distribute it in the new world quite contrary to the ways in which they found themselves now making a distribution of it for purposes of

23

their own private and socially unequal enjoyment, as if it were still the old world.

The emblematic face of government changed all at once.

Each successive administration brings to Washington a new composite face. There is, of course, no such thing definitely as a Republican face or a Democratic face. A composite profile made up of all the official faces of one Republican administration would differ from the profile of another Republican administration; and yet very much less than the face of any Republican administration would differ from the composite face of any Democratic administration. However, here suddenly was a face unknown. It was not Republican; it was not Democratic. It was not a political face at all. Its character was academic, and not positively masculine, owing to the admixture of so many feminine faces, also of the intellectual cast.

Such would be the effect of a sudden extension of bureaucratic government on ideas that were provided, not by the politician, not by the statesman, but by the scholastic mentality, acting upon a sympathetic President.

The boom in government belittled the politician. He might go and bulge his political eyes as such a bulletin as this: "Notice of Civil Service examination. One Senior Social Economist, $4,600; one Social Economist, $3,800; one Associate Social Economist, $3,200; one Assistant Social Economist, $2,600." Or he might go and buy himself a leather briefcase to carry around, thinking to associate himself with the rising new intellectual power in government, yet he would deceive neither himself nor anyone else. It is not the briefcase alone; there is a manner to go with it.

The boom in government was for social, economic and administrative scientists who for years had been writing what they knew in books or teaching it in classrooms to others who would in turn write it in books or teach it in classrooms, because there was nothing else to do with it. To these the

24

astonishing expansion of bureaucratic government, in the spirit of their own frustrated ideas, was the opening of a new world. It meant not gold, not land, not oil, but refuge, career, power, access to achievement.

The rush to seize the opportunities in the spacious world of new government created in Washington a famine of small dwellings. The ancient capitalistic myth of supply and demand acted upon the supply of habitations. There was the irony of bureau workers engaged in the Federal program of slum clearance and subsidized housing for low-income people in New York, Atlanta and elsewhere, themselves seeking slum dwellings in Washington, and trying, in a spirit of social adventure and with the aid of exterminators, to make them do. There was the irony also that with its employees groaning under the rise in rents, the Government itself was competing with them for housing space, even putting them out of second-class hotels because it needed the hotels for more Government bureaus.

Garrett was a gentleman. He wrote volumes on the New Deal, almost all of it harsh, but almost nothing of the man he respectfully called "the President." In the next piece he attends a White House press conference.

At His Ease

From "A Washington Errand," the *Saturday Evening Post,* January 22, 1938

I don't know why I am doing this," said the Old Reporter to himself. "I see no copy in it. But since I am looking at Government, I may as well go to a White House press conference." And he went.

The President sat at a large flat desk, under a strong light, smoking a cigarette in a holder. He was greatly at ease. He called the newspapermen by their first names, launched quips and sallies at them, and they answered back, though never with too much point, and never in a way to turn the laugh on the President. Every moment of it was his show.

It was all very agreeable. Too agreeable, perhaps? The Old Reporter had learned to note laughter, because laughter is very often an unconscious statement beyond words. The laughter that went back and forth here was not on an equal plane, as everything else was made believe to be. On one side was laughing up; on the other side it was laughing down.

This happy access of the press to the head of a great Government—what did that mean? Some would say it was democracy working in, perhaps, its best informal manner. But the Old Reporter no longer knew what people meant by the word "democracy." He was not cynical, but he had known men who called themselves great democrats, and who were believed to be, because they spoke always in the name of the people. He had never noticed that these men were marked by any particular kind of manner, either informal or austere. What did mark them was an imperious nature. They were invariably men who distrusted the people and would be scandalized to hear you say so. Their faith in the people was a faith in themselves. Proof of their distrust of the people was their passion to save people from themselves, to do for them and to them what was good for them, to reform them by law.

The Old Reporter had heard that the President secretly entertained a great contempt for the press; exempting, of course, the individual newspapermen for whom he conceived a personal liking. However that might be, it was obvious here that the press was not exploiting the President; to the contrary, the President was exploiting the press. With one sentence—and it might be a sentence that was not to be quoted—he could make big headlines on the front page of every newspaper in the country, saying, the Government may, the Government will, the Government is about to, do a certain thing.

Just then the Old Reporter was thinking of a paragraph that had appeared in Arthur Krock's *New York Times* column.

The paragraph was: "In the press's Government, the President is supreme. He who said, in trying to guess the industrial prospect, 'The answer is with one man, the President,' spoke the exact truth."

One man responsible for the industrial prospect of the country. How could that be? And that was the man who sat there facing the newspapermen, chatting with them, exchanging pleasantries with them, laughing down to them, smoking a cigarette in a long holder, greatly at his ease.

The next piece is about Federal Loan Administrator Jesse Jones. He was the opposite of the young intellectual trying to make over the world. He had an eighth-grade education. He was a self-made entrepreneur, the big man of Houston, banker, builder and the biggest money man of the New Deal. Hoover had appointed him head of the Reconstruction Finance Corp. in 1932; Roosevelt kept him on and made him a kind of second federal Treasury. "We know that the Government cannot lend money to itself—not really—and yet that is what it seems to be doing," wrote Garrett in the Post of Dec. 7, 1940. "What happens is that the RFC writes its IOUs and sells them to the banks. Then it has credit in the banking system. And this credit in the banking system is what it lends to the Government. Having borrowed from Jesse Jones the credit he has borrowed from the banks, the WPA, the PWA, the CCC, the Secretary of Agriculture and all, write their checks and send them out, and the people who receive the checks go straight with them to the nearest bank and deposit them and the bank is then ready to buy more of Jesse Jones's IOUs."

The month before Garrett wrote that, the Saturday Evening Post called Jones the second most powerful man in the United States.

The Yes Principle

From "The Yes Principle," the *Saturday Evening Post,* June 28, 1941

Each time the Reconstruction Finance Corporation appears before Congress asking for more power, its creators regard their creature with feelings of awe and amazed paternity. Then for an hour they debate their retreat from responsibility, agree to withhold something as a token of their authority, and end happily by congratulating themselves and the Government on the fact that the Federal Loan Administrator is Jesse Jones. He is the stone of truth, his manners are respectful, and, as Senator Taft[5] naively says, "I think it is a very good thing that when such additional powers are wanted, Mr. Jones should come back to Congress."

This instructive little scene occurs annually. It has just now been re-enacted. With one billion still free in its drawer, the RFC wanted authority to borrow one and a half billions more. As concerning the sum, there was no difficulty whatever; but always before, the RFC had indicated in some general way what it meant to do with its billions. This time it was saying merely that the money would be used for anything that might promote the national defense. Suppose it should get into its head that things the Congress had considered and rejected, such as Passamaquoddy or the Florida Ship Canal,[6] would be good for the national defense. A Senate committee asked Mr. Jones if he had anything like that in mind, and he replied that he had not; and it was then suggested that he might write a letter to say the RFC was not going to do anything the Congress had specifically said not to do. A letter of promise to the Congress of the United States!

Even so, it might do things the Congress had never imagined and would vote against if it thought of them. "I am satisfied," said Senator Adams,[7] "that under the bill the RFC could enlist and drill an army... if they assert it is in the interest of national defense."

Beyond this, the Senate debate turned principally on what the RFC had done with an innocent power granted the year before. It had been represented to be a power of convenience only. Until then, when the RFC needed a separate corporation to transact a certain kind of business, like the Export-Import Bank, it had to go over to Delaware or Maryland and get a state charter, which was a nuisance. Please, would the Congress give it the power to charter its own corporations? The Congress did.

After that, the RFC, as a creature of Congress, could and did create creatures of its own; and the extraordinary fact was that since there was no limitation upon its genetic power, it could create creatures of its own with more power than Congress had yet conferred upon the RFC itself, and create them in perpetuity.

Staring at this biological phenomenon, the Congress could scarcely believe its eyes. The Senate committee put the question squarely to Mr. Jones. "Can you or your organization create a corporation with a life beyond that of the RFC, and with powers in excess of those of the RFC?" His answer was yes. In fact he had done it, not once but four times, and that was all Congress knew about it. Nobody had ever seen the charters of the RFC's creatures. They were nowhere on file; they might be in Mr. Jones' hat. And since the powers conferred by the RFC upon its creatures were unknown and probably unlimited, the possibility followed that these creatures might create other creatures, to the third and fourth generation.

What is the Reconstruction Finance Corporation?

Under the Hoover Administration, at the blackest moment of the depression, it was created by Congress and provided with a revolving fund of half a billion dollars to make distress loans to agriculture, business and banking—for that and nothing else, and for the duration of the emergency only.

The New Deal took it over. It has now outstanding more than $2 billion in loans and investments, with $2.5 billion free in its drawer. Itself, through its creatures and through its creatures' creatures, it is interested directly and indirectly in nearly every kind of business there is; it lends money to the Government for farm subsidies, for relief, and for other purposes, some of which it gets back and some of which is from time to time wiped out by bookkeeping; it enters into financial relations with foreign governments and makes loans to foreign governments; it finances works and industries in foreign countries—sugar industries in Cuba that compete with American sugar growers, and steelworks in Brazil that compete with the American steel industry, according to an international policy of its own.

It has a kind of sovereignty of its own. With blanket authority delegated by Congress to borrow money on the credit of the United States, it borrows billions and lends them in its own discretion, subject only to the will and discretion of the President. The Congress and the Constitution are bypassed. The Constitution says that only Congress may borrow money on the credit of the United States and that no money may be spent but in accordance with a law of appropriation enacted by Congress. It authorizes the RFC to borrow them, and it is the RFC that appropriates them.

It is more than a matter of money. The decisions and activities of the RFC affect not only financial, economic and social policies within the country; they affect also foreign relations. Without the consent or previous knowledge of Congress, this agency of executive government, this nominal creature of Congress, may commit, and has committed, unneutral acts, at the discretion of the President alone.

More significant than anything the RFC is or does is its abstract meaning. It is the sign of the triumph of the executive will over the parliamentary principle.

In many ways and many times during these last eight years we have said that government is the natural enemy of freedom. That was the great American truth. Thomas Jefferson was its zealot. He was a radical republican before the word "democrat" was acceptable, keeping feud with the Federalists, who were for strong government; and yet this truth was never in dispute between them, really; the American Government in the republican form was a constitutional, representative, limited government, with the emphasis always on the limited.

If people cannot limit government they will not for long be free. There is in government a living impulse to extend itself indefinitely; and there is in freedom a necessity to resist that impulse. The natural tendency, as Jefferson said, is for government to prevail and freedom to give way.

Purposely to limit the ambitions of executive government, the Constitution invested the Congress with very great powers, the first of which was the ultimate power—namely, control of the purse. These powers Congress has surrendered and delegated in a progressive manner, first in the state of emergency and then in the name of national defense.

In time of war or great emergency it becomes necessary to give the President extraordinary temporary powers. All the more in such times should the Congress be jealous of the power it delegates, take hostage for it and make sure of its return intact. But what happens is that there is formed a habit of surrender.

Jones raised some $20 billion for the war effort, some of it through satellite companies such as Defense Plant Corp. and Defense Supplies Corp. During the war he got into a turf fight with Roosevelt's left-wing vice president, Henry Wallace, and he resigned in 1945. The RFC was shut down in 1956 after a favoritism scandal.

CHAPTER TWO NOTES:

1 Hilaire Belloc, 1870-1953, was an English Catholic novelist, biographer, poet, historian and political philosopher. He wrote *The Bad Child's Book of Beasts* (1896), *The Path to Rome* (1902), *The Servile State* (1912) and *The Restoration of Property* (1936). He criticized socialism and industrial capitalism and advocated a pastoral state.

2 Andrew Mellon. A conservative, he pushed hard to pay down the national debt, and during that time did pay it down by more than a third. He also pushed to lower the top rate of personal income tax from 73% to 25%, which stayed until the Depression.

3 It wasn't, though an argument is made today that a flat-rate tax would have that effect.

4 William Patrick Connery, 1888-1937, Democrat of Massachusetts, went on to be the co-sponsor of the New Deal's labor law, the National Labor Relations Act of 1935.

5 Robert A. Taft, 1889-1953, Republican of Ohio, son of President Howard Taft, was elected senator in the anti-Roosevelt tide of 1938 and served until his death. Leader of the conservatives, he opposed economic controls under the New Deal and FDR's efforts to get into World War II. Taft tried for the Republican presidential nominations in 1940, 1948 and 1952, but was edged out by more liberal candidates each time.

6 Passamaquoddy and the Florida Ship Canal were New Deal projects rejected by Congress. At Passamaquoddy, a bay at the border of Maine and New Brunswick, a civil engineer proposed to make a power plant using the tides. Roosevelt, who had a summer house near there, favored it, and in 1935 used relief funds to begin work on it. Congress refused to appropriate follow-on money and the project died. The Florida Ship Canal, a proposed sea-level channel, was also begun but abandoned during the war. Work began on a fresh-water canal in 1964 but was canceled in 1971 when it was one-third finished. It is now a park.

7 Alva Adams, 1875-1941, Democrat of Colorado, senator 1923-24, 1933-41. He died six days before the bombing of Pearl Harbor.

Chapter Three
A FINISHED WORLD

*Garrett once summed up the mantras of the New Deal—
ever-normal granary, balanced abundance, planned economy,
social security and stability—as "all the ideas of a finished
world." In this piece, written just before the New Deal began,
Garrett sniffs those ideas in the air, and denounces them.*

To Stabilize Industry

From "Unemployment—What Is It?" the *Saturday Evening
Post,* January 21, 1933

Time: One hundred years ago. The mechanical era is in the
gristle. There is steam power. Machines have been
hitched to steam engines, and there are factories and coal
smoke and tall chimneys, but no railroads, no steamships, no
electricity, no telegraph. The world's commerce is moved by
wind power and animal power. And yet there has been already
a great industrial crisis that people name over production,
causing poverty, hunger and unemployment in the factory
towns of England and France. Already a school of antagonists
is denouncing industrialism. The economist Sismondi[1] says
machinery increases competition among workers, extending
their misery.

Others of the same antagonistic school, like Fourier,[2] are
saying "Back to the land!"

Time: Fifty years ago. The mechanical era is in the bone.
Population has doubled, and yet there is food in plenty and
running over, because now railroads are walking all over the
continents of Europe and North America, and steamships are
parting the seas, so that not only may grain flow as by gravity but the cost of moving it is almost nothing. The ocean
freight rate from New York to Liverpool that was twenty cents
a bushel now is two cents, and the railroad freight rate has
fallen from three and a half cents per ton-mile to seven-tenths
of a cent. For the first time on this side of the world fear of
famine is banished. There is a price to pay. New and far-away
lands have acquired value, but at the same time the near, old
lands have been wrecked in value.

This is the beginning of the steel age. The price of steel has
fallen from eighty to seventeen dollars a ton. Large-scale
machine production has cheapened the cost of all goods. The
telegraph has altered time. There is chaos in all values. A price
structure has fallen. Old profits and old capital have been
swept away. Of everything there seems suddenly too much,
and no profit in it. Agriculture, industry, transportation—all
are frightfully depressed.

Much of this change has happened suddenly; and because
it has happened suddenly, a sense of relation and rhythm is
lost and there is a worldwide economic crisis, in fact and in
feeling. There is terror of the machine that never needs to
sleep or to rest. What will society do with its surplus labor—
with people who cannot be employed because the machine is
doing their work and who cannot buy because they cannot be
employed?

A new school of antagonists is denouncing the industrial
system, free competition, anarchy of production, uncontrolled
change. They are demanding that the state shall interfere, and
saying, if it doesn't, civilization will perish. They propose,
variously, that prices shall be restored by inflating the currency, that production shall be controlled by law, that work shall

be spread by an edict to limit the hours of labor to eight in one day, where it has been ten and eleven, and that the government shall redistribute wealth.

The problem is not how to produce anything more. It is how to divide existing production. Therefore divide the work until everyone has a job.

The world at this time is still lighted by the gas flame and the coal-oil lamp; it is warmed at the stove and open fires. There is no oil industry but for kerosene, and there is no such thing as an automobile. No concrete highways, no radio, no telephone system, no aviation, no movies, no electrical appliances, no elevators, no subways; and the word "automatic" still had to be looked up in the dictionary.

Time: Now. The mechanical era is in its third age. There are machines that act by seeing, hearing and feeling; machines that seem to think. For example, an automatic loom that stops when the thread breaks, mends it, and starts itself again. People are beginning to speak of the manless factory.

All this time population has been increasing. In this country it has much more than doubled in the last fifty years. And yet there is an abundance of food—a surplus of it. Industry and science acting upon agriculture have revolutionized it, increasing the product per hour of manual labor.

And now again a grave economic crisis. Another price structure has fallen. Old profits, old capital, old methods are going over the dam, for all any government can do to save them. There is chaos in values. The rhythm is broken, all relations are abnormal, a sense of continuity is lost. And this again is from what we continue to name overproduction. Of everything there is suddenly more than can be sold—a surplus of food, a surplus of goods, a surplus of raw materials, a surplus of machines, and, in consequence, a surplus of labor. The evil of unemployment returns. The actual extent of it is so much greater than before that the mind of the world is appalled. But it is the same old evil, wearing the same face, and we are saying about it the same things we have said before.

An eminent British scientist is saying, "Let us declare a science holiday, until the world can catch up." Echo of the Swiss economist Sismondi, who, before railroads and steamships, was saying: "Let inventions cease, at least for a while."

We are saying, as Sismondi said, and as others said fifty years after him, that human misery is from machines that devour employment, and from free competition that results in anarchy of production, that is to say, from uncontrolled change.

We are saying now, as people said one hundred years ago, and again fifty years ago, "There is already wealth enough if only it can be divided." We shall have a static society. Change will trouble us no more.

Suppose invention had ceased, suppose production had been limited and change restrained, suppose all wealth had been divided into consumption one hundred years ago, before railroads and steamships; or again, fifty years ago, before motor cars. Or suppose—and it comes to the same result—that at either time the total amount of work had been divided by the total number of workers, to determine how much less everybody should work. That might have seemed to solve the problem of unemployment, but, in fact, it would have brought universal partial employment, as if industry had been a worn-out land unable to reward the full human exertion.

Yet this now is one of the proposals. There is a national propaganda, suggested by the Government, for "spreading the work." As a mitigation in a time of emergency there may be nothing to say against it. But back of that is the idea of a five-day week and a six-hour day as a cure, so that everybody may be employed. Fifty years ago, in a similar crisis, the eight-hour day was proposed instead of the ten-hour day, on the same ground. The eight-hour day did come. But not then. It came later; it came with the return of prosperity, and not until science, technology and a tremendous increase of mechanical power per worker had made it possible for people to produce in eight hours not as much as they had been able to produce in ten, but more—much more!

From the beginning of the mechanical era until now, the hours of labor have been shortening. They have been almost halved. And all the time wages have been rising. They have doubled and doubled again. But no step in this progress has ever been made by dividing a given amount of work into a greater number of hands. Each step has been made possible by creating new work for the labor released from old jobs.

What else we are saying in this crisis is nearly all borrowed from the past. Let the Government restore prices by inflation—that is to say, by debasing our money. Industry must be stabilized. Production must be controlled by a plan beforehand. Some say, very earnestly: "Prices do this to us. Therefore, let us abolish prices." Others say: "Money does it. Therefore, let us a invent a new kind of money." Some say: "The banker does it. Let the Government take over banking and control credit in the public welfare." Others: "It is the profit motive. Away with the profit motive." And many are saying, as Fourier said one hundred years ago: "Back to the land."

To denounce one part of the system involves many debatable particulars, but to denounce the system as a whole, as now is the high fashion to do, involves only an attitude and a conclusion. The only new thing in this is that many who may be supposed to speak for the industrial system now join with others to denounce it.

Leaders of industry themselves are proposing to do what only the antagonists proposed before—namely, to stabilize industry by coercion and restraint, to limit production by a plan beforehand, to control change. A planned economy hereafter. There is a passion for planning the economic future in a rational manner, so that prices, values, supply, demand, employment, production shall never be in this state of chaos again. But who could have planned railroads and steamships before they appeared, or what plan could have anticipated the change they brought? Who, fifty years ago, could have planned a motor-car industry, and what would any plan have been worth that did not include the agency of uncontrollable change? Is there a plan that will secure to us all the benefits of change without the price?

The price is what is hurting us now. It is the price of further progress in material well-being. But the price itself is all we seem to be thinking of, and we treat it as an indictment, not of our own vast and collective follies, but of the anonymous industrial system.

It is a terrific indictment, certainly. In this country alone, more than one-fourth of the people who might be employed are out of work. In the social body these are not as dead cells. They are devouring cells. They must be fed and housed and clothed, and what it costs to do this is a total loss. There is also a loss of morale and the political liability of creating in millions of people the habits of economic dependence and the expectation of refuge in public credit. And there is a total inability of industry to guarantee that this will not happen again, as it has been happening for one hundred years.

There is a saying that if industry had had only the vision to see the road ahead and the chasm there, it need not have gone over the edge. It might have put on the brakes. But who is industry? What shall personify it? Who shall see for the whole of it? Then we say that if industry is nobody in particular, or nobody that can be held responsible, it is time that the state should do the seeing, keep its hand on the brakes and set them in time.

Well, the state may have eyes. This Government's financial eye is the Federal Reserve Board. A year before we went over the cliff, it did have some glimpse of the danger and tried to throttle down on the gas. The gas was credit. And with what result? Not industry alone, not business alone, not Wall Street alone, but popular opinion also turned on it with animal ferocity. By what right did it propose to hinder prosperity? Where was its certificate of wisdom?

The road was clear. Never had there been a road so clear and straight. This, you will recall, was in the time of great delusion. Everybody was profit-mad and money-mad and buying-mad. And if the Federal Reserve Board had suddenly arrested the momentum and had saved us from going over the cliff at the cost of only a few bad bumps, and then nothing else had happened, we should now be saying that nothing else would have happened, and, perhaps, be passing a law forbidding the Federal Reserve Board ever to reach for the gas or the brakes again.

Concerning the indictment, there is the possibility that it is unsound by reason both of things left out and things assumed. For example, it is explicit in the first premise that machine industry is to blame for unemployment. That we take this for granted shows how little we know about unemployment, and how easily a new word persuades us that we are gazing at a new thing. The word is new. But unemployment is historic. The pyramids, perhaps, are monuments to unemployment. The public bread and the public circus were to quiet the unemployed and unemployable of Rome, called the mob or the rabble. In England, two or three centuries before the mechanical era, there were the poor, the paupers and the beggars. The word "unemployment" was not used as we use it, yet the misery of the unemployed was such as nothing we can now imagine.

By 1700, unemployment relief in England, called poor relief, had become a staggering social and moral problem. There were too many people in England; there was a surplus of people and not enough work. That seemed to be the trouble. What else could it be? It was Defoe, creator of Robinson

39

Crusoe, writing economics before there was a word for it, who first challenged that idea. He wrote a pamphlet, beginning: "I humbly crave leave to lay these heads down as fundamental maxims, which I am ready at any time to defend and make out. 1. There is in England more labor than hands to perform it, and, consequently, a want of people, not of employment."

How right he was! For the work that lay just ahead of her, England would need ten times as many people as she had then. Her work was to bring the mechanical era to pass and then to lead it for one hundred years, to found an empire, to colonize and tame wild continents, to take possession of the seas, to become the principle of stability and magnificence in the trade and commerce of the world. All this she did, never knowing beforehand how, only the way of it when the time came; but never did she get rid of unemployment.

There is bound to be unemployment in a society in which change takes place at a rapid rate. And then this curious matter: that under any conditions whatever, there is a kind of person who will be never unemployed, and at the opposite end of the scale the kind of person who will be always unemployed; between these are other kinds, such as those who are inconstant to employment, and others who, though they may be constant to it, live, nevertheless, near the periphery and are certain to be cast off when anything happens.

This is not to look away from the facts of human misery. It is to suggest that we are still primitives in this new economic environment, behaving toward it as a savage behaves toward Nature. In a season of plenty, we gorge and dance and spend in a spirit of uncontrollable extravagance. One lean year gives us trouble; two or three in a row involve us in disaster, no matter how many fat seasons may just have passed in succession. The more of them, and the fatter they were, the greater will have been the extravagance and the worse will be the disaster when it comes. Think how many famines there had to be, and that for thousands of years a helpless, superstitious dread of them was constant, before the race learned to adapt itself prudently, intelligently and with foresight to the rhythms of Nature. These rhythms have never been conquered; they are as unpredictable now as they ever were; only famine and the fear of it have been done away with. It may be we shall have to learn from depressions how to adapt ourselves to the rhythms of this economic environment.

Do you say that whereas the rhythms of Nature are beyond control, it is not so with those of industry? We make industry; we make its rhythms; therefore we can control them. But are we sure? Invention and change, in this artificial world we have created, are as unpredictable as natural events. Whence come the ideas that lead to discovery? No one can say more than it happens. Theoretically you might hothouse industry; so also you might hothouse agriculture and remove it entirely from the hazards of Nature; but if you did, the cost of food and the cost of industrial goods would rise enormously, and that process of cheapening them which has been acting for one hundred years would come to an end.

Suppose we had never rightly understood what industry was for—and this would not be strange, in view of the fact that it began with no history at all. We do not complain of nature that it knows no social function. Simply, it rewards human exertion, not at a fixed wage, not without seasons of unemployment and disaster, but in the average as well as the labor deserves. Try supposing that neither has industry any social or paternal function. Try judging it as if its only function were to multiply divisible wealth in a progressive, prodigious manner.

It has been the particular genius of organized labor in this country to regard it somewhat from that point of view. In the philosophy evolved by the American Federation of Labor, there was a deep distrust of any political interference with this primary function. The relationship between capital and labor was conceived to be neither political nor social; it was strictly economic. Give the wage earner his right wage. That was all he asked of industry. In every other way he would take care of himself and live as he pleased.

In a time of extreme depression, there arises a demand that industry be required to foresee the social consequences of its function and assume moral responsibility for them, on the ground that people are increasingly helpless. Recently the American Federation of Labor, contrary to the philosophy it had so jealously built up, voted for compulsory unemployment insurance to be imposed by the state as a social charge upon industry.

A time may come when the cost of free progress in material well-being will be intolerable. Many believe that time is present. This is a painful thought, inseparable from the fears and anxieties of depression. We have had it before, only to forget it.

Suppose it had been possible, one hundred years ago, to present a picture of the world as it is today, and say: "All this will come from that anarchy of production, planless competition and uncontrollable change you are beginning to denounce. The convulsions from time to time will be terrific. Everything will have to be destroyed and made over again four or five times. There will be depressions, such as now you are complaining of, each one wider and deeper, only each time there will be relatively much more wealth with which to absorb the disaster. You may be able to stop it now. But if you let it go on, you will be unable to control it. For all it costs, will you have it?"

They might have been so terrified as to say, "Stop it now." And if they had stopped it, at least one-third of the people now existing in the world, and certainly one-half of those existing on the western side of it, where most of the industry is, would never have been born. Simply, life could not have employed them.

So now, what, if anything, is to be concluded?

In any previous major depression, all of the obvious conclusions were wrong, as to say society was already rich enough, that there were too many people, that there was not enough work because machine industry had devoured it. These were appearances only, but so tall and dense that people could not see their way out. Never were they able to see their way out. Always they have had to feel themselves out.

As a conclusion from experience, we do not advance from peak to peak; neither do we simply recover from a depression. The advance proceeds from depression. In a time of depression, necessity acts. What is that necessity? A necessity to accommodate oncoming change. The measure of depression is the measure of necessity, and the measure of either is the measure of the first power of change, which is destructive. The second power of change, which is creative, will be in proportion to its first. This is not a law. It is all the experience we have. Simply, the greater the depression is, the greater the next advance will be. If the change were toward a static condition, or toward retrogression, it would not produce a violent disturbance, for that would be the change of decay, slow, amiable and painstaking with the ruins, to make them soft and lovely.

It should follow that the accumulated forces of creative change are at this moment greater than was ever the case before. They probably are. How and where will they spend themselves? In a world where at the present state of knowledge three times as many people might be contained in the web of life, where even yet one-half of the existing population is not within reach of the industrial standard of living, the sudden release of these creative forces is bound to prepare much more work than leisure.

Trying, one hundred years ago, to project the consequences of machine industry, the political economist arrived at the celebrated image of one man producing everything by simply turning a winch. Then what? There would be employment for only one man in a whole kingdom.

You see what was wrong with their image. They were projecting the logical consequence of machine industry in the world as it was then. They did not see that machine industry would give man the power to transform his environment and extend it prodigiously. They supposed that the quantity of work to be performed was limited by the range of human wants at that time, so that labor-saving machinery could mean only leisure to be divided, or unemployment. It means neither one nor the other. Each new machine did release labor from old employment, but at the same time it was like a blast in a quarry of unknown and invisible possibilities, bringing down an avalanche of new material to be acted upon.

Well, there is less excuse now than there was then to suppose that the economic world is finished. We have seen what happens. We know better.

Wealth redistribution was another idea of a finished world. Garrett hung the following piece on a tax bill President Roosevelt sent to Congress June 19, 1935. It proposed an increase in inheritance and income taxes, pushing the top rate of income tax, already raised to 63% under Hoover, even higher. Attorney General Homer Cummings summed up the theme when he blurted to a Senate committee: "I cannot understand why it is immoral to stop people from becoming rich."

The Wealth Question

From "The Wealth Question," the *Saturday Evening Post, August 31, 1935*

The demagogues who excite the minds of the many complain about the unequal distribution of wealth. And yet in 1932, fewer than 2 million people out of 125 million paid any Federal income tax at all. The tax was graduated according to income. Those who had incomes between $5,000 and $6,000[3] paid an average tax of less than 2 percent, whereas the few who had large incomes paid up to more than 50 percent of their income, following the doctrine that people shall be taxed according to their ability to pay.

Of the total personal-income tax paid in 1932, 47 percent was paid by fewer than 8,000 persons. This is by the will of the majority. The poor tax the rich, and, where the majority rule, there is no limit to what the many may take from the few simply by voting it.

A visitor from another time viewing all this might say: "In such a system the poor are bound to destroy the rich. You may tell them that in the end they will thereby increase their own poverty. They will not believe you. If they did believe you they would not care. The end is tomorrow; they live today. I cannot see what principle restrains the many."

There is a sense in which a democracy is like a great family, and in that sense all the wealth belongs to all the people. They may do with it what they will. If a majority is resolved to divide the total wealth in equal portions all around and consume it, that can be done. There is no physical force to prevent it. If there is a law to forbid it, the law may be changed to make it legal.

And where is any political restraint? The demagogue, the social hero, the altruist, the ameliorist in romantic revolt against the disparities of human existence—all these unite their sayings. The poor are poor because the rich are rich. The way to abolish poverty is to abate the rich. Therefore, divide the wealth. To overcome the moral difficulties, if any, it shall be declared that social justice is the first law of morals, and this is social justice. It is for the greatest good of the greatest number. Moreover, the many will be taking back only what the few have despoiled them of.

So what is the answer to the question?

That the rich are few and the poor are many is true. Abolish it as an economic fact, and still it would be so as a biological fact. That 3 percent of the people own 95 percent of the wealth is not true. Yet suppose it were. Reverse it and see what it means. It means that 95 percent of the wealth has 3 percent of the vote—and this in a democracy where a majority may do what it will, where the many, if they are so resolved, may freely divide among themselves the wealth of the few.

In that case, obviously, the rich are helpless, and the question is acute. Why have the many not destroyed the few? What has restrained them? What until now has defeated the misgivings of Lord Macaulay,[4] written in 1857 to an American? He said: "I seriously apprehend that you will, in such season of adversity as I have described"—he had just described a depression in England— "do things that will prevent prosperity from returning. There will be, I fear, spoilation. The spoilation will increase the distress. The distress will produce fresh spoilation. There is nothing to stop you. Your Constitution is all sail and no anchor."

The answer is important. For all that has been said, the restraints are powerful. What are they? The first and perhaps the most powerful of them is not rational. As it is deeper than a principle, so it is deeper than reason. There is no exact name for it. In a further sense, far beyond that sense of total proprietorship in the total of things, a democracy is again like a family. So long as it is alive at the core and obedient to the law of its destiny, it will have a feeling for its own future strong enough in a crisis to overthrow all other feelings. If this were not so, civilization could not advance, nor without that feeling could it ever have arrived. It is not an individual feeling. On the contrary, from the individual's point of view, it must seem irrational. Moreover, the individual is bound to resist it, because he is obliged to make sacrifices for it. Why should he sacrifice present satisfactions for a future in which he will not participate? Who can tell him what the future is? Who knows for sure there will be a future?

46

The individual is for a little while and discontinuous; the society is for long and continuous. Thus the demands of the present and the claims of the future are in conflict, and it is one of the remorseless realities, everywhere touching life.

Imagine a people suddenly seized with the conviction that the life of society and the lives of all existing individuals were coterminous; that both society and the individuals comprising it would perish together, and after them, nothing. Why then would every idea of wealth be altered? Why would it be folly to save, to store, to invest, to invent a machine, to build a durable thing, to withhold anything from present desire? Because the claims of the future upon the present would cease. The first impulse of those having more than they could consume would be to give the excess away. The passion for progress that now costs us so much would no longer act. The standard of living would rise, because it would be safe to consume the whole product of labor, to wear out the machines without replacing them, to use up the place, even meaningless to do otherwise. But suppose the conviction should turn out to be a delusion and that, after all, society had to go on. Then the fall in the standard of living, the misery, the privation, the doing without in order to go on again would be appalling.

Why did the patriarch of old go on to the end of his days increasing his flocks and herds, his lands and stores, his responsibilities and troubles? Not for himself. He needed but ease and one fig tree for himself. It was for the family he did it, and for the seed of the clan that was in the family and the seed of a nation that was in the clan. And why did the patriarch impose on the members of his family a rule of self-denial, require them to forgo many present enjoyments and with ruthless authority put down such a thing as a divide-the-wealth movement? Because the future of the family, the clan to come after the family, and the nation to come after the clan, demanded that sacrifice of the individuals composing the family. Some make it willingly, some with passive discontent

47

and others under the threat of revolt, saying, "There is enough. Why not enjoy it while we may? Let those who come after us toil as we have." But if these prevail, the character of that family will soften, its habits of industry will be forgotten, its substance will be devoured, and together with its substance, its future.

This conflict between the demands of the present and the claims of the future, between the immediate desires of the individual and the family that in some measure must sacrifice the individual in order to bring its own future to pass, is one of the great tensions of civilized existence. It is with a society as it is with a family, only that in a society the individuals appear as classes and the struggle becomes political. A corporation, regarded as an artificial family with a limited motive, has the same kind of problem. One may be ruled by a hard patriarch, who limits his wailing stockholders to a moderate dividend and keeps returning the profit to the property. That is a corporation that will weather any kind of storm. Another will be unable to resist the clamor of the stockholders to divide the whole profit, and the end of that one is foretold.

But observe that this conflict, in any aspect, will arise only where there is much to divide. A poor family has nothing to divide but poverty; hence no quarreling over division. A share-the-wealth movement occurs only in a rich society. How does a society get rich? Not by the exertions alone of the individuals that today compose it. A little they have done, but much less than they think. They were born into a world already equipped with wonderful means and tools that cost them nothing. These wonderful means and tools did not naturally exist. They had to be provided; and they were provided by the greater toil and self-denial of those to whom the now living were the unborn, the unknown. Our present is that future in which they could not participate.

Every proposal to share the wealth or to redistribute it downward out of the hands of the few into the hands of the many is, in fact, a proposal to dissipate the accumulated assets of society. If it does not mean that, it has no popular meaning whatever. With no greater exertion than before—indeed, with less—the many shall have more to consume and enjoy, not by increasing production, but by dividing among them more of what is. The struggle for existence shall be thereby suspended. The disparities shall be reduced or wiped out.

The disparities are represented to be a consequence of the concentration of wealth in the hands of the few. But what if the concentration of wealth in the hands of the few were a consequence of the disparities inherent in the human material? And it is. The exceptions are fortuitous and impermanent. Suppose all the wealth of the country were divided equally on a per-capita basis. What then? In a little while, there again would be the poor, the moderately well off, the well-to-do and the rich—all as before, and in the same proportions.

The many live today and pay tomorrow. The many spend and the few save. And it is not that the many have nothing to save. For look: The proportion of the total national income received by employees as wages and salaries increased from 53 percent in 1900 to 65 percent in 1929. If all employees as one person had invested this increase—only the increase—they might now possess the entire corporate wealth of the country and be receiving the interest and dividends. They would have had to endure for only two or three years the standard of living they had in 1900, and then they would have begun to be rich.

To the concentration of wealth in the hands of a few there is but one alternative. If the few do not save, the government must. That is to say, a government then must withhold from present enjoyment that costly proportion which the future demands. That is what the government does in Russia. But if the government does it, that is the beginning of tyranny and the end of democracy. And that is something democracy knows. In a people who have cherished extreme personal liberty, and who, under a free economic system have made themselves the richest people in the world, there are other restraints. This the New Dealers have discovered, to their amazement, carrying benefits to people who resent them in the act of receiving them.

Why are people resentful? Because it is an exchange of freedom for status; the greater the temptation the more hateful the choice. They are asked at first to surrender only a very little freedom, a mere raveling; and yet a raveling caught in the great Washington gears may take suddenly the whole garment along. But the gears have a wonderful song.

When the divisionists, seizing the helpless statistics, find that the total annual production of goods and services may have a value, say, of $90 billion, and divide that figure by the total number of families, they say: "There it is. We produce enough to give each family $3,000 a year, and, as the Government's experts tell us, that is the minimum of income to support the average family in a decent way, only the necessities and a few little luxuries. Yet there are millions of families with less than $1,000 a year, millions of families below the line of bare subsistence. What becomes of our national income? Who gets it? Not those whose labor produces it. Profit takes it. The rich get it. To abolish poverty we need only to distribute the wealth so that everyone shall have enough and no one too much!"

Thereupon a naive fantasy begins to rise in the popular mind. A sum of $3,000 divided by 52. Roughly sixty dollars a week to be received as due. But how? Supposing the figures are right and that the rich have it and that it may be taken away from them without wrecking the system of production from which all income is derived—still, what will the procedure be? The Government will not allot to the rich man a list of those with whom he is to divide his income and direct him to send each of them a check every Tuesday. That will not happen.

First, the Government will tax the money into the Treasury. There will be the cost of collecting it, then the cost of planning its redistribution down to the many, and a great bureau for that purpose; then the cost of many bureaus to search out the beneficiaries and to punch for each one an index card showing the status and condition and what the income already is and how much will have to be provided by the Government to bring it up to standard, and then a great disbursing machine minded by thousands of clerks. When all of this cost has been deducted, the sum that was to have been standard will have to be squeezed. It may have to be reduced from sixty dollars a week to fifty dollars. Say it is fifty dollars. Well, then, what shall be done with millions of families to whom fifty dollars a week would mean only taking it easy— very, very easy? Shall these be made to work? Who will say how hard they shall work, and see to it? Moreover, they have been told that this standard of income is something that they are entitled do, whether they earn it or not, on the ground that as a matter of public policy every family shall have the means to live in a minimum state of comfort.

Beyond any of these difficulties there is this: that merely the receipt of fifty dollars a week does not guarantee the economic security of a family. It may go wildly into debt; it may spend and consume a year's income in three months, and so be ruined and destitute. Shall the Government mind them to see how they spend their money?

Absurd as this may sound, a problem of exactly that nature has been faced in the flesh. The Senate was passing the Farmers' Home Corporation Bill. That is a bill creating another Federal corporation, with authority to borrow $1 billion for the purpose of abating farm tenancy. This corporation shall provide farms of average size, complete, equipped and stocked, for tenant farmers and wandering sharecroppers whose only claim to them will be that they have been unable to provide farms for themselves. Waiving such a difficulty as

51

that a billion dollars would not be enough to provide a farm for everyone who might have that claim to it, perhaps not enough to provide farms for only those tenants and share-croppers who have been displaced by the curtailment programs of the AAA, the Senate earnestly debated this question: What if a man for whom the Government had provided a farm should get into debt and lose it, or be unable to pay his taxes and lose it? Would he not become again a tenant or wandering sharecropper? He would. So it was written in the bill that when the Government had provided such a man with a farm, it should be legally inalienable. That is to say, it could not be taken from him for debt or taxes.

Now what do you see? Such a man has a farm. If he cannot pay the Government for it, he need not worry; the Government, having provided him with a farm only because he could not provide a farm for himself, is not going to dispossess him. If he cannot pay his taxes, let the county worry. He still has the farm. No one can touch it. It is his, and yet again it is not his. He cannot do with it what he likes. He cannot borrow on it. He cannot put a mortgage on it. He is free only to walk off and leave it, and he will not do that, because if he does, the Government may not take care of him again. He is safe. He is protected against himself. He is tied to the land. But so was the Old World serf tied to the land and protected against himself.

Why are farmers divided on the AAA program? It was designed to redistribute the national income in favor of agriculture. To redistribute the income is the same, of course, as to redistribute the wealth itself. A special tax was laid upon the consumers of food, the proceeds of the tax to be handed over to the farmers, provided the farmers would agree in writing to curtail their crops.

This was all to pass more of the national income from industry to agriculture. There was at first no objection, or hardly any, because agriculture had become the underdog and people were willing to tax themselves to increase its share. Only, how would it work?

In the beginning and for the first year it was emphasized that, between the farmers and the Government, all arrangements were voluntary. A farmer could sign up to cut his production and receive cash benefits from the Government, or he could stay out of the plan, just as he pleased. But in the second year the cotton farmers were laid under compulsion. Each one was allotted by the Government a quota; he could raise so much cotton and no more. And the way of compelling him to stop at his quota was to put a prohibitive tax on any amount above his quota. Thereafter each bale of cotton had to bear a Government tag, indicating that it was permitted to be grown.

Wheat farmers, corn farmers, hog farmers and others, signing up with the AAA and beginning to receive United States Treasury checks for what they did not produce, were generally pleased until they began slowly to reflect on what they had done and to reread the papers they had signed in the office of the Government's county agent. They had signed away the right to do as they pleased with their own land. They had bound themselves to obey any rules and regulations, issued as law, by the Secretary of Agriculture, or by any one of the many bureaus authorized to stamp his name on a piece of paper.

Many of them still were a little dim about what was happening, until they read in the newspapers the account of the President's interview on the Supreme Court's decision in the NRA case.[5] He was speaking of the possible effect of the NRA decision on the AAA. If the AAA also turned out to be unconstitutional, then would the Government, he asked, be obliged to withdraw its hand from agriculture and go back to the old policy that every man was a lord on his own farm?

But if a farmer is not a lord on his own farm, what is he? Would he give up being lord of his own land for a difference of forty or fifty cents in the price of wheat? Whether he would or not, he has done it. And so far, that has been his experience with the redistribution of wealth, though it was meant to be all in his favor.

As the wealth of a democratically constituted society increases, there is bound to take place a redistribution of it downward in terms of extra division. The social sense, those altruistic feelings that only a rich society can afford, public policy—all three require it. The pressure is irresistible. That explains the appearance and extraordinary growth during the past thirty years of "social expenditures" as a charge upon public funds, for health, education, recreation, mass culture, relief, pensions and so on, accompanied always by an increase of taxation upon the well-to-do and the rich. The graduated income tax, begun in 1914, taking more and more of very large private incomes, means simply a redistribution of wealth by taxation. It may go very far and still be economically feasible, but only so far as the total wealth of the country may be at the same time increasing. If it goes further than that, the public treasuries first go into debt and then begin to default.

It had gone already very far, and perhaps too fast, when in time of great economic trouble the New Dealers arrived, with but one consistent idea among them. That was to redistribute the wealth in a grand manner, according to social-science theories that worked out infallibly on charts, like pieces of mechanism working in a vacuum.

It has been a mistake to regard the New Deal from any point of view but this, because from any other it is incoherent, with such inscrutable contradictions as that of limiting production and raising prices in order that people should be able to buy and consume more, and so bring themselves back to prosperity. But from the point of view of that one idea, everything is clear. Every major undertaking of the New Deal has contemplated directly or indirectly a redistribution of the national wealth and income. Debasing the dollar and repudiating the redemption clause in Government bonds was to ease the debtor by giving him cheaper money with which to discharge his creditor. The AAA program was to redistribute the national income in favor of agriculture. The Blue Eagle was to increase the share of labor, although at the same time it limited the production of goods out of which real wages are paid, and this in order that prices might rise in order that the debtor class should be relieved and in order that the farmer's share should be increased, and so on.

One short question: Has it worked? To ask that question is like setting a serpent free in a menagerie.

The public debt is one answer. The Government deficit is another. And at a time when all the capital we possess ought to be acting in a dynamic manner, freely, to increase the production of divisible wealth out of which all wages, all debts, all income and all deficits must be paid, what is the case? Wealth is looking for holes in which to hide itself; it is running to and fro in the world, seeking places of asylum, and willing to pay for them. A rich man says: "Your proposition may be attractive, but the fact is I would not walk across the street to make a million dollars. Why? Because, in the first place, I have to risk three or four millions to make a million. If I lose the money, it is my loss. If I make a million, nearly two-thirds of it belongs to the Government. If I put aside on my books the two-thirds that belongs to the Government and then die before my income tax is due, the inheritance tax goes on everything I possess, including the two-thirds of a million that I have set aside on my books as belonging to the Government, and in that case it will cost my estate maybe $75,000 actual loss for me to have made a million."

What of the many? On the whole, for the greatest good of the greatest number, how has the great scheme of redistribution worked? One answer to that has been running in the news. If on the whole it had worked well, if only, for example, unemployment had been halved, a revolt of an overwhelmingly Democratic Congress against the President and his brain trust would not have occurred. Such was the meaning of that Washington drama.

Taunted on his extreme and sensitive left by those who had kept saying he had not gone far enough, suddenly the President sent his share-the-wealth tax message to Congress, suggesting that the tax power of the Government be employed for three purposes at once—retribution, reform and revenue. Higher taxes on the few, on the ground that they had enjoyed an unfair advantage at the expense of the many who had helped them to get rich; higher inheritance taxes, on the ground that it is not good for large fortunes to be handed on; and penalty taxes on the profits of big corporations because of their bigness.

Taunted still by those who said it was a political gesture and that he really didn't mean it, the President called a conference of his principal supporters in the Senate and the House. When the conference was over, the announcement was made on the White House steps that the President's share-the-wealth tax program would be annexed as a rider to a bill already pending in the Senate, called the nuisance-tax bill, which was only to renew certain emergency taxes that were about to lapse. This nuisance-tax bill had to pass by the next Saturday night, otherwise the taxes would discontinue and the Government would lose the revenue. Thus it was clear that the intention was to enact the President's share-the-wealth tax program in haste, with no time for discussion. The news writers so understood it and reported it. The President's soothfast supporters so announced it on the floor of the Senate. A bill began to be written under great pressure. The chairman of the Senate Finance Committee sat up all the next night with the Treasury experts, working on it.

But on the second day there was a sound from the country such as the New Dealers had not heard before, saying nothing on the merits of the thing proposed to be done, but very positively that it could not be done that way.

The sound was unmistakable. The brakes went down hard, there was a bad smell of rubber, and the skid was embarrassing. To the news writers, assembled again at the White House, the President said it was not he who had been running the traffic light. The idea of haste was not his. The newspapers had made that up. But even while he was saying this to the news writers, his personal supporters at the Capitol, sleepless from trying to get a law ready, were saying positively on the floor of the Senate that a law must be got ready and passed immediately because that is what the President said he wanted.

Only enough of this to shape the point. The rest of it may be found scattered in the pages of the Congressional Record and in the newspapers of the latter part of June.

What restrains the American democracy is a study now added to the intellectual perplexities of the New Deal. Who could have supposed that it would have made that sound against the way of doing a thing? Yet that is very significant. What the Supreme Court said in the NRA case was that the Congress, under the Constitution, could not surrender its legislative power to the President. Above the Supreme Court is a voice that is sovereign when it speaks, and now of a sudden that voice says: "The people themselves will make up their minds. The President shall not do it for them." And this is the instinct of self-preservation acting in a democracy.

Government by discussion therefore continuing, there was time to debate retribution and reform, and time also to weigh the solids. The President had said that the social amends he proposed would have a material issue. There would be revenue from it, and the Government needed the money to balance its budget. How much revenue? There was time to ask that.

The popular idea of how much may be got by holding the feet of wealth to the fire is absurd. After the President's loyal supporters in Congress had been up all of one night with the Treasury experts, acting under the delusion that they had heard him say he wanted the law immediately, they brought forth a tentative schedule of share-the-wealth tax rates. The rates went up to four-fifths of a very rich man's income and three-quarters of his whole fortune when he died, and not quite one-fifth of a big corporation's profits because of its bigness; and yet when the amount of additional revenue the Government might reasonably expect was calculated, it was only $340 million, whereas the Government had just spent in one year $7.3 billion and its deficit was more than $3.5 billion.

The President had particularly mentioned million-dollar incomes, indicating them for sacrifice. Let the rich bear more. Certainly. Almost nobody cares how much of the burden is put on million-dollar incomes. If by making a burnt offering of all of them we could propitiate our gods of evil, or solve any major social problem, or greatly reduce unemployment, most of us no doubt would join a procession to the hill of ritual.

In 1933, however, the last year reported for, the number of such incomes was forty-six and the total of these forty-six incomes was $81,558,981. Suppose the Government confiscated them entirely. To what extent would that relieve the burdens of the many? With Federal expenditures running at $7.3 billion a year, this sum of $81,558,981 would have supported the Government for about 98 hours. But as the Government had already received from these forty-six incomes the sum of $25,848,046 in taxes, all it could get by confiscating them entirely would be an amount to run the Government about 66 hours.

The arithmetic is disgusting. All share-the-wealthers possess an extreme facility with prodigious statistics and a corresponding infirmity with arithmetic. A statistical picture of the wealth of the nation and the distribution of its income is a new thing, and still imperfect. They focus on what they want and need of it to make an emotional case. It may be a statistical fact, true in itself, and yet in relation to the whole picture it may be false. When they divide a figure to represent the total annual product of divisible wealth by a figure to represent the total number of families, they do not consider what the divisor contains. It contains millions of Negro families living in cabins, and millions of hillbilly families, and all the ineffectives in a population of 125 million. These may be all below the line of bare subsistence, which is another statistical fiction, meaning the amount of income an average family should have to live as an average family should. But there is no such thing in fact or truth as an average family, and never was.

Last year, under the title "America's Capacity to Consume", the Brookings Institution produced a study of the national income, who gets it and what happens to it. Here the treatment is not of the taxable income, but of the nation's aggregate gross income, regarded as the total product of divisible satisfactions. One of the findings was that in 1929, the high year, 21 percent of the families received only 4 1/2 percent of the national income, and that rich families, who were one in 1,000, received all together as much as all the poor families in the country with less than $1,500 a year each, and the poor were 42 percent of the total.

And one of the conclusions was: "There has been a tendency, at least during the last decade or so, for the inequality in the distribution of income to be accentuated. That is to say, while the incomes of the masses of people were rising during this period, the incomes of those in the upper income levels increased with greater rapidity."

For such findings and for that conclusion—these among others—the book has been petted by divisionists and much quoted among them to prove that the concentration of wealth in the hands of a few is a growing social affliction.

The book proves nothing of the kind. A "decade or so" is a very short time. What the distribution of wealth was thirty, fifty or one hundred years ago, no one knows. There are no comparable statistics. Moreover, this "decade or so" was one ending in 1929, therefore a boom decade, in which speculative profits would be high in the high-income levels. So would the losses on the same levels afterward. According to the Government's figures, the number of individual incomes of $1 million or over in 1929 was 513, but in 1932 the number of them was 20.

Inequalities in the distribution of wealth may be, and probably are, as constant as the inequalities in the distribution of human faculties. Any intelligent person's guess would be that the concentration of wealth in this country is less than in any rich society that ever before existed.

The share-the-wealthers allege both the facts and their implications. They speak of the power of concentrated wealth. This, too, must be exaggerated. Wealth is not able by any might of its own to save itself from being divided. Is that power? For fifty years the statute books have been fattening with laws to limit and control the powers of great wealth and great incomes and great capital, such as the Interstate Commerce Commission, the Federal Trade Commission Law, the Antitrust Acts, innumerable laws of regulation, the Income Tax Law, compensation laws, minimum-wage laws, and so on. Have these been passed in spite of wealth? If in spite of it, where was its power?

In the book of the Brookings Institution there is a glimpse of a whole like this:

In 1929, how did the total product of divisible wealth, estimated at $81.9 billion, divide itself? Those receiving wages and salaries got 65.1 percent of it; individuals in business, including farmers, got 17.3 percent; investors and property holders, receiving rents, interest and dividends, got 14.9 percent, and the amount saved by business and corporations and added to capital was 2.7 percent—total, 100 percent.[6]

The share of employees—that is, the share of those receiving wages and salaries—was nearly one-tenth more than what it was in 1910; the share of property holders was a little less than in 1910.

The divisionists who quote the book will not quote that. They will not quote this paragraph from the fundamental conclusions: "No matter how much we may increase wage rates with a view to expanding purchasing power, we will not find available in the market places the goods which minister to the satisfactions of human wants unless they are produced. Whether we live under a wage, price and profit system, or under a completely communistic method of economic organization, it will always be true that the level of consumption or the standard of living can be raised only through the production of food, clothing, shelter, comforts and luxuries."

Which reduces to the truth, also, that you cannot raise the standard of living by dividing the wealth of the few. What is it that can be divided? Not the wealth really. Its great forms are indivisible. You cannot divide a railroad, or an electric-power system, or a pipe line, or a motor industry. It is only the income of the few that can be divided. And how much of that? Really all that can be divided is the amount the rich consume in living more than is consumed by an equal number of poor. And the amount of that, actually large, is yet relatively so little that if it were divided among the many, it would be despicable. Beyond this, what disposition do the few make of their large incomes? They provide a great deal of direct employment in their way of living; that may not be very important. They pay already the greatest part of all income taxes received by the Government. What of the remainder? The remainder is saved for reinvestment. The Brookings Institution went into that also. Roughly, half of all the large incomes is saved, which means one-half is invested again in the means to the further production of divisible things, and necessarily so, for this is a scheme in which wealth that does not work, and work in that way, is lost. Now, if the Government takes these large incomes entirely, which is the more likely—that it will itself save the half which hitherto has been saved and invest it effectively, or spend it?

Nor can the cost of the New Deal be paid, any more than the standard of living can be raised, by the simple practice of dedicating thereto the wealth of the few. After 1929 there was a broken boom to pay for. We had almost paid for it when the New Dealers arrived. Now what had been paid on account of the broken boom stands recapitalized in the debts and the deficits of the New Deal. Its deficits cannot be paid, its debts cannot be met, its budget cannot be balanced, except by a terrific increase in taxation. That is clear. But the necessary taxes cannot be paid except by a terrific increase in our productive exertions. This is a truth that nobody wants. It is a truth the divisionists conceal. There is nothing in their language about it. They tell only of a softer living from a redistribution of what already is. The more they are believed the harder it will be for everybody, rich and poor alike; and, if there is history, the many, when they find this out, will destroy their darling Gracchi.[7]

Congress raised the top rate of income tax to 79%, raised the estate tax and put in a graduated corporate income tax, but still did less than Roosevelt wanted. Raising taxes in a depression cost Roosevelt some of his political support.

The first federal pension plan had come in 1920, and then a federal pension for railroad workers in 1926. The Social Security Act was the big step—a compulsory plan for private industrial workers. The original plan, passed in 1935, envisioned "full reserve" funding, with a huge trust fund invested entirely in Treasury bonds—a prospect Garrett found appalling.

The Promise of Security

From "Security," the *Saturday Evening Post,* September 19, 1936

Hardly could there be a right more potent or elementary than the right of the individual to receive the whole of what he earns and to do with it what he likes. Industrial workers no longer possess that right. In the name of social security, it has been taken from them. Agricultural workers, Government employees, domestic servants and sailors are not included.[8] But if you are an industrial worker, the Social Security Act imposes upon you a law of compulsory thrift, and there is nothing you can do about it. Each week the Government puts its fingers into your pay envelope and abstracts a certain percentage.

It says: "The Government does this for your own good. When you are old, it will give the money back to you, with interest."

There may be an industrial worker who says: "I do not wish the Government to take it from me and give it back when I am old. It is mine. I have earned it. I want it now."

The Government says: "But this is our old-age insurance. It is social security."

The worker may say: "I will take care of my own old age."

The Government says: "The actuarial evidence is that you do not take care of your own old age—at least, not very well. Now the Government is going to do it for you."

The worker may say again: "Nevertheless, it is mine. I have earned it. I want to save it myself. I want to invest it myself."

The Government says: "The evidence is that you cannot be trusted to save it, or invest it, for yourself. Too often, when you invest it yourself, you lose it. The Government will now invest it for you in Government bonds."

The worker may say: "I would sooner buy a house. Nobody knows what Government bonds will be worth forty years hence."

The Government answers: "Social security is a house for everybody. Moreover, it is the law."

And the industrial worker is obliged to accept the law, to accept a status, to accept a card and to account for his time to the Government, for, whether he does or not, the Government each week will put its fingers into his pay envelope to abstract a percentage of what he has earned, and only by accepting can he get any of it back.

Besides old-age insurance, the Social Security Act provides also unemployment insurance for industrial workers. For this purpose the Government does not directly invade the worker's pay envelope. Instead, it lays a tax upon the total payroll. Who pays this tax? The employer writes the check, but he does not pay the tax. He only calculates it. Indirectly and finally, the wage earners pay it. Not that the amount of the tax will be cut out of wages. But a tax upon the payroll will be a weight upon wages. The incentives quickly to dispense with labor in bad times and slowly to reemploy it as times improve will be increased by the amount of the tax.

Come to it in principle: What is a tax on payrolls? A tax on payrolls is a tax on employment. It cannot be anything else. The trouble is unemployment, isn't it? The first problem of all is how to increase employment. Well, then, how a tax upon employment can conceivably tend to increase employment is a question that must be left to the brilliant young doctors of the new economics who say that all the old principles are obsolete, that we were fictitiously bound by them, that we must now learn to make new ones as we need them. They have not yet had time to answer it. Their solution may be to pass a law, saying: "New Principle No. 1: It shall be hereafter contrary to public policy for a tax upon a thing to affect the demand for it in any other way than to increase it."

Of the popular unguents, social security is the best seller. The demand for it is so insistent that no political store can afford not to stock it. The article that bears the New Deal label is the one most widely advertised. Since there is neither a pure-food-and-drug law nor a fair-trade-practice act that applies to political advertising, social security may be represented to people as a blessing conferred upon them by a warm-hearted Government. But there is no such thing. No government can provide social security. It is not in the nature of government to be able to provide anything. Government itself is not self-supporting. It lives by taxation. Therefore, since it cannot provide for itself but by taking toll of what the people produce, how can it provide social security for the people? The means of social security must first have been produced by the people themselves. All the Government can do is to take it from them and give it back, minus the cost of administration, which is to say, minus the increased cost of its own living.

There is no conceivable scheme of old-age insurance that does not require the sacrifice of present enjoyment for future comfort, nor any scheme of unemployment insurance that does not require less to be consumed in good times in order that there may be a reserve to live upon in hard times. Under any scheme of Government insurance, the young will support the old, as they always have, because there is no one else to do it; the employed will support the unemployed, because there is no way to feed and clothe and house the unemployed but by dividing with them the products of employment. The only difference is that, instead of people doing this in their own way among themselves, the Government will do it for them. The Government will take from the young and give to the old; it will take from the employed and give to the unemployed.

The argument is that when people do it for themselves, there are many failures and widespread human suffering. It is a responsibility the people discharge very unevenly. Let the Government do it for them and it will be done systematically, and people will be happier to know that they are relieved of the responsibility, and need not worry.

So the 20,000-word Social Security Act was invented. First, what did people want, almost more than anything else? Security. Having suffered from their failure to provide it for themselves, they were bound to welcome the thought of receiving it from a beneficent Government. Well, then, since it was so much wanted there had to be a way of doing it. The idea of doing it by forthright taxation—that is, by taking it out of the stream of current production, what was the only place it could ever come from—that was too simple. That would be no invention at all.

The invention turns out to be an enormous reserve fund—such a fund as was never imagined in the world before. This fund rises from a tax laid upon wages and payrolls. But for a period of years the fund will pay out less than it receives, so that it will grow; as it grows it will be invested at interest, and a time will come when the income of the fund from its own investments, plus the tax on wages and payrolls, will provide complete social security with no appropriation of public money by Congress at all. Social security self-sustaining!

The size of the fund is incredible. By 1965, the old-age insurance fund will amount to $36 billion and by 1980 to $47 billion, when its own earning power from investments will be nearly $1.5 billion a year.[9] What the unemployment insurance fund will amount to, nobody knows. It cannot be calculated because its disbursements cannot be foretold.

And how will funds of such magnitude be invested? They will be invested entirely in Government bonds. What is a Government bond? It is the promise of the Government to pay at some future time; it is, simply, the Government's promissory note. There is one little difficulty to be cleared up. The inventors have not mentioned it. How can the Government earn money by investing money in its own promissory notes? In one hand it holds the gigantic insurance fund; in the other hand it holds its own promissory note. These are shifted. The promissory note passes from the right hand to the left and the money passes from the left hand to the right. What has happened? The Government has given its promissory note to itself for money which it promises to return to itself with interest. Where will the interest come from?

Noah was going on the water, but he was not going to sea. Therefore, the critics who stood around telling him the ark was absurd were right only about the ark and not about Noah. There was something else they didn't know. Criticism has that limitation. It may be a mistake, for example, to take the Social Security Act in its obvious aspect. Regard it, instead, as a new instrument of Government power, and the light suddenly changes. Not only does it enormously extend the authority of the Federal Government to administer our everyday lives and well being; it delivers free into the hand of the Federal Government a fund that may very well represent the capital resources of the country. What form of government might survive after that would not matter. Its economic power would be absolute.

Conservatives in Congress grew alarmed at the prospect of an immense fund of Treasury bonds. They teamed up with New Dealers who wanted a quicker ramp-up of benefits and in 1939 passed the Federal Insurance Contributions Act (FICA), which made Social Security pay-as-you-go.

When Garrett wrote this, the total tax, employer plus employee, was 2% of the first $3,000 in income, and would remain unchanged until 1950; in 2008 the system, which had grown to include disability insurance and Medicare, took 15.3% of the first $102,000 in income.

The next selection is about the birth of another idea: that some workers have a right to bargain for themselves and some do not. Those who do not are covered by the National

*Labor Relations Act of 1935; those who do are said to be
"exempt." That distinction continues to this day. Here Garrett
writes of it when it was new.*

Status for Labor

"Status by Law," the *Saturday Evening Post,* November 30,
1940

Formerly in this country there was labor. If you were writing about it you would speak of wage earners, never of work people, as in England. This distinction was important. American labor was not a class in the Old World sense. Labor legislation was not class legislation. It concerned itself with economic relationships, in which the wage earner had that position just as the employer had his position, and there was no caste in it.

The great leader of the American labor movement was Samuel Gompers, to whom the thought of status was intolerable. All that he wanted for labor was a fair field in which to conduct its struggle for an equitable division of the product, and this, he said, was an economic struggle, not political. He resented the idea of government conferring benefits upon labor as such—anything, that is to say, in the current meaning of social gains. Let the division be just and let the wage earner do what he would with his wage, spend it, waste it or save it. Then he was free. But give him a serial number and a card in a grand social scheme devised for his security and benefit, and what was he? Rugged individualism was not a trait of the capitalists only.

All of that belongs to a past that was both wonderful and imperfect. There is now a working class, and its status is defined by law. This does not result from the fact that the law fixes a standard week and a minimum wage, nor from any law or legislation that touches all wage earners alike. All work people are wage earners; all wage earners are not work people. Some are exempt. That is to say, the law makes a distinc-

tion between citizens by dividing wage earners into two classes, one protected and one unprotected. For one class there is
the protection of a standard legal week of forty hours and pay
at one and a half times the regular wage for overtime; the
other class is free.

And the basis for this distinction is what? It is the kind of
work performed and the amount of wages received. Such is
the beginning of what Hilaire Belloc calls servile legislation,
toward a servile state.

The curious fact in our case is that legislation of that character was not intended. The history of it, therefore, is instructive; we recite it briefly to show that a step is the beginning of
all departure.

In the crisis of depression there arose the thought of fore-
shortening the hours of labor, with no change in the wage per
hour, as a way of spreading the work. Later the Blue Eagle
adopted it, not as a social doctrine but as a balance to what it
was doing for business and industry, which was to spread the
profit by limiting competition and regulating production.

Then came the vivid word image for it: "A floor under
wages and a ceiling over hours." And after that it was established as one of the irreversible social gains. When the Blue
Eagle died, and with it government by code, the Congress
passed the Fair Labor Standards Act, commonly called the
Wage-Hour Law.[10] Proceeding upon the constitutional right
of Congress to regulate commerce among the states, the law
says that in the production of goods that enter interstate commerce the standard labor week shall be forty hours and the
standard minimum wage shall be 30 cents an hour until 1945
and 40 cents thereafter.

This is the basic law. Public opinion very generously supported the obvious purpose of it. Anyone who objected on
grounds of abstract principle was silenced by reproach, or
smeared. Was he defending the sweatshop? Did he begrudge

to labor the niggardly reward of $12 for forty hours of exertion?

Moreover, the basic law did not make the class distinctions we speak of. Its terms were general; even the exceptions were general. For example, if agricultural workers were exempt, they were all alike exempt. But a general law has to act in particular cases. Congress cannot imagine beforehand all the practical problems that will arise. Therefore the law has to be administered, and to administer it was created a great bureau with power.

The name of this bureau is the Wage-Hour Administration, and it is invested with power to make rules and regulations having the force of law. Thus you come to the new thing, which is administrative law, not enacted at all, but promulgated by a bureau; and yet it is, in this case, a law that deeply touches the lives of the people, regulates their hours and wages, and fixes their status.

Having dealt for more than two years with a great variety of "impractical situations," meaning any situation in which it is clearly absurd to confine a man's work within a rigid frame of hours, the Wage-Hour Administration now promulgates that body of law under which wage earners are divided into two classes, by a distinction based upon the kind of work and the amount of reward.

As a wage earner, if your work is "predominantly intellectual," if it requires the "exercise of discretion and judgment," if the product is such that "cannot be standardized," if your knowledge is from "specialized intellectual instruction" and not "from apprenticeship," and, if your wage is $200 a month or more, then you are exempt. The law touches neither your hours nor your wages. You are free to make any bargain you like with any employer, on the ground, presumably, that you are not such an employee as could be easily exploited.

But, as a wage earner, if your work is "routine mental, mechanical or physical," if your product is such that it can be standardized, if your work is such that it can be performed by one who is endowed by only "general manual or intellectual ability," or "from training in the performance of routine mental, manual or physical processes," and if your wage is less than $200 a month, then, and for these reasons, the law gives you the status of a working-class person liable to be exploited; therefore, it will mind your hours and wages.

Belloc wrote his treatise on the servile state nearly thirty years ago. The tide making for it was already very strong, he said, even in England; yet he could hope it could be defeated by the reaction of free societies, especially one, "where a recent attempt to register and insure the artisans as a separate category of citizens has broken down." That was France. It was a universal tide. It went on rising in England, it engulfed France, and the kind of free society he trusted to counteract it has quite vanished from the world.

In 1947 Garrett argued that public housing also divided Americans into two classes.

Status for the Poor

From "Status for the Poor," *American Affairs,* April 1947

In a marble temple of classic design on the Washington Mall sits the heroic figure of a man who was born and raised in substandard housing. He never knew what substandard housing was. The term had not been invented. But he knew poverty, which is an indispensable part of the Lincoln legend, and he knew the proud American maxim that every schoolboy wrote in his copybook. The maxim was: *To be poor is no disgrace.* In the whole civilized world that was only true here, and it was true here because no stigma, no hint of caste, no sense of status attached itself to the condition of being poor.

But if it were today, the Lincoln family would be certified as underprivileged. The government at Washington would calculate its minimum budget. Several years ago the Farm Security Administration might have moved it to a decent house with a TVA icebox and an electric light. The life of the boy Abe would be minded by the public authorities. The Child Labor Law would probably forbid him to work—it certainly would if anything that he helped produce went down the river as interstate commerce. And at school, with a hot public lunch in his middle, he would be writing in his copybook, if copybooks were still in use: *The first of the Four Freedoms is freedom from want.*

Certainly the Lincoln family would be better off. Whether or not you would have had the eternal mystery of human greatness enshrined on the Washington Mall is a question that has no answer. Only the social fact is present. All the Lincoln families are better off, and if this is owing less to their exertions than in the welfare works of a benign government, they need to feel no humiliation on that account.

The welfare programs of benign government are at first impersonal. They are put forth in terms of public policy. The poor shall be acted upon not because they are poor but because they happen to be numbered among the underprivileged. One may belong with no feeling of shame, no sense of dependence and no loss of pride. There may be indeed a sense of injury, as if one had been deprived of something to which one was justly entitled.

But as the form of the Welfare State begins to rise, this fiction about the underprivileged as a product of social injustice, subject to grand measures of correction, begins to be unwieldy. There is more and more the impulse to act upon the poor as such. Amelioration is not enough. It is both false and unscientific. As a social idea the poor must have security; and since they are unable to provide it for themselves, or since they do not provide it for themselves, the government must see to it.

Then you get compulsory social insurance. This is something that must be done for and to the people for their own good. Compulsion, however, is not laid upon all alike. It applies only to those who live in the lower brackets below a certain level of income. Those in the higher brackets are exempt from compulsion and will be taxed for the benefit of the others. So now there are high-bracket people and low-bracket people and it is the law that makes a distinction between them. You may say still that the distinction is economic, not social, and this is for a while a supportable fiction. But it holds only until you come to public housing, which is the next step. There the line is struck, and now definitely a social status attaches to the condition of being poor.

Public housing never went far in the United States, outside of a few big cities. The status of being poor is now certified by other things, such as free breakfasts for your kids at school.

CHAPTER THREE NOTES:

1 Jean-Charles-Léonard Simonde de Sismondi, 1773-1842, French historian and socialist, argued that industrialism hurt the poor. He opposed Jean-Baptiste Say and the classical economists.

2 Charles Fourier, 1772-1837, French utopian socialist, proposed that traditional villages be replaced by "phalanxes" of 1,620 people each, living in communal quarters, forming what one fan called "a society of lovers and wild enthusiasts." Several U.S. utopian communities, including Oneida, were inspired by Fourier. All of them failed.

3 Multiply by 14 to get 2008 dollars (but not 2008's standard of living).

4 Lord Thomas Macaulay, 1800-1859, British pundit, member of Parliament, author of the five-volume *History of England*, which offered a Whig version of history.

5 A.L.A. Schechter Poultry Corp. v. United States, 295 U.S. 495, decided May 27, 1935, invalidated Roosevelt's main industrial control law, the National Industrial Recovery Act, as an unconstitutional delegation of legislative power to the executive branch. The ruling was 9-0, the liberals going against the New Deal—one of the few times they did.

6 Between 1930 and 2000 the share going to wages, salaries and employee benefits increased from 62% of national income to 72% (Bureau of Labor Statistics).

7 Tiberius and Gaius Graccus were the radical leftists of ancient Rome. Tiberius (d. 133 B.C.) pushed through land redistribution, and when the tribune Octavius vetoed it, Tiberius illegally had him removed. Later Gaius pushed through a law requiring grain to be sold at half-price. Tiberius and Gaius each died in riots, and their laws were repealed.

8 In 1950 Social Security was extended to farm workers and domestics, and soon after to self-employed farmers. State and local worker groups were allowed to opt in or stay out. When Garrett wrote, it covered about 60% of workers; by the late 1950s, it was 90%.

9 Multiply by 16 for 2008 dollars. Social Security's Old Age and Survivors Insurance Trust Fund on Dec. 31, 2006, was $1,844,304,000,000, all in Treasury bonds. It seemed a gargantuan sum, but it was small compared with the system's liabilities, and in any case was not a net asset of the government.

10 Passed in 1938, the Fair Labor Standards Act is still the federal law that requires payment of time-and-a-half to non-exempt employees after 40 hours in a week.

Chapter Four
ON THE LAND

A Kept Industry

From "Notes of These Times: The Farmer," the *Saturday Evening Post,* November 12-19, 1932

OMAHA—As you might start with agriculture in the extreme east of the country and pursue it westwardly, you would notice that the farm problem has certain topographical features. Toward the west it rises, very gradually at first, then faster, then suddenly, as you approach the Mississippi River regions, it rears to its utmost political and social climax.

There is agriculture in New England. There, as elsewhere, it is the most important activity of the human race; and yet you almost never hear of New England agriculture. There is agriculture in Pennsylvania, in many respects the finest in the world. It has its misfortunes and disasters, too, as when once its best cash crop, which was tobacco, went out from under it. It adopted potato culture instead, and so saved itself with no benefit of government. New York State, for all its urbanity, is one mighty farm, subject to all the vicissitudes of agriculture; you might say the same of Ohio. In neither of these states does the farm problem trouble the national mind.

In Indiana and Illinois it begins to do that, and from there it rises wildly to the proportions of a national calamity in

Iowa, Minnesota, North Dakota, South Dakota, Nebraska and Kansas. If you ask the Western farmer why this is, he will say it is because the Eastern farmers are so much nearer to the great city markets. They have that advantage. But when you talk to Eastern farmers, they complain that in the markets of Boston, New York, Philadelphia and Pittsburgh they compete desperately with Western produce.

You may think of other explanations. Although agriculture in the East is older, or perhaps because it is older, more of the tradition of self-containment has survived; much more than Western agriculture it sets its own table, never having quite forgotten that the only way a farmer can realize the full value of what he produces is to eat it himself. A pound of butter on his own table is worth just as much as a pound of butter on a city table, but for the pound of butter he sells he will receive that value, less the cost of packing, shipping and selling it to the city consumer.

A further explanation is that in Eastern agriculture land values are more settled. A farm is valued not as a speculation, not by what it might have brought in the late land fever or may bring again if the fever returns, but by what it may be expected year after year to produce in the way of sustenance for one family and a by-product for sale. Above everything else, the Eastern farmer knows some reasonable limit to what land will bear in the way of capital, debt, equipment and taxes.

Take an Iowa farm and consider the burden that has been laid upon it in the last twenty-five years by the farmer himself. The farm is the same or better. Its fertility has not declined. The regal corn, the fattened hog, the steer in the feed lot—all this is as fine as ever. Twenty-five years ago this farm was worth $100 an acre and could be easily made to pay a handsome dividend on that valuation. On the great rise in agricultural prices that began after 1900, continued for nearly twenty years and touched a dizzy peak in wartime, the price of that

76

farm rose to $400 an acre. There the fortunate owner sold out, for part cash and part mortgage, and retired to California.

Then came the deflation of agricultural prices. Now, with corn at twenty cents a bushel where it was two dollars, oats at ten cents where it had been forty-five, and hogs at four cents a pound where they had been fifteen, the owner of that same farm, having paid $400 an acre for it, part cash and part mortgage, may be unable to pay interest on the mortgage, to pay even his taxes. And with agricultural prices so low, the land is worth again only what it was twenty-five years ago—that is, $100 an acre, which may be less than the face of the mortgage.

If this were all that happened, it would be enough. But consider what a burden has been laid upon this land since that time twenty-five years ago. By taxation there has been laid upon it the cost of building and maintaining concrete roads, and in the same way the cost of a magnificent consolidated high school with its athletic field and tiled swimming pool. For this alone—the school—taxes have been increased as much as one dollar an acre. There has been laid upon it directly by the man who paid $400 an acre for it, the capital weight of a motortruck, a tractor, tractor equipment, electric light and power, and at least one automobile. And besides all this, where formerly the land supported one family, it must now bear the weight of two—namely, the family that acts upon it and the one in California that holds the mortgage. Although it may be the best agricultural land in the world, simply, it will not bear such weight—not so suddenly, at any rate. Neither the farmer saying, "it should," nor the Government saying, "it must," can so oblige it.

It is true that the farmers in Pennsylvania and New York have concrete roads and consolidated schools, but the land does not bear the whole weight, as it does in Iowa. It bears no more than it can afford, and the rest is absorbed by the urban and industrial people. The Western farmer asks: "Are we then condemned to do without these things, having no urban and industrial people with whom to share the cost of them?" This question, however, is too simple. As well ask why people cannot equally afford all things, why the soil of Iowa is richer than the soil of Vermont, or why South Dakota was not put where Pennsylvania is.

The Western farmer has at least this political advantage— that in his region the farm vote is dominant, whereas in the East it is swallowed up by the city vote. That is another reason why the farm problem rises to a great peak west of the Western Reserve. Yet with all these rationalizations to account for it, there is still a residue unexplained. You might almost suppose it was a chemistry from the soil or a subtle inheritance from the natural environment. As you drive from southern Iowa northwest toward Sioux City, the corn, the hogs, the cattle, the types of agriculture, are all the same, but the mood of Nature seems to change from tranquillity to brooding, with touches of slight weirdness in the landscape; and going only from one part of the state to another part is like climbing the hill of the farm problem. In southern Iowa there are areas— whole counties—where nine-tenths of the farmers, even in these times, are getting on; these are very little interested in the idea of a farmers' revolt, nor can they imagine that agriculture is going to perish with or without Government relief. But in northwest Iowa it is very different. There the sense of injury, disadvantage and impending disaster runs high.

Ask in Sioux City why this is so, why in this neighborhood the farm problem flares so easily into violent feeling, and they cannot say. In every state it is the same. Sore-minded areas and tough-minded areas, counties radical and counties conservative, unaccounted for by any thing correspondingly different among them as to the land, its opportunities or the diversities of character the people brought with them.

ST. PAUL—In about 1900 there arose in this country an anxiety about food. There was no more virgin land to be exploited—at least, none that was then supposed to be arable. Grain yields were declining because we had been mining the soil instead of farming it. Population had been increasing at a terrific rate, a million a year by immigration alone; and these immigrants, settling in the cities instead of going to the land, were consumers of food, not producers of it, as they had been in Europe. They were deserting agriculture for industry. So were many of our own people. The rural population was declining.

Our destiny was industrial. Our industry for the first time was invading the markets of the world, and we were wonderfully excited about it. Nevertheless, it gave us concern to think the time would soon come when, like Great Britain, we should be exchanging manufactured goods for food. This country, that had been so long feeding Europe, itself to become a food-importing nation! That was in many ways an undesirable sequel.

To postpone it as long as possible, the Government undertook as a matter of national policy to aid and promote American agriculture by means of education, propaganda, credit, indirect subsidy and science. This it did with unanimous approval. Congress freely appropriated money for a Federal organization of county agents to teach farmers better farming, for scientific research on yields and soil and blight and pest control, for loans, direct and indirect, to agriculture through Federal banks and revolving funds, for enormous reclamation works whereby rivers were made to irrigate deserts. Then costly experiments with dry farming on semi-arid land hitherto thought to be fit only for grazing, but which turned out to be fairly thirsting to grow wheat.

All this seemed intelligent at the time. Every new extension of agriculture was hailed with satisfaction and delight. And it was intelligent, probably as intelligent as any economic planning may be. We were planning our future food supply. No one could imagine going too far. Too much food?

Impossible. If we had a surplus we could easily sell it. We thought so. The whole world thought so. The anxiety that was moving us was more or less general in the world. Europe was wondering where she should get her food when the time came that this country would need its entire production for its own use.

What no one could foresee was change. And that is what no economic plan will ever be able to anticipate. If nothing unexpected had taken place, we should now be congratulating ourselves; we might even be erecting monuments to those who began, in 1900, to urge the promotion of American agriculture as national policy. Since then immigration has ceased, the birth rate has fallen, agricultural method has been so revolutionized by mechanical power that one man now does the work of three or four. The Wheat Belt has been pushed farther and farther north, countries that were unthought of competitors then, now are producing enormous quantities of food for export—and how to limit agriculture has become our national anxiety. Surplus is its ruin.

Agriculture having been stimulated in all other countries, the world does not require the American surplus, or so little of it that it will not pay above the cost of production to have it.

The farmer says—and not without reason—that since the Government inflated the body of agriculture, extended the area of it, intensified the competition within it by encouraging people in excessive numbers to remain on the soil, increased the debt upon it by enormous injections of credit, and so on, it now has some moral obligation in respect to the surplus. He says the Government must find some way to get rid of it. Well, but the Government does not know what to do with the surplus. It cannot eat it. As a last resort, it tried buying it up with public money, hoping meanwhile to persuade the farmers to produce less, but the farmer finds himself in a momentum of production and does not know how to produce less, and presently the Government had to stop buying the surplus for fear of breaking the United States Treasury.

It is interesting, even though without profit, to wonder what would now be the state of facts if the Government had never touched agriculture, to subsidize or promote it. That is to say, if instead of trying to plan our future food supply, we had left it entirely to the natural event, what would have happened? All the unexpected things that have happened would have happened just the same, so that in no case had we anything to worry about. We only thought we had. There would still be plenty of food. But if the Government had not interfered, it is probable that the movement of population from rural to urban life would have been naturally greater. With what effect? Probably the pressure of population upon industry would have been enough greater to check the extraordinary rise of industrial wages which created the disparity between the people of agriculture and the people of industry. The industrial population might now be greater than it is, and the rural population smaller, with a better balance of consuming power. Perhaps.

It is certain, however, that the United States Treasury would be better off by some four or five billions to represent the cost of promoting, assisting, extending and financing agriculture; it is certain, also, that there would have been much less speculation in land and much less debt upon it now. All the forces of land speculation assisted the Government to promote and extend agriculture. They were not thinking of the food supply; they were interested only in the fact that a farmer brings value to the land, whoever he is, however he gets there, for whatever reason he stays. A great deal of the money spent by the Government in aid of agriculture was captured at last by the speculators who sold the land either direct to the Government for its reclamation works or to the hundreds of thousands of people fostered in agriculture by Federal policy.

DES MOINES—The economic plight of agriculture at the present time is no worse than the common lot; in all human terms it is better, for, whatever else happens, it will have shelter, food and warmth within its own resources.

Possibly a few years hence it will appear that what now is taking place was necessary. Land was overcapitalized. When prices were high, it was valued up to the hilt and mortgaged accordingly. Now land is in a process of devaluation, which means that agriculture is scaling down its debt. In the individual case it may be harrowing.

When a piece of land that was valued at $300 an acre and mortgaged up to $150 is foreclosed under the mortgage, what happens? It goes to another farmer, or it may go back to the same one, at a deflated value. Suppose every mortgage in the state of Iowa were foreclosed. You could hardly imagine anything worse. Yes, but what, then, would the mortgagees do with the land? They would have to sell it back to the farmers; there is no one else to buy it.

SIOUX FALLS, S.D.—If there are two problems that may be said deeply to concern agriculture as a whole, they are, first, excessive debt; second, excessive competition. And both have been intensified by the Federal Government. For twenty years the Government has been competing with private agencies to pump credit into agriculture. First it set up a Federal Farm Loan Board and under it a system of Federal land banks and a system of joint stock land banks. These between them have loaned more than two and a half billions on the land. Next it set up a system of intermediate-credit banks and a system of agricultural credit corporations. Then it created the Federal Farm Board, with a revolving fund of $500 million, which was to be employed for any helpful purpose. The two purposes for which, mainly, it was employed were most extraordinary. First the Federal Farm Board loaned money to the farmers to enable them to buy their own crops, with intent to impound them and so stabilize prices; and second, when prices were still not stabilized, the Federal Farm Board itself went into the wheat market, the butter market, the cotton market, and elsewhere, and bought up the surplus at the Government's risk.

If it had done nothing more than to inject enormous quantities of public credit into agriculture, the Government would have responsibility enough for the excessive competition now so bitterly complained of; Federal credit did undoubtedly enable a great many people to remain in the margins of agriculture who would otherwise have been squeezed out by the law of survival. But in other ways the Government was acting to intensify competition. For twenty-five years it has been promoting and extending agriculture by every means it could think of, and stressing always the commercial side of it. Agriculture as a business. Low-cost production. Profit.

Whether it had been better or worse for those sustained in agriculture by Federal assistance to be squeezed out is another question. Some would have abandoned agriculture entirely; others might have retired only from the competition of commercial farming, for a self-contained life on the soil.

In any case, having sustained them there, the Government now does not know what to do with them or for them but to go on sustaining them. Having once begun to interfere, it has never been able to stop. And the dilemma to which it must have come is already present. The Reconstruction Finance Corporation now is lending public money, with one hand, to the Federal Farm Board to enable it to continue withholding a surplus of agricultural products, and, with the other hand, to the Department of Agriculture for distribution to farmers who need to be assisted to plant more crops. That is to say, public money is being loaned to agriculture for two purposes at one time—namely, to impound a surplus of agricultural products and to increase the production of them—literally.

No wonder the farmer is bewildered. Nor is he grateful. His feeling against the Federal Farm Board and against the beneficent Government ranges from indifference through cynicism to bitterness. The Federal Farm Board has become the goat for all the disillusionment there is about Federal farm relief. What it has cost the Government is not what bothers him. But when he reads that the Cotton Stabilization Corporation, created and financed by the Federal Farm Board, paid its president $75,000 a year, and that the Farmers' National Grain Corporation, also financed by the Federal Farm Board, to stabilize the price of wheat, pays its general manager $1,000 a week, the disgust is untellable. And he makes a curious further indictment—curious as coming from the farmer first—that the Federal Farm Board became a paying refuge for too many professional farm leaders, now derisively called "farm reliefers." Wherein are both reason and unreasonableness; wherein, besides, it is becoming apparent that what now overtakes agriculture, to everybody's dislike, is the common fate of a subsidized industry.

Then came the New Deal. Six years before that event, in the Saturday Evening Post of April 2, 1927, Garrett had written that any attempt to guarantee farm incomes would entail crop controls. "It would mean that a farmer could not break open a new field or change the character of his production without a permit." And he was right.

A Kind of Progression

From "Plowing Up Freedom," the *Saturday Evening Post,* November 16, 1935

It may appear that there is a disability in the point of view of those who criticize what the President calls "the kind of farm program under which this nation is operating today." They take certain premises for granted, such, for example, as that we believe in minority rights, that a man who owns a farm in fee simple is lord there, and that we live in a free system.

But suppose the principles these critics take for granted—principles hitherto inviolate in our system—are taken by the other side to be worn out, and, for purposes of a new system, obsolete. In that case, what we are debating is not a farm program, or whether it will work, but a philosophy of government of which the farm program is a singular manifestation. Let that idea be applied to the contradictions and see what happens.

There is at first the AAA program to control production. The basis of it was to be voluntary. Every farmer should be free to sign or not to sign. No one was to be coerced. Well, handlers, middlemen and processors, perhaps, but farmers no. Or, at least, if there was to be any coercion of farmers, it should be the farmers doing it to themselves, by the democratic process of majority consent. Such were the representations.

But how could anyone suppose that a scheme for limiting production to raise prices, with millions of free farmers involved, might be managed on a voluntary basis, everyone at liberty to come in or stay out? The very success of it generates its failure, for as it begins to succeed and prices improve, a free minority will increase production until there is a surplus again.

"As is well known," says the Secretary of Agriculture,[1] "participation in any acreage-adjustment program was originally voluntary. Later, under special legislation relating to cotton and tobacco, features penalizing non-cooperation were introduced. Farmers themselves demanded this change."

Not all farmers demanded it. A minority did not want it. A majority of the cotton farmers did not vote for it until the representatives of the AAA program had been through the South exhorting them to demand a law of compulsion, for unless they did, the Government could not continue to hold up the price of cotton and they would all be ruined.

Once resort has been made to compulsion, there is a kind of progression in it. Before the law of compulsory limitation was laid upon cotton, the AAA referred it to cotton farmers and was able to assure Congress that a majority wanted it. But when it came to potato control, this year, the method was first to impose the law of compulsion and then provide that after one year of it, farmers may vote on how they like it.

This extraordinary law was enacted last August as an amendment to the Agricultural Adjustment Act. The device employed is the same as used to limit the production of cotton and tobacco. The law does not forbid you to grow potatoes. Nothing so direct and simple as that. It assesses a tax of three-quarters of one cent a pound, amounting to 45 cents a bushel, upon the first sale of potatoes, all alike, everywhere. The law then goes on to say that the Secretary of Agriculture shall guess how many potatoes the total population can afford to buy in one year at a reasonable price; and when he has guessed and proclaimed the quantity, he shall apportion it among farmers who apply, and say to each of them like this: "Your share in the total crop, determined according to Sections 204, 206 and 207 of the law, is so many bushels. For that number of bushels, and no more, you may receive tax-exemptions stamps, which, when they are affixed to a standard Federal package, will indicate that your potatoes are tax-free." A sale of potatoes will require either this stamp or proof of tax paid. The penalty for bootlegging potatoes will be a $1,000 fine, and for the second offense, fine with imprisonment, both to seller and buyer.

That is the law. It is the law of potatoes for 1936. As the law stands, it will be a crime next year for a farmer, on his own land, to grow a potato and sell it but by permission of a Federal bureau, in a Federal package, bearing a Federal stamp. It will be a crime for you to drive out to a farm and buy an ordinary sack of potatoes for the cellar bin. If you do it once, and get caught, it will cost you $1,000. If you are caught a second time, you will be imprisoned, along with the farmer.

Thus production control brings its own absurd and logical sequel to pass—so absurd that the AAA had no sooner received the Potato Control Act from Congress than it began to think of ways of not enforcing it, and yet logical, because 6 million farmers will not voluntarily, all as one, bind themselves to sell only so many potatoes each; 6 million farmers cannot trust themselves not to forget their agreements if the price of potatoes goes up; and, provided it were otherwise, then what of those who would go to the land and begin raising potatoes if access to the land were free? So, if you are going to raise the price of potatoes where there is already a surplus of potatoes, a surplus of labor and a surplus of land, you must resort to compulsion. And what is true of potatoes is true in due time of any other crop.

The whole AAA is founded upon a price obsession. It proceeds upon the theory that the principles that are supposed to govern industry may be applied to agriculture. Kill the surplus. Limit production. Raise the price.

It is true, of course, that industry stops producing when it cannot sell. It is true also that industry sometimes limits production to control the price, but this can never be for long in a free economic system, because the profit at that price will attract competition. Never in modern times could the idea have occurred to industry, when it has had to stop producing for want of demand, that the way out would be to produce still less and raise the price. Never did it get itself out of a depression by that magic. On the contrary, when demand falls, its first thought is to reduce costs, and then prices, in order to increase demand. And that is the way it would have worked itself out of this depression if the Government, through the NRA, had not interfered.

But even if the AAA had not got the principles that govern industry upside down before trying to apply them to agriculture, the fact would still remain that agriculture is not industry. If the principles that really govern industry were applied to agriculture, at least one-third of the people in it would be eliminated. Then what?

Commercial farming is one thing; it requires capital, skill, enterprise and business management of a high order. Farming as a way of life is another thing. Probably one-third of the cultivated land is owned by people who produce only one-twentieth of the commercial product. These are the people with little or no capital; poor renters, poor tenants, sharecroppers, and then the small owners of lean and hilly land who in a peculiar sense belong to the soil and abide with Nature on minimum terms. They are the marginal and submarginal people. They would be marginal and submarginal in any situation. In industry they would be the first to lose their jobs and the last to get them back. The soil is kinder. It never disemploys them; it only cuts their wages.

In a third aspect, agriculture is an emergency refuge. When industry begins to fail, the unemployed who can and remember how instinctively go to back to the land. That was happening. Between 1929 and 1933, 2 million people left the industrial centers to find subsistence on the soil. In Illinois the number of farms increased 18,000; and most of this increase, amounting in some southern counties to as much as 25 percent, was on poor land, of course, because that was the cheap land.

Here were people taking care of themselves, with no benefit of Government, even though on a low standard of living; but in the act of taking care of themselves they were interfering with the program for Government to take care of agriculture. The AAA was leasing out of production 40 million acres of land, thereby creating idleness of land, idleness of equipment, even unemployment on the farms, in order to limit production; and here at the same time were people making new farms on poor land.

Said the Secretary of Agriculture, "Here is a dilemma. On the one hand, the progress of agriculture absolutely requires a limitation of farm production and, therefore, of farm employment. On the other hand, national expediency forbids closing the rural country to the urban unemployed."

At the base of this dilemma was this obvious fact—that it is impossible really to control agricultural production unless you control also the surplus land and the conditions under which people may have access to it.

Observe, therefore, the rise of the great land program. Having undertaken to remove a surplus of agricultural commodities, it becomes necessary for the Government to remove a surplus of land.

A land program had been already initiated in a casual way. In his book *New Frontiers*, the Secretary of Agriculture says that in a moment when the President was struck by the "foolishness of spending millions in public-works money to irrigate new land while at the same time the AAA was taking land out of use," he said let the Public Works Administration use $25 million of its money to buy and retire enough poor land to offset the new land it was bringing in; and that was done.

To buy millions of acres of surplus land was a thought that crystallized later. No such land program was ever formulated by Congress. It evolved in the bureaus. The authority for it is found in bills whereby Congress delegated general policy-making powers to the President. The controlling idea is one that Congress would probably have been unable to seize in the pure form. Land is a collective asset. The right of private ownership is limited. That is the pure idea. Unrestricted private ownership, a man being lord of his own land, is a kind of anarchy.

"Our system of unrestricted private ownership," says the Secretary of Agriculture, "developed in a reaction against the restraints of an earlier tenure." That is to say, the American people wanted land to be free, but having it free, they wasted it and wasted themselves. They cannot be trusted with free land, really.

"Complete license to buy and sell land, and use it in any manner that seems desirable," says the Secretary of Agriculture, "ultimately burdens the farmer with heavy fixed charges... On overcapitalized farms, even a small decrease in the income from products sold may bankrupt the farm operator; it will certainly make his farm ownership illusory."

However illusory ownership may have been under a system of free agriculture, when the Government comes to lay its hands upon the surplus land, every piece of it is owned, and is owned by people who cling to it. To remove the surplus land from agriculture, it is first necessary, therefore, to remove the people. The land shall be added to the public domain. But to what shall the people be added? Where shall the Government move them? To other and better land. That is the only answer. But they cannot take their houses with them, nor can they afford to build new houses and new barns on the better land. The Government must do all that.

Thus the land program entails a resettlement and colonizing program of which the limits and responsibilities are still unknown. It involves the regrouping of masses of the rural population; it involves changing the lives and habits of all those marginal and submarginal people, and the task of minding them afterward. So there is a Resettlement Administration, with a program that contemplates the purchase of 10 million acres of land and the responsibility to transplant and rehabilitate millions of human beings.

The ideality of it is dramatic. To abolish the rural slums, to save hopeless farming from itself, though it were only for the sake of the children; to reestablish the broken third of agriculture on good soil and to put the lean and miserable land to grass and forest and parks.

Unfortunately for the ideal intention, it is bound to get distorted in the execution. The difficulties of doing for people what rationally is good for them are very discouraging. This you will come to realize when you come to look at resettlement transacting on the ground.

Let it be Southern Illinois. The project you are going to see is in Pope County, and it involves all the typical problems of resettlement.

First the Federal people, in collaboration with the state authorities, select the area to be acted upon. An area of 7,000 acres is demarked. Some of the land is good, some of it fair, some of it poor, and people are farming it indiscriminately. Naturally, the Government will have to buy all of it. The bad land it will keep and put to forest; the poor land it will keep also, and put it to grass for purposes of controlled communal grazing; but the good land will be made into model farms, of just the right size, each with a suitable house and proper equipment; and these farms will be sold back to the people on easy terms. There will be a community center, of course; and good roads and recreational facilities, a school, bus service for the children, and forever a good life.

The next step is to get options on all the land. Agents are sent out to get them. They are salesmen. Their only business is to come back to headquarters with the options. With an owner who is unwilling to sell, they try threats and then promises. The threat is that if the owner does not sell, the mighty Government will condemn his property and take it anyhow, probably at a lower price; or the threat that if the owner does not sell, the Government will buy out everybody else and forget him and he will be left there all alone. The promise is that one who signs will receive each year 100 days' work at cash wages on the project—work such as road building, park making, forestation and erosion control.

Nearly everybody does sign. In a lovely log cabin with a shaded porch, flowers and vines around it, is a woman who says no, they have not signed. She likes to show it to you. Her man built it. She was born on this ground. It may not be much, but she is attached to it. Can the Government take it from them, really? She asks you. Maybe, if you are a lawyer, you can tell her what to do.

In a neat frame house is a woman, seventy, who helped her man clear the ground by taking herself one end of a cross-cut saw. There is her man on the porch, ill. That is their only trouble. They need a little relief for that reason. But why does the Government want their land? It says it wants their land because it is no good. The land she helped her husband clear is no good! Why not? All these years they have lived on it. There is nothing the matter with it, only that it has been a little overcorned.

A young man plowing corn in a creek-bottom field says he has signed. Will he buy one of the new farms? He says: "How'd I know? There ain't no new farms yet. Ain't nobody seen one and ain't nobody knows what they will cost. Looks like I'd get out and find another piece of land." Cheap land, he means. Land like this again, if the Government leaves any of it free.

On one porch, the Federal agents argued from eight in the morning until nearly dark, the man wavering and his wife saying all the time, "No." They had come from St. Louis, back to the land they knew, and they were doing well, owing nobody, saving a little money. Their land was good. But the man signed. Then, when they took their copy of the contract to read it by candlelight, they found a sharpness in it. All Government contracts are sharp. The sharpness in this one was that while they had bound themselves on a certain date to deliver title, the Government had not bound itself to pay at any particular time.

"And look at what the Government is going to tear down and throw away," the woman says. "This house. Come in and see." She is right. It is a nice house—a parlor, a dining room, spare bedroom, running water in the kitchen. And yet not so charming as the little log cabin that will be destroyed by the

92

mighty Government if the women whose man built it weakens.

Well, then, having signed their farms away, these people apply for the work that was promised. There is already some road work going on. But before they can go to work, they have to sign a pink paper in small print. That was not in the bargain. All the same, they have to sign it to get the work; and when, at night again, by lamplight, they read the small print, they discover that they have applied for rehabilitation, whether they wanted it or not, thereby achieving the dependent status of rehabilitation cases, each with a file number. Moreover, they have signed a binding contract to abide by all the rules and regulations that may hereafter govern the project.

The consolation is that they have the work. Presently the wages are due. But when a man goes to get his wages, he is asked to sign one paper more; and this one, if he signs it, will be an agreement to leave half his wages with the Government as a down payment on an ideal farm that no one has seen because it does not yet exist; and no one, not even the Government, knows what it is going to cost. If a private real estate company did business in that way, it would encounter the law. That is, perhaps, a trifling reflection. Motives and intentions are not in question. Particularly, there is no profit motive.

The trouble is people. The administrators of the resettlement program are still innocent of one of the old agricultural maxims—namely, that poor land seeks the poor farmer. There is such a thing as a good farmer on poor land, or a poor farmer on good land, but it is most unnatural. The assumption that a poor farmer translated to good land will become a good farmer is bound to provide many disillusionments; on the other hand, if and as it happens, you return to the dilemma. If he increases his production he becomes a liability to the AAA program of saving agriculture by limiting production.

Such is "the kind of farm program under which this nation is operating today." Regarding it as one program of several parts, it is inconsistent with itself. The question is whether the inconsistencies are of principle or of the action only. The answer is determined by the point of view. If you assume the existence of a free economic system, they are of principle; if you assume the end of the free system, they are of action only, and all confusion may be thus explained. You cannot expect to see a new order created without confusion.

In the latter point of view, observe how the contradictions disappear. Observe that the farm program is entirely consistent with the idea of a totally regimented agriculture. Observe how consistent it is with a deistic theory of government—a government, that is, all-seeing, all-powerful, all-wise, undertaking to administer the lives of its people, to mind them in their occupations, to arrange their incomes, to correct their past individualistic mistakes, to absorb their troubles, to regroup them on the land, to admit them conditionally to agriculture, to appoint what they may grow to eat and what they may grow to sell.

But this is happening. The Government is doing it. The freedom of American agriculture is trapped.

It cannot be done to agriculture alone. It cannot stop there. If the writing of the new order is more legible in agriculture than elsewhere, as it is, that is only because agriculture has been less resistant than industry.

In U.S. v. Butler, announced Jan. 6, 1936, the Supreme Court decided in a 6-3 vote that the Agricultural Adjustment Act was unconstitutional. But it was reenacted in a different form, the court changed, and much of it survived.

Never a Prayer

From "Give Us This Day," the *Saturday Evening Post,*
June 24, 1939

YAKIMA VALLEY, Wash.—The Reclamation Bureau has already brought water to 3 million acres of desert land in the eleven Western states. On its thirty-four irrigation projects, where before there was nothing but sagebrush, cactus and reptiles, there are now 50,000 farms, 257 cities and towns, nearly 1 million people, 900 schools and 1,000 churches. There was no economic necessity for it. All of this wealth might have been created where it rains, with much less outlay of original capital. We did not need the agriculture, really, and in any case it contributes less than 2 percent of the country's total annual crop values.

But what is one saying? There was no economic necessity for skyscrapers, either. If reclamation is an economic mirage, so is the New York skyline. Let it be the oasis motive. Each of the Government's reclamation projects as it comes to view gives rise to the oasis emotion and you forget your economics.

Here is one of them—the Yakima valley, with a record of twenty years of tree fruits, quality vegetables, dairy products, poultry and eggs and sugar beets. The Reclamation Service is proud of it. If you like irrigated agriculture it is lovely. Whether you like it or not it has a rich surface. Living is in the good sign. The shops are stocked with New York styles and the best merchandise. The life has an insular feeling, which may seem strange at first; then it occurs to you that an oasis is an island.

The only security the island has is the certainty of crops. In the 1,000 churches on the Reclamation Bureau's thirty-four projects there was never a prayer for rain. All agriculture under the irrigation ditch has, of course, that advantage, but to the winds of economic hazard it is no less exposed than agriculture under the rainfall, and it has some liabilities peculiar to itself. Partly, the rich surface it presents to the eye is owing to the fact that it is, of all agriculture, the most expensive. Those engaging in it, besides requiring special skill, must have capital. Thus, it will be able for a while to absorb a great deal of distress without showing it to every stranger. The overhead is very high, owing to the capital investment in dams and canals, and to the cost of maintaining them and minding the water.

Always the Bureau of Reclamation has underestimated the expense and overestimated the profits of irrigated agriculture. In the beginning it expected the settlers to pay back to the Government the cost of the works in ten annual installments, principal only, no interest. That was more than the settlers could pay. The time was doubled, making it twenty years; and that was still too hard. Then a plan of payment based on the annual value of crops was tried, and when that did not work out so well the period of payment was extended to forty years. Even so, in 1932 there was need for a general moratorium.

Now, if you ask, "Is this farming profitable?" you will find profit even here to be the faithless flit-jade that is so bitterly complained against in all farming whatever; and even more fickle and suddenly vanishing here, owing to the highly specialized character of the farming, the expensiveness of it and the fact that so much of its product is exotic. You will find farmers borrowing money from the Government to spray their fruit trees, others tearing out their trees because there is no money in the fruit, and borrowing from the Government again to go into something else. In short, this irrigated agriculture, basically subsidized by the Government in the first place, has become dependent upon Government aid and subsidy, like agriculture everywhere else.

Certainly the expenditure of public funds on reclamation, whatever else may be said for it, bears not in any way toward a solution of the agricultural problem. But there is found for it a new significance. It will solve, at least in part, the problem of resettlement.

"We are now engaged in the greatest construction program in the history of the Bureau of Reclamation," says the commissioner. "When these projects are completed, opportunity will be provided for a total of 825,000 on 41,600 farms and in cities and towns as yet unlocated."

Looking at Grand Coulee Dam, the President said: "There are thousands of families in this country. . . who are not making good because they are trying to farm on poor land, and I look forward to the day when this valley is dammed up to give the first opportunity to these American families."

The need is critical and exceeds the means of satisfaction. The Commissioner of Reclamation says: "If it were possible by some engineering legerdemain to complete overnight the network of canals in order that we might deliver water to each farm in the 1.2 million acres to be served by the Grand Coulee Dam, we would not be able to provide farms for more than three-fifths of the families which are now refugees from the Great Plains drought alone."

It seems then a pity to speak of the unsentimental realities. The people who are on poor land are poor people, and that is why they are on poor land. If they had that amount of capital which would be the least one could start with in irrigated agriculture with any hope to succeed, they would be already on better land. There is plenty of good land under rainfall, costing much less per acre than irrigated land—so much of it, in fact, that in order to keep millions of acres of it out of production the Government is paying the farmers who own it an annual subsidy; and the amount of that annual subsidy is greater than the total capital cost of the Grand Coulee Dam.

As for the "refugees from the Great Plains drought," to whom the commissioner holds out the Promised Land, when you see them in California, where they are called dust bowlers, you are reminded that if your aunt could wear your uncle's boots she might be your uncle. If they had the capital that is necessary to make even a start in irrigated farming under Grand Coulee Dam, they would not be refugees on public relief. Where will they get the money? If the idea is that the Government is obliged to restore them to the land and settle them on it, providing not only the land but all the means, under a great social program of resettlement, then it would cost far less to buy them land in Indiana and settle them there.

SAN JOAQUIN VALLEY, Calif.—Prunes have been selling at nine dollars a ton as feed for hogs, raisins at five dollars a ton as feed for cattle, and very good feed they are. Not so long ago, land in prunes and raisins might be expected to yield a profit of $400 to $500 an acre. That was bonanza. And what happened to it? Many things happened to it, but mainly one. The profit was mobbed; and the valley turned to cotton, of all things, for a cash crop.

Not so long ago, an orange grove in Southern California was thought to be a competence forever. Now the Surplus Commodities Corporation buys one part of the crop, on condition that another part will be cast into the sea; the third part is sold under the state pro-rate law, and the owner of an orange grove is lucky to be solvent.

I was once in Fresno, talking to the fig growers who had been in trouble with too many figs; but they were happy again and starting all over under a self-imposed agreement to pool their sales and limit the quantity, which would permit the price to rise and bring the profit back.

I said: "What is all that empty land I see out there?"

"That?" they said. "It's what you call it. Empty land."

"Will it grow figs?"

"Of course it will grow figs."

"Then," I asked, "how are you going to keep people from putting fig trees on it if you make fig growing profitable again?"

98

They did not know how. And again the fig profit was mobbed. Since then a state law has been passed under which, although a man cannot be stopped from planting trees, the amount of fruit he may legally sell can be limited by a vote of two-thirds of the producers.

The "newest horticultural specialty of Southern California" is the avocado. Anywhere in the ten southernmost counties you will see big board signs like this:

Do You Need Money? Grow Avocados.

It is as simple as that. And it is a sight to see young avocado groves running away with the hillsides.

It will be remembered that the Agricultural Department of the Los Angeles Chamber of Commerce put forth a booklet, and then another one, entitled, What You Should Know About Avocados—first all the hard, unromantic facts that were known for sure, and then the warning to bonanza seekers. Either the price of the avocado will decline to a point at which the profit will be disappointing, or, if not that, then the price of land will rise to absorb the profit.

The price of avocado land now is from $400 to $500 an acre. Everybody knows what will happen. Yet many think they can beat it before it happens. Let the profit continue for a little while and the avocado business will be overdone; and when it has been overdone and the demand for avocados is choked, two-thirds of the growers will ask the state for a pro-rate law. The Commissioner of Agriculture will take thought and say yes. Then an Avocado Crop Board will be set up to tell each avocado grower how many pounds of the fruit he may send to market. If he wants to produce more, that is all right, but he may not sell more. Maybe he can eat it.

This liability of the profit to be mobbed is acute in California, probably because here, more than anywhere else, land and crops are as dice in a game for high stakes; but the same liability besets agriculture generally. It is true that in business a high profit attracts competition and will, in time, be worn down. The difference is that a man in business is generally working with his own capital, or, if he borrows, must prove the economic case for it, whereas the farmer, since he turned from the tough country banker to the Government for credit, has been so overwhelmed with it that very often now it is literally true that his only capital is debt.

First the Government set up for the farmer a system of land banks to make mortgage money cheaper and more plentiful; then a system of intermediate credit banks to make short-term credit easier; then a system of banks to lend money to farmers' co-operative credit associations, and a Central Bank for Co-operatives.

There is a Production Credit Corporation that made, last year, 243,000 loans to enable farmers to produce crops. There is a Commodity Credit Corporation that lends money to the farmer who wants to store his crops on the chance that prices will rise; if prices fall, the Government takes the grain or the cotton, and takes also the loss. There is a Surplus Commodities Corporation to buy up surplus quantities of staple crops and dispose of them somehow.

The farmer may now borrow money from the Government for all purposes of farming—to buy the land, to equip it, to buy fertilizer and seed, to hire labor, to harvest the crop. It is only another riddle, the Government with the right hand paying farmers to diminish production while with the left hand it lends others the money to enable them to produce.

There are still farmers, many of them, who own their land outright and work with their own capital. These are obliged to meet the competition of those who, if they fail, have nothing to lose.

What would be the effect upon any trade, let it be the grocery trade, if it were declared that any man who wished to do so were entitled to open a grocery store and borrow money

100

from the Government to do it? Would there be any profit in the grocery business, or a living even?

If the annual agricultural production that is directly enabled by Government loans were eliminated, there would be no surplus problem—no problem, that is to say, of surplus commodities. There would still be the problem of surplus people on the soil, but that is not the agricultural problem.

TUCKAHOE, New Jersey—For years I had been running my own farm on a share-profit basis, plus a guaranty to the manager. But there was never any profit to share. This year I rented the farm to him—the land, the buildings, the power equipment, the livestock, the orchard, the house he lives in, and all, for the total consideration of one dollar plus maintenance. Everything he makes will be his and I shall be saving money.

If my advice will only keep him away from the Government-lending agencies that are tempting him to go into debt, I dare say he will make some money. As I watch him I notice that he uses the tractor much less and the mules much more, having learned already the three-mule hitch. Only once have I seen him use the truck to haul cornstalks to idle mules in the pasture, and then I called his attention to it. I notice that he is buying less fertilizer in bags, whereas formerly, when we were halving the cost, he was lavish with it; instead, he has bought from a bean grower in the county a great quantity of rotted bean vines at a few cents per ton. Lastly, he hires less labor and puts his own hand more heavily into it.

From going to and fro in agriculture and from looking at my own bit of it, I come to no solution to the agricultural problem, but to a hard and simple conclusion. For the farmer who has a reasonable amount of capital to begin with, and will be content to operate within his resources, who will stay out of fixed debt, who will borrow on his note only what he would lend of his own money on the same security if he were a cold-hearted country banker, one who knows the work and will not spare himself, there is a living in it and a fine way of life, pro-vided only that he will hang on his wall and read twice daily the reminder:

IT IS NOT WHAT A FARMER SELLS THAT RUINS HIM; IT IS WHAT HE BUYS.

This, you see, is upside down. Generally the statement is that the farmer is ruined by what he sells, because of the price, and that a way must be thought of to increase his buying power. Generally the nation concerns itself about the farmer chiefly as a customer. But one of his troubles is that he is his own worst customer.

The share of American workers on the farm has shrunk every decade for more than a century. In 1920 it was 27%; in 1930, 21%. All the efforts of the New Deal only slowed the plunge. In 1940 it was 18%; in 1950, 12%; in 1960, 8.3%; in 1970, 4.6%; in 1980, 3.4%, in 1990, 2.6%, in 2006, 1.4%.

CHAPTER FOUR NOTES:
1 Henry A. Wallace, the man who brought crop controls to America. In 1940, Roosevelt put him on the ticket as vice president, and in 1944 Democratic kingmakers booted him off because he was too left-wing. Wallace left the Democratic Party in 1948 to run for president under the banner of the Progressive Party, which favored friendship with the Soviet Union.

102

Chapter Five
REPUDIATION

To Garrett, the most appalling thing Roosevelt did during the 1930s was to walk away from the government's promise to pay its obligations in gold. Here he tells the story.

'At All Hazards'

From "Two Chapters in the Story of Gold," the *Saturday Evening Post,* March 3, 1934

In the last presidential campaign, sound money became unexpectedly a subject of partisan debate; and the Democratic Party was on the side of sound money. One of the planks of the Democratic platform was this:

"We advocate a sound currency to be preserved at all hazards."

The Republicans were expected to say, as they did, that the Democrats had been playing with the idea of inflation, and this was the Democratic Party's reply beforehand. Sound currency had then a definite meaning. The Democrats repeated those two words again and again, as if everybody so well understood what they meant that no definition was necessary, and that was so. They went on to say that the Republican Party, false to its traditions, had become unsound about money; specifically, that the Hoover Administration, with its desperate use of public credit, had been on the road to unsound money.

Then, on Oct. 4, Mr. Hoover made his Des Moines speech. He told there the perils through which his party had been steering the nation. One was the peril of vanishing credit, and the cause of its vanishing was the draining away of the gold base. Besides enormous withdrawals of gold by foreigners, there had been domestic hoarding. At one point, said Mr. Hoover, "The Secretary of the Treasury[1] informed me that unless we could put into effect a remedy, we could not hold to the gold standard but two weeks longer."

The implication was clear. The Republican Party had saved the country from the disaster of going off the gold standard.

This produced a fury of indignation among Democrats. Had not the Republican Party involved the country in a series of disasters? Now here it was inventing one disaster that had not happened to prove it had saved the country. The President of the United States himself willing to injure the credit of the country by saying publicly, for the whole world to hear, that we had been about to go off the gold standard. It were bad enough if it were true. But it was untrue.

To answer Mr. Hoover as he deserved, the Democratic Party put forward Senator Carter Glass.[2] He had been Secretary of the Treasury in the Wilson cabinet and was expected to be Secretary of the Treasury again in the Roosevelt cabinet if the Democratic Party won the election. Moreover, having written and moved and carried, with acid integrity, more money and banking legislation than any other living man of either party, his words were bound to be deeply respected by the whole country.

Accordingly, on the night of November 1, over a nation-wide radio hookup, came the authoritative money speech of the campaign. Carter Glass speaking. Virginia Democrat. Member of the Banking and Currency Committee of the

United States Senate. He ought to know. He himself wrote into the Republicans' emergency banking bill such safeguards as Mr. Hoover's people at the Treasury ought to have thought of, and then, with some distaste, had helped to pass it.

"I assert," said Senator Glass, "that those of us responsible for legislation never had the remotest intimation from the Administration that the gold standard was in danger... Anybody who says this country was within two weeks of being driven off the gold standard actually impeaches the official integrity of the President of the United States and of the Secretary of the Treasury. The latter official, from January 1 to June 30, 1932, with the approval of the President, sold to the banks and private investors in the United States $3,709,213,450 of Treasury notes and certificates of indebtedness, redeemable in gold at the Treasury. If the President and the Secretary of the Treasury had knowledge of the fact that this country was faced with imminent disaster by being driven off the gold standard in two weeks, and failed to so advise the banks and private investors who purchased nearly $4 billion of these Federal securities, they were guilty of amazing dishonesty. They were cheating the investment public."

This was an official party speech, and lest there should be any doubt about it, Mr. Roosevelt in a speech, November 4, at the Brooklyn Academy of Music, said: "Senator Glass made a devastating challenge that no responsible government would have sold the country securities payable in gold if it knew that the promise, yes, the covenant, embodied in these securities, was as dubious as the President of the United States claims it was..."

"One of the most commonly repeated misrepresentations by Republican speakers," said Mr. Roosevelt, "including the President, has been the claim that the Democratic position with regard to money has not been made sufficiently clear. The President is seeing visions of rubber dollars. That is only a part of his campaign of fear. I am not going to characterize these statements. I merely present the facts. The Democratic platform specifically declares, 'We advocate a sound currency to be preserved at all hazards.' That is plain English."

Thus the Democratic Party came into control of the Government plainly committed to uphold the gold standard, and moreover to the following propositions:

First, that for anyone to suggest that in the hands of the Democratic Party the country might be driven off the gold standard was a political indecency, a dangerous calumny, and not far short of treason; and

Second, that for the Government to engrave the words, "Payable in gold coin of the present standard of value" on the face of its bonds and notes and certificates of indebtedness and sell them to investors while knowing that the gold standard was in danger would be an act of amazing dishonesty.

In so far as the popular vote that delivered the Government to the Democratic Party was touched by thought of monetary principles, it was a vote for sound money and for the gold standard. What followed was without suggestion of a mandate from the people.

And what was it that followed?

First, gold payments were suspended. Next, the gold standard was forsaken, though, as it were, temporarily. Then it was flatly repudiated by law, the President thereafter referring to it as one of the "old fetishes of so-called international bankers," now to be replaced by the idea of planned currency. "The United States seeks," he said, "the kind of dollar which a generation hence will have the same purchasing power as the dollar value we hope to obtain in the near future."

And again, October 22, 1933, disclosing the gold-purchase plan, wherein the idea was to cheapen the dollar by manipulating the price of gold, the President said: "We are thus continuing to move toward a managed currency."

106

To take the currency off the gold standard, certain steps had been necessary.

It did not happen all at one stroke. The time it took altogether was three months; and during these three months the Government sold to banks and investors $1.4 billion of securities, all of them bearing the engraved words, "Principal and interest payable in gold coin of the present standard of value."

On March 9, the Congress enacted an emergency law investing the President and the Secretary of the Treasury[3] with absolute power to control money and banking, including the power to require all private owners of gold to deliver it up to the Treasury in exchange for paper money. Then, as the banks began to reopen, they were forbidden to pay out gold. The country was still on the gold standard. To suspend gold payments in an emergency is by no means the same as to abandon the gold standard.

On March 12, the Treasury sold $800 million of short-term bonds, called certificates of indebtedness, and on each bond was engraved the promise to pay "in United States gold coin of the present standard of value." On March 15 it sold $100 million of Treasury bills, also payable in gold.

On April 5, the President ordered all private persons and banks to deliver, by May 1, their gold and gold certificates to the nearest bank in exchange for paper money, under penalty of fine and imprisonment. After that time it was a crime to have more than $100 in gold or gold certificates in one's possession.

A gold certificate is, or was, simply a Treasury receipt for gold coin, reading on its face: "This certifies that there have been deposited in the Treasury of the United States ten dollars in gold coin, payable to the bearer on demand." This had been, for longer than anyone could remember, the finest money in the world. And now, suddenly, both as money and as faith, it was broken.

Still we were not off the gold standard. The Treasury said we were not. This was something the Government was doing to its own people. A foreigner who held any amount of gold certificates might still expect the United States Treasury to honor them; and a foreigner owning a U.S. Government bond might still expect the Treasury to keep its contract.

As for the American citizen, taking his gold to the nearest Federal Reserve Bank and exchanging it for paper money, he supposed, first, that it was all a matter of emergency, and, second, that the money he received was as good as gold. Indeed, the Government gave him that impression. On April 5, parallel to the President's order commanding privately owned gold to be surrendered, the Secretary of the Treasury[3] issued a statement: "Those surrendering gold, of course, receive an equivalent amount of other forms of currency, and other forms of currency may be used for obtaining gold in an equivalent amount when authorized for proper purposes." That is a fairly good statement of what gold-standard currency is. It is paper money that may be exchanged for gold when one wants the gold for any purpose for which gold may be properly required. The Secretary of the Treasury added: "Gold held in private hoards serves no useful purpose under present circumstances. When added to the stock of the Federal Reserve Banks, it serves as the basis for credit and currency."

Thus people understood that they were surrendering gold in time of emergency only to strengthen the banking system, and that the paper money they received was the equivalent of gold. There was no suggestion that the Government intended to devalue the dollar or repudiate its gold contracts.

On April 19 the President proclaimed an embargo on exports of gold. That meant the Government would suspend gold payments abroad. Foreign holders of U.S. Government bonds could no longer expect to receive the principal and interest in gold—at least not for a while.

All over the world the value of an American dollar began to fall. And yet only in the sense of payment were we off the gold standard. We had stopped paying gold, yes, but that is not the same as to repudiate the gold standard. Once before for nearly two decades the American Government had to pay with paper money. That was during and immediately after the Civil War. But it held all that time to the gold standard and ultimately restored all its paper money to a gold parity. And what now immediately followed gave many people the idea that such was the case again.

On April 23, the Treasury sold $500 million in short-term bonds, called three-year notes. It made them in small denominations and recommended them to small investors; and in the Treasury circular offering these bonds the Government said: "The principal and interest of these notes will be payable in United States gold coin of the present standard of value." People bought them on that representation, unaware that the Government was then writing a law to repudiate that contract.

On April 28, the Senate passed the inflation law—namely, the Thomas[4] amendment to the Agricultural Adjustment Act, authorizing the President to debase the dollar by reducing its gold content by one-half, to print and issue $3 billion of fiat money, and to exchange $3 billion of paper currency for outstanding Government bonds. Even that was not final. There was one more step.

On June 5, responding to the wishes of the Administration, the Congress repudiated the gold clause in every form of public and private contract. This included the $900 million in Treasury bonds and bills sold twelve weeks before and the $500 million sold six weeks before, which were declared payable in any kind of paper money the Government might see fit to print.

Thus in three months the Democratic Party had not only thrown the country off the gold standard; it had repudiated the gold standard entirely. It had repudiated the contract on every existing Treasury gold bond, gold note or gold receipt. The only thing left was the silver certificate, redeemable in silver coin on demand. That had not been repudiated, but the right to repudiate it had been reserved.[5]

What ensued was still strange enough to be incredible. The dollar, off the gold standard, did not fall fast enough. The Government was acting on the theory that the way to raise prices was to depreciate money, and it was very anxious to raise prices, especially agricultural prices. Accordingly, it adopted an aggressive method of cheapening the dollar. It began to buy gold with paper dollars, and to buy it above the world price, day after day increasing in a progressive manner the number of paper dollars it would give for an ounce of gold—one day $32 for an ounce of gold, the next day $33, the next day $34, and so on. It neither needed nor wanted gold. It wanted only to cheapen the dollar, and said so.

But while this was going on, the Treasury again needed money, by the hundreds of millions, to meet the enormous expenditures of the RFC, the PWA, the CWA, the AAA, the CCC and all the other agencies through which the Government was pouring money into the hands of farmers, into the banks, into public works and into relief. Thus, after June 5, the oblique spectacle of the Treasury selling its bonds and notes and IOUs continuously, while at the same time the Government was openly engaged in cheapening the money in which those bonds and notes and IOUs would be redeemed.

In the apologia the first statement will be—it already is— that the Democratic Party did not do it. Necessity did it. There existed a national emergency.

Well, in the first place, the emergency was not new. It was present during the campaign, when the Democratic Party was passing upon others the moral judgments that now return to embarrass it. Secondly, if necessity be the justification, then necessity must be proved. An idea of it will not do, for the idea may be wishful.

What of the alleged necessity? It was never proved. It was asserted. But it was also denied. And the man who most bitterly denied it was the one who during the campaign had been the Democratic Party's chosen authority on the morals, principles and facts of money.

This is the most dramatic part of the story. The senior senator from Virginia, Carter Glass, did not become Secretary of the Treasury in the Roosevelt cabinet. He declined the office, saying he could be more useful in the Senate. But his private reason for declining it was that after the election in November and before the Democratic Party took control of the Government in March—an interval of four months—he began to be deeply troubled by certain signs and omens in the party household. During the campaign, all who spoke for the party said the same things. What they said was what he believed, and he was persuaded that they believed it as he did. Suddenly he could not be sure. Men whom he trusted said that strange ideas about money were rising. Reluctantly he decided to stay in the Senate.

On April 27, when the inflation law came before the Senate, Mr. Glass appeared, not to oppose it, for that was hopeless, but to characterize it. He was ill and very weak. In a low voice he said:

"I have not deserted my party.

"I wrote with my own hand that provision of the national Democratic platform which declared for a sound currency at all hazards.

"I was unable, because of illness, to make more than one speech during the entire presidential campaign. And in that one speech, with all the righteous indignation that I could summon, and in terms, perhaps, of some bitterness, I reproached the then President of the United States and Secretary of the Treasury for saying that this country was within two weeks of going off the gold standard.

"The reaction to that speech—and I do not say it in any boastful way—was that I now have bound in excess of 5,000 telegrams and letters from people, mostly strangers to me, commending that utterance. The first telegram in the first bound volume is one from Franklin D. Roosevelt, now President of the United States, who said the speech was to him an inspiration...

"This simple recital will indicate that I have not deserted anybody or any party in opposing the bill. I am simply consistently maintaining an attitude of earnest conviction...

"We are proceeding on the assumption that nobody hereafter will desire credit; that farmers hereafter will not want credit or need it, because we are destroying credit and largely have done so. No man outside of a lunatic asylum will loan his money today on farm mortgages, because we have destroyed the market for farm mortgages and for almost all types of mortgage.

"I cannot in any circumstances, painful as it is to me to differ from the occupant of the White House and from my party colleagues, support the second provision of this bill, relating to the devaluation of the gold dollar. England went off the gold standard because she was compelled to do so, and not from choice. She had less than $1 million in gold left after paying her indebtedness to the United States...

"Why are we going off the gold standard? With nearly 40 percent of the entire gold supply of the world, why are we going off the gold standard? ...To me the suggestion that we may devalue the dollar 50 percent means national repudiation. To me it means dishonor. In my conception of it, it is immoral."

"Repudiation" is an honest word for an ugly thing. The inflationists want the result without the word. Already, in their flight from it, they had made a confusion of reason. With the air of having discovered it, they brought forth the fact that there never was gold enough, and never would be enough, to redeem all the public and private bonds that were payable in gold. They counted them up—Government bonds, state and local bonds, corporation bonds, and so on, to a total of maybe $150 billion. "Look," they said, $150 billion in bonds payable in gold and only $4.5 billion of gold in the country. All that Congress has done has been to face for the first time the reality in fact. Why pretend that $150 billion in bonds are payable in gold when it is physically impossible for them to be paid in gold?

The total amount of money of all kinds then—gold, silver and paper combined—was $10 billion. By the same reasoning, the promise to redeem the bonds at all is preposterous. Why not a resolution in Congress to annul the promise to pay, on the same ground—namely, that the contracts cannot be performed?

It is an elementary fact that bonds payable in gold are not actually paid in gold. Bonds are paid out of income, and the same piece of money may be used to measure a quantity of income again and again, just as one bushel basket may be used again and again to measure a quantity of grain. Money is a measure, not wealth; and to say that gold bonds cannot be redeemed in gold money because the aggregate is many times greater than the total amount of gold is as absurd as to say a year's wheat crop cannot be measured because there are not enough bushel baskets to hold it all at one time.

During the ten years from 1920 to 1930 the Government redeemed more than $9 billion in gold bonds. Probably not a single bond in all this $9 billion was actually paid in gold coin or gold certificates. The Government, like everybody else, redeems its bonds by mailing out a check. On receiving a Treasury check, you take it to a bank. You may deposit it there or you may take it in paper bills.

You say, "But that Government bond was payable in gold." The bank says, or it did say, "All right. Here is the gold in place of the paper money. How will you carry it?" But you did not want to carry it. You only wanted to know you could get it, for if you could get it you knew your paper money to be the equivalent of gold. It was not until people begin to distrust the value of paper money that they want the gold itself and are willing to carry it into hoarding.

The hoarding episode was in two phases. First it was simply a hoarding of money, in distrust of banks. Probably not one person in ten thousand knew the difference between a gold certificate, a national bank note, a greenback, a Federal Reserve note or a silver certificate. All kinds of money were equal.[6] Never was there any doubt about the integrity of money.

The second phase opened when this faith in money began to weaken. Then people began to ask and to distinguish between the different kinds of paper money and to select out the gold certificates; they began also to demand the gold itself, wishing to hoard it. But the gold certificate was even better for purposes of hoarding. It was an absolute receipt by the United States Treasury for gold coin, payable to the bearer on demand, and nobody could imagine the circumstances under which the United States Treasury would ever refuse to honor it.

The Treasury continued to vacuum up gold in the 1930s, and there was little inflation. Then came World War II.

The Paramount Money

"Gold Marbles," *Saturday Evening Post* editorial, November 16, 1940

We are hearing a lot of erudite nonsense on the subject of the American gold hoard. Nearly three quarters of all the monetary gold in the world is now in this country. We got it in four main ways, namely:

One. We sold more than we bought in world trade and took the balance in gold.

Two. In the first year of the New Deal, an agronomist with a money thesis sold it the wonderful idea that recovery could be produced by a series of financial manipulations.[7] The scheme was to raise the price of gold in terms of the American paper dollar, whereupon the value of the paper dollar would fall, all commodity prices would rise accordingly; with rising prices the ecstasy of prosperity would return—and there it was! So, where the price of gold had been less than $21 an ounce, the United States Treasury suddenly offered to buy all the gold in the world at $35 an ounce in paper dollars. The effect of this fantastic performance upon prices was much less than the agronomist said it would be, with the curious result that the world began at once to swap gold for dollars, because there was a profit in it. We got the gold.

Three. Owing to that, European governments, especially Great Britain and France, seized the opportunity to create in this country a very large war chest. With gold they bought dollars, and then they either invested the dollars in liquid securities or put them in banks against a time when they should need them to buy armaments, machine tools, food stocks and all the things they were going to want in war. They knew that when war came they would be unable to borrow money here as they did in World War I, because they had defaulted on their own war debts and the Congress had passed a law saying that defaulting war debtors could not borrow any more. Hence their anxiety to create a war chest here, and they did it to much advantage, because the American dollar was undervalued in gold.

Four. As the war drew near, there was a flight of gold from Europe to this country, because here was refuge, not a perfect refuge but the best one left in the world.

So, we have the gold. We are six percent of the world's population, doing normally two-fifths of the world's total business, and yet we have nearly three-quarters of all the money gold there is. The Government controls it entirely. It is illegal for private persons to touch it. There is not a dollar of gold money in circulation. Even banks that speak of gold reserves have only certificates from the Government, representing the gold—just such certificates as the Government repudiated in the first year of the New Deal in order to get possession of the gold. Much of it is buried in a bombproof cave at Fort Knox, Kentucky. The rest of it is in Federal Reserve Bank vaults, under Government lock and key. The Government now is bereft of monetary ideas. It has no intelligible monetary policy. What to do with the gold is a conundrum. The agronomist who invented it was unable to solve it and died.

But the nonsense we speak of is the saying now current that all this gold may turn into pig metal on our hands. The rest of the world may agree to demonetize gold altogether, simply refuse any more to treat it as money, whereupon it would sink to the value of a commodity like lead or copper.

That thought did not begin here. It came from Europe. The American economists who have accepted it are now busy to elaborate it. First it came from Great Britain when she was trying, a few years ago, to form what she called a sterling bloc, off the gold standard—a block of countries that would trade together in the medium of the British pound sterling and forget gold. That, of course, was to challenge our gold supremacy, and we were stupid enough to let it scare us off the gold standard.

It comes now from Germany. Herr Doctor Funk,[8] Hitler's Minister of Economic Affairs, threatens a blitzkrieg against gold. The gold game, he says, is over because the Americans have all the marbles, or nearly all. Under German dictation, Europe will become one economic bloc, with a currency of its own, which shall be a reichsmark with a value assigned to it by an all-intelligent Reich; and then, if the United States wants to trade with Europe, or in foreign markets at all, against the competition of Germany, it will have to adjust its money to that perfect medium of exchange, representing not gold but value according to Hitler.

What all this means, very simply, is that the United States has in its possession the most fabulous bunch of sour grapes that has ever existed.

Forget everything you may think you know about economics and let your common sense act. When Hitler conquers a country, what does he first look for? Its gold. When a country sees Hitler coming, what is the first thing it tries to put beyond his reach? Its gold.

Ask yourself a question. Above all the kinds of money now current in the world, including the dollar, what would you take if you could get it? Gold money, certainly. And why? Not because gold is a habit, a fetish, a superstition, but because it is the only kind of money that cannot be debased or repudiated. Where now in the world is a great country, saving not even our own, that has not debased its paper currency, or one that has not repudiated the word engraved upon its bond?

Only a few weeks ago the British Government repudiated for the duration of the war all British paper money held in non-British hands, which is to say that if you happen to possess a pound-sterling note, it has for the present no value; and yet, only a little while ago, that was the premier money of the world and no one could imagine it would be ever repudiated. This, as a war expedient, was probably necessary. What we point to is that it could not have happened to the old British gold piece.

Gold is not the ideal money. There is no such thing as ideal money, nor ever will be, until the state of the world is such that between individuals and between nations there shall exist perfect faith and perfect integrity. The gold obligation, engraved upon money or written in a bond, is man's hostage to himself for the word he knows he will be sometime tempt-

117

ed to break, if he can. And when he has broken it so far as to become cynical about it, where there is no longer any faith to be kept in money or bond and the whole world is in a state of such moral and financial insolvency that the only thing any-body will trust is the gold itself, then those who have too lit-tle gold want to abandon the gold standard and begin all over. But what will they begin all over with?

True, trade may be conducted without gold, without gold-standard money. If you come to that, you may trade with no money of any kind, by a system of barter, exchanging goods for goods; but so you may hitch horses to automobiles, as they are doing in Scandinavia, and travel still. Germany has been conducting trade by barter for several years, not by choice but by necessity, because she had so swindled the world with German money, and had then so upset her balance of exchange by importing war materials, that she was obliged to resort to barter.

Those who talk of conducting international trade by barter as a normal method, or of conducting it with fiat money such as the reichsmark, having a value assigned to it by the gov-ernment, must have forgotten nearly all the history there is. Much of the greatness of Greece for half a millennium was owing to the famous integrity of the Attic owl, which went beyond the Mediterranean world and was good in the hands of the barbarians. The curious fact is that if you found a pot of Attic owls today, they would still have monetary value. You could take them to the mint and get current money for them. The Attic owl was a silver piece and was never diluted. For Greece, silver was more convenient than gold. The superiori-ty of gold over silver in our time is that it expresses more value in less bulk.

The point we are arriving at is simple. This gold, though we paid too much for it and though the handling of it has involved the Government in a stupid riddle, is nevertheless a very great economic asset. When the war is over and the mind of the world inclines to restoring peaceful trade, the very first want of all will be for a kind of money everybody can trust. No fiat money can be trusted. The word of no government can be trusted.

But if there were then one country—and it could be only this country—with gold currency resting not upon the engraved word but upon gold itself, the money of that one country would be the paramount money of the world. All values in the world would be priced in that money; all banking in the world would be related to it. What that would be worth to the United States in terms of exchange and banking profits and in the trade that would be bound to gravitate to the one system of sound money, might be a billion dollars a year. And the only way Hitler could keep his own people from trading their reichsmarks for American dollars would be to shoot them.

The dollar became the paramount money anyway, because the American economy was the largest and most open there was. But the dollar did not keep its value. Gold did.

119

1 This was Ogden Mills, 1884-1937, who was Hoover's final Treasury secretary, Feb. 1932-March 1933. Mills was the last Treasury secretary to support the gold standard and became a critic of the New Deal.

2 Carter Glass, 1858-1946, as a Representative sponsored the Federal Reserve Act of 1913 and was Secretary of the Treasury 1918-1920 under President Wilson. As Senator from Virginia, 1920-1946, he sponsored the Glass-Steagall Act separating investment banking from commercial banking, but opposed federal deposit insurance.

3.William Woodin, 1868-1934, was Roosevelt's first Secretary of the Treasury, but resigned for health reasons.

4 Elmer Thomas, 1876-1965, Democrat of Oklahoma, was in the Senate 1927-1951.

5 The Treasury stopped redeeming silver certificates 35 years later, on June 24, 1968, under President Johnson. The government had begun replacing the $1 silver certificates with Federal Reserve Notes in 1963. The last 90% silver coins were dated 1964.

6 These looked different until the Treasury shrank bills in 1928 to their current size. National currency was issued by national banks and had the bank's name and signatures. Gold and silver certificates were issued by the Treasury, with metallic backing; and until 1928 the reverse of the gold certificates was in yellow ink. Federal Reserve Notes were issued by the Federal Reserve, but said on the face, "Redeemable in gold on demand." United States Notes, issued by the Treasury, were the descendants of the Civil War greenbacks and had no metallic backing, but in practice were as good as the others.

7 This was George Warren, professor at Cornell University, who convinced Roosevelt that the price of commodities could be raised by raising the price of gold. Writes Gary Dean Best in *Pride, Prejudice and Politics* (1991), "It seemed manifestly another instance of Roosevelt's confusion of cause with effect... Many of those who advocated the Warren plan did so not from any confidence that it would work, but from a desire to see Roosevelt move in the direction of a flexible, commodity-based dollar."

8 Walther Funk,1890-1960, was convicted of war crimes and imprisoned until 1957.

Chapter Six
Entanglements

To Garrett, capitalism and constitutional government in the American form were expressions of a culture molded on the frontier and seeded from northern Europe. Here he considers the American effort to inject that system into a different culture, turning the Philippines into a colony of America.

Sentimental Imperialists

From "Our Asiatic Attribute," the *Saturday Evening Post,* January 24, 1931

As you enter Manila harbor, there is a possessive thrill in the thought that you are about to land on American territory, ten thousand miles from Washington. Black bones of the Spanish fleet destroyed there by Admiral Dewey, May 1, 1898, are still showing above the water. Lean gray ships of the United States Navy lie at anchor in a row. The city of Manila from this point of view is exceedingly fair.

You will remember that when the Americans came, this was one of the plague spots of the earth, dreadful for diseases of filth, such as cholera. The Americans introduced sewers and sewage disposal where the immemorial way with waste had been to cast it into the street or let it fall through the bamboo floor to pigs below. They brought drinking water from the hills. They drained the pestilential canals. Now parks, palm trees, boulevards, white club buildings.

Then, at landing, everything turns suddenly strange. There is no feeling at having arrived on American territory. The customs is Filipino, the health service is Filipino, the police is Filipino. The newspaper reporters are Filipino, all speaking book English in an acquired, overexact manner, with some odd disasters to the free meaning of words. You wonder at this. For thirty years the Americans have been implanting the English language here; all that time it has been the language of instruction in the free public schools. These reporters, therefore, must have got it in their childhood. Why do they use it as a foreign tongue?

To the hotel is a short drive along the bay front. Immediately at the hotel a collision with hearty Rotarians may temporarily efface your pier impressions, or, if they return, you will remember that the Filipino's progress in self-government under American sovereignty must in itself be regarded as an American achievement. When it comes time to go calling on the Governor-General to pay your respects, you are feeling more at home.

At the door of the palace Filipinos receive you. Filipinos take down your name and business. Filipinos ask you to be seated. They have all a way of seeming strange with you and very observing, which makes you to be strange with them and unobserving. The Asiatic eye, besides that it is impenetrable, cannot be embarrassed. A Filipino conducts you to the Governor-General.[1] Passing through the executive offices, you note that the entire personnel is Filipino. The first American face you see is that of the Governor-General's aide in the antechamber. He takes you to the Governor-General. You do say "Excellency" to a man from Missouri. Then the door shuts behind you and the form is forgotten.

Hours later you will still be trying to say what gave the interview its singular character. Not that it was in the least unsuccessful. It was very agreeable and the talk was free. Yet there was a certain air of constraint about it. Why? Lest anything that was said should be repeated? Yes and no. More as if it might be overheard. And you recall that with the American members of his staff there was a common trick to look around before speaking—that is, if the words were to be of any conviction—and always a drop in the pitch of the voice.

If it were not absurd you would say the representatives of the American sovereignty behave as if they were afraid of the Asiatic ear.

You feel it again with an American you find in one of the executive departments. You ask him broadly some question touching the nature of Filipino government, and he answers it lightly. But when two or three Filipinos around him are gone and the door is closed, his manner changes and he says, "Now I'll tell you what you want to know."

A few repetitions of this experience will set you to observing Americans. They may well for a time become your first study. The official group is very small. In all the Philippines there are not more than seven thousand Americans among thirteen million natives. Generally, they are in business. You meet them at the Chamber of Commerce, in the clubs, in their homes, at the Manila Hotel; and that mark of inhibition is on all of them. It is as if one great area of fact and opinion were always guarded. You may yourself say anything you like with no offense whatever, but the coin you get in exchange is small and often rings false. Yet, except only in this one area, the American tongue is itself and reckless.

The most interesting group is that of the thirty-year men. These are they who came with the army of occupation and stayed to raise the Filipino. When the military job was done they went over to the civil side as executives, organizers, founders, teachers. Much of the American achievement is actually their work. Now you find them on their own, in sugar, hemp, coconuts, industry and trade.

You would hardly take these men to be afraid of anything—Filipino, Malay or earthbound. So only the more strange. At a dinner with eight or ten of them in private surroundings, you will have the typical experience. Here again the guarded area of speech. It may occur to you that an American in the Philippines is very seldom out of Malay hearing. Almost never.

If you had not already remarked that on one subject the American tongue is heedless and violent in any hearing, you might find yourself a little dazed at the way the thirty-year men handle the Government at Washington. For these occasions they keep it in the form of a stuffed effigy. Their pastime after dinner is to eviscerate it, let out the sawdust, and trample it. Who gathers up the sawdust and restores the effigy for the next occasion? The Filipino servant.

After such a dinner it happens that one of them will accost you to say: "I'm sorry somebody didn't open up last night. You were not interested in anything we could say about the American Government at Washington. You know more about that than we do. But there were two or three men there who might have given you the very low-down on what you were after here. I was hoping they would."

"Why didn't they?"

"You've been here long enough to know the answer to that question. We are afraid."

"Afraid of something I might write?"

"Hell, no. We don't care what you write, as long as you don't quote us by name."

"Well then, what are you all afraid of? Americans afraid in the Philippines! It's incredible."

"That's exactly what General Wood[2] said when he was Governor-General. I knew the general very well. I said to him, 'Governor, the truth is these people have got us buffaloed. We

124

are afraid. And I'll tell you something else. Before you are through here, they will have you buffaloed.' " A pause. "They did buffalo him, too. I was sorry afterwards I said it. He reminded me of it later when he was at an impasse here. The Malay won."

"It's the Malay, then?"

"Yes, it's the Malay. The longer you study him the less you know him. I've been here thirty years and I don't know him. It's the Filipino Government. You ask the Governor-General how far he can protect an American who, from a point of principle or for any reason not a wrong one, gets himself on the wrong side of the Filipinos. Do you know what he will say? He will say that although he may be able to protect him in a specific instance, he cannot keep them from taking it out of his hide in a hundred and one other ways. Then there is the situation in which no power can help. I was saying, about that dinner last night, that somebody might have opened up to you. One man there I was sure would not. He did it once, among friends, all Americans; yet the things he said somehow got out. The Filipinos took them badly, and what it cost him in his business I'd hate to tell you."

So there it is. In the Philippines—one place on earth—the American is afraid to speak his mind out loud even under the sign of American sovereignty.

The American official has two reasons for minding his speech. One is a reason of tact. The Filipino, being Malay, is extremely sensitive. He is cursed with a sense of inferiority, and although he may have a mind so cultivated as to be able to admit it, still, that does not alter the fact. Even more, perhaps, than other Asiatics, he has a face to save.

The second reason is that official Filipino-American relations have come to rest wholly on Filipino goodwill. Least of anyone is the American Governor-General independent of it. The American Governor-General does not govern the Philippines. The all-Filipino legislature passes the laws; the

American Governor-General administers the laws through executive departments, all of which are Filipino in personnel and all but one of which is Filipino at the head. So long as the Governor-General is in the good will of the all-Filipino legislature there is cooperation; if he falls under its displeasure there is no cooperation; no cooperation, no government.

Given these facts and the nature of the Malay, with his extremely injurable face, all the rest is clear. The slightest saying from an American official unacceptable to the pride of a Filipino explodes like a bomb in the Filipino press. One overt saying from the palace, direct, overheard or repeated, may wreck a Governor-General's administration.

The Filipino has a pure appetite for this kind of situation. The Malay mentality is perfectly suited to exploit it. The American mentality is stultified by it. The power is all on one side, and it is the power to exercise an all-pervading moral terrorism.

The recent Roosevelt instance was convincing. The President of the United States appointed Nicholas Roosevelt to be vice-governor. The governor-general and the vice governor are the only two representatives of American sovereignty who may be legally appointed without the consent of Filipinos. Actually they, too, must be possessed beforehand of the Filipinos' good will. And that is what the Filipinos proved. Mr. Roosevelt had written a book on the Philippines in which the Filipino found something to hurt his face.[3] Instantly, therefore, a specious bonfire of Filipino indignation—specious because Mr. Roosevelt himself was not the main point. Probably not fifty Filipinos in a population of 13 million had read his book, seen it or heard of it. Apparently there was some difficulty about finding a copy of it in Manila for the ceremony of public burning. Moreover, every intelligent Filipino knows how impossible it is for a vice governor to act injuriously in Filipino affairs. He cannot act upon them at all but by suggestion and counsel and with the consent of the Filipino legislature.

Simply, it was a grand occasion for the exercise of moral terror. And it worked. Mr. Roosevelt did not go to the Philippines.

Here authority acquires no merit by grace alone. It is the Malay nature of the Filipino to be contemptuous of Americans in proportion as his power increases to make them walk softly and fear their own tongues.

Not long ago the American principal of a provincial school untactfully refused to permit his wife to dance in public with a Filipino student. Another bonfire. The student body threatened to go on strike. In the Filipino press appeared a propaganda for expunging the last of the American teachers from the Filipino school system. Later a Filipino official of that province, on receiving some American visitors, speaks not of the incident itself but of how tactfully it was handled by the provincial Filipino authorities so that nothing really disagreeable came of it. He tells this with an astonishing inflection. You are to understand that he and his associates have in a very considerable manner saved your American face.

This strange American. Having brought to the Filipino his sausages, his ABCs, his tools, a standard of living two or three times higher than now existing in any neighboring Asiatic country, and then a ready-made government as a political gift, where does he stand? He is a foreigner under his own flag.

The American in the Philippines—this sentimental imperialist—is not the least of the riddles of the East. His sovereignty is an oblique thing, both real and unreal. His responsibility in it is unlimited; therefore, it is real. But he has no more rights in it than a foreigner. Therefore, it is unreal.

For more than thirty years he has been building here a self-governing Malay state in the Anglo-Saxon pattern, with a most vague idea of why or what he should do with it if he succeeded. There was no economic or political necessity for a self-governing Malay state, either here or anywhere else. No such thing had ever existed in the world. Nor was there any moral obligation.

When the American raised his flag in the Philippines his title to them was absolute and clear. The whole archipelago was American territory, ceded to him by Spain; the only reason for not treating it as incorporated territory, like Alaska, Texas or California, and giving the inhabitants citizenship, was that the inhabitants were Asiatic; and Asiatics, we think, are not desirable to be assimilated. So, first, it was saying to them that under American sovereignty the Philippines would be governed with the happiness and well-being of the Filipino people in mind. Then from much paternalistic feeling and thinking came a second saying, which was: "The Philippines for the Filipino."

As Americans we cannot imagine happiness and well-being for any people without the institution of popular self-government. We were bound to press that blessing toward them, and we did. Almost unawares, a Malay state has been created. The all-native Filipino legislature is the supreme law-making body. The sovereign American right to make laws in American territory has been surrendered to it. The American Congress, it is true, could abolish the Filipino legislature and the whole Filipino government, but that now is unimaginable. It has reserved to itself the right to annul any law enacted by the Filipino legislature; it reserved also to the American governor-general that right. But the power to annul is but the one-sided power to say no. The Filipino legislature also may say no. That is, it may in its pleasure refuse to function, and bring government to an absurd impasse. This it once did. What results in practice is that the governor-general is reduced to suggestion, persuasion and barter. Nominally he is the supreme executive power to administer the laws. In fact, the Filipino legislature controls also the administration of its laws, from the fact that the heads of the various executive

128

departments appointed by the governor-general are subject to the approval of the Filipino Senate. Thus the executive power, too, has been practically surrendered.

The heads of all executive departments, with one exception, are Filipino. The bench is Filipino, up to the Supreme Court, where five Americans survive against four Filipinos; the chief justice is Filipino. The attorney general is Filipino. The prosecuting attorneys are all Filipino. In the whole government of the Philippine Islands fewer than two officials in each one hundred are American.

With the Filipinos now demanding absolute independence, because the thought of it has been held out to their pride, and demanding it immediately because they want it now, and a great many Americans for both sentimental and selfish reasons saying, "Give it to them," the situation is growing worse. The American Government must either cede away the last of its sovereignty and be done with it, or find some working alternative that will be acceptable to the Filipino government.

"And it is my conclusion," says one who represents American sovereignty here, "that the sooner we see this and make terms with them, the better bargain we shall be able to arrive at."

What he means is that as American prestige and authority decline, the hot spirit of Filipino nationality advances. With it, and perhaps more deeply inspiring it than anyone suspects, rises also a morbid, resentful feeling of racial self-consciousness.

That wind is blowing in all of Asia. In the Philippines it has certain eccentricities of direction and effect. To begin with, even in his own world, the Malay has a sense of racial inferiority. Other Asiatics put it on him through centuries of conquest and overbearing.

The Filipino, therefore, is under a special necessity to assert his self-esteem, by a law of psychic compensation. That the keenest edge of his new racial vanity should set itself against Americans seems at first thought quite natural. Their presence is a constant reminder of the low estate in which he recently lived. But the Spaniards represented tyranny, and this feeling we are speaking of seems to have risen much less against them.

The Spaniard's superiority was an basic assumption, always implicit in his behavior. In that case the inferior race suffers one shock to its pride, which is thereafter numb, and there is no journal of minor injuries. Subsequent relations have the merit to be free of make-believe.

Then came the Americans with their sayings about equality, their faith in education to level people up, their ideal of democracy, and a notion among them that in dealing with an inferior people you must take pains to flatter their self-esteem and treat them as if they were equal. But as every American in his heart does know his superiority, and as every Filipino does feel his inferiority, all suavities to the contrary are in a sense false. The inevitable facts of behavior break down the fiction, and this slip of the mask in sudden and unexpected ways is very hurtful to the Filipino's pride.

All contacts now are embarrassed by the rising sensibilities of the Filipino. Everyone feels it, and everyone knows that the difficulties are increasing, and yet the subject by its very nature is taboo. The glimpses are often painful. For example, at a dinner of journalists and publishers, purposely arranged to prove the amenities between Filipinos and Americans in the presence of a visitor, the editor of an important Filipino newspaper is making a speech on the theme of understanding. He is telling how deeply he respects the American, to the point of loving him, and how well Filipinos and Americans get to know one another from daily contact. Pointing to one American at the table, he says: "We have known each other for fifteen years." There is a pause. His color changes. It is evident that something has suddenly occurred to trouble his thoughts. When he speaks again, his voice is altered. "We have known each other for fifteen years," he says once more. "I like to think we are friends. All that time I have been seeing him every day. But he does not know my wife."

The last seven words are uttered with intense feeling. What he is saying is that an American who treats him as an equal in the daytime does, nevertheless, reject him socially in the evening. Then he recovers his poise, goes to the end of his speech, and everybody pretends to forget one more slip of the mask.

At a formal dinner, under the auspices of the American sovereignty, the seating will be two Filipinos, then three Americans, three Filipinos, two Americans, and so on, around the table of thirty or forty places. The Filipinos are rigid. They speak in low tones to one another; seldom to an American right or left; the initiative must come from the American. When it does, the Filipino responds politely, very correctly, and immediately drops back into his well of reserve. In what goes lightly back and forth across the table he takes no part. This may be mentioned afterward to a cosmopolitan Filipino who was once a newspaper reporter on Park Row.

"That only shows," he answers, "what new eyes may see. I did not notice it. Yet now that you speak of it, I know it was so. It is always so. We take it for granted and no longer see it as you have. Nobody is to blame. It simply cannot be helped."

Garrett finished his series on the Philippines by asserting, "Independence would mean a government of the Filipino-Malay masses by a caste of Filipino mestizos, tending to become oligarchic. There is no positive evidence that a Malay state in the American design is possible, very little that it is wanted."

In 1954, in The American Story, he said it had been folly to take the Philippines in the first place. "The moral argument for keeping them was that the natives were unprepared for self-government," he wrote. "It was a specious argument."

That peacetime Europe might default on its war debts was not a new idea. Garrett had gone to wartime Germany in 1915 to do a series for the New York Times, and had reported:

"A shrewd-minded German economist asked suddenly this staggering question: 'What would be the effect if in the conditions of peace it were stipulated that all the belligerent countries should repudiate their war loans?' After some reflection, the answer of a neutral was: 'It is a very immoral thing to consider... The obvious effect, of course, would be a relocation of wealth so sudden as perhaps to be very disastrous.' "

A few years later that neutral was writing about it at the Saturday Evening Post.

Give, Forgive and Lend

From "On Saving Europe," the *Saturday Evening Post,* February 24, 1923

Like thistle in a wind the idea has run all over the place that what this country was unwilling to do for political reasons it will be bound to do for economic reasons. Not, as was once said, that it turned back from Jericho;[4] but now for its own sake, for the sake of its prosperity, it must put forth its hand in Europe and save civilization again.

What is it that now threatens civilization? The enemy is prostrate. There is no Hun at the gate. There is only a state of mind—a state of the collective European mind. There is a quarrel over material things, like reparations, debts, advantages and guarantees. And in the attitude of being about to commit economic suicide the nations of Europe all with one

132

voice call upon the United States to restrain them from the deed.

Why do they call? Is it because we are wise? They are contemptuous of our wisdom. Is it because we are just? Among themselves they call us Shylock.[5] Then why? Because we are rich.

They cannot say this out loud, bluntly. So they say: "You think you can live in isolation over there in America. Well, you can't. You cannot prosper without us. We are your customers. If we sink we shall drag you down. Your prosperity will wither. There will be nobody to buy your goods. Moreover, we can never pay our debts to you."

They have said this so incessantly, so plausibly, with so much hypnotic orchestration, and it has been so little challenged, that it is imposed upon our thought. We almost believe it. Wall Street says it. The United States Chamber of Commerce says it. The Administration says it. The farm bloc says it. The harmony is international, but there are two distinct themes:

The American theme is foreign markets. The European theme is give, forgive and lend.

Europe knows precisely what it wants; it is never off the tune of its own purpose. On our side, among the interventionists, there is only a nebulous idea that there is something we could do, both happily to save Europe from itself and preserve our foreign markets. Senator Robinson[6] says: "We are impelled by motives of common humanity to act. Would you stand idly by and see Europe destroy itself? Moreover, our farmers are suffering. While Europe is in this state of mind it cannot buy our agricultural surplus."

That is what so many people say. We must do something. What? Give, forgive and lend.

One would think that since the doors of the United States Treasury were closed to Europe we had done nothing. Well, then, let us raise some facts to view.

Everyone knows that on account of the war the American Government loaned to the Allied governments of Europe, on their I.O.U.s, $10 billion,[7] which sum by now, through accretions and interest, amounts to about $11.5 billion. What everybody does not know is that since the war the American people have put abroad, to help Europe directly or help to take up her load, $9 billion or $10 billion more. This includes foreign loans through Wall Street of $2 billion and nearly $1 billion of German marks, now worthless. There is also unpaid interest on the Allied debts, which the American people are taxed to pay. This item will be explained later.

If the figures worry you, behold it in the shape of goods. All this giving, forgiving and lending was simply to enable foreign peoples to buy American goods. In four years since the end of the war our exports of goods have exceeded our imports by more than $10 billion.

The Comptroller of the Currency, D. R. Crissinger, in reply to those who "persist that this country has not done and is not doing its full part," recently calculated that from August 1914 to the end of 1922, our contributions of credit and things to the world had been nearly $22 billion. And our national wealth in 1914 was estimated at $200 billion. Imagine it! Take a full minute! In eight years we have given, forgiven and loaned away an aggregate of things equal to one-tenth our total estimated wealth when we started.

Yet we are wrung by propaganda. We must do something for Europe. We are almost persuaded that we owe her something on account of civilization, and that if we do not recognize this moral obligation, we shall lose our foreign markets. And we are in danger of being quite persuaded that what Europe owes us is beyond her power and means; that although this country, with $200 billion in national wealth, could and did in eight years give, forgive and lend away more than $20 billion worth of things, the United Kingdom, France and Italy, with a combined national wealth estimated in 1920 by Edgar

Crammond before the London Bankers' Institute at $248 billion, cannot in 25 years pay the $10 billion they owe the Treasury of the United States.

Well, that is because we have not been thinking our own thoughts. We have been thinking the thoughts of Europe. We have been too willing in the international chorus.

One speaks lightly of propaganda in order not to become too serious about it. It is a kind of twentieth-century sorcery in which a few are extremely skilled, or it is a systematic delusion, like fifteenth-century witchcraft, concerning which one is likely to be absurdly mistaken.

You are speaking to a senator in his private chamber. You happen to say propaganda; not with any emphasis at all, just naturally in a certain place. He makes a sudden startled gesture.

"You need not tell me anything about propaganda," he says. "Don't I know? They—"

There he stops. The gesture is abandoned. After a moment of silence the conversation moves on. Who are they? He does not know. If you ask him he says he doesn't. But that gesture was involuntary. You think he is excited, perhaps, or morbidly suspicious, as statesmen often are. Still, this same thing may happen four or five times in one day, with senators of different habits, and then with a member of the Cabinet.

It is an Old World art. That we know. It is assiduously practiced on us. That we know also. How much of it is spontaneous, how much is organized, how much of it we naively do to ourselves through a press that is wide open to foreign viewpoints, more than the press of any other country, we do not know. And if we knew, what could we do about it?

In four years we have used up a forest to print the basic European formula: "Every day, in every respect, our condition gets worse and worse."

You might suppose they were hysterical and believed it themselves, except for the fact that it is greatly to their advantage to make us believe it. Purposeful hysteria, possibly. We are mesmerized. We do not even wonder if it is true. We take it for granted. Facts in support of it receive constant publicity. Facts in contradiction receive much less, not being fanned by the breath of propaganda. If you question it, voices are raised against you. What? Do you deny that there is malnutrition in Europe, that infant life is suffering, that the American embassy in Berlin finds it very difficult to procure milk for its own babies? No! That is all true. Only, there is another side to the picture.

While committing intentional financial bankruptcy, and while selling worthless marks by the bale all over the world, Germany has been building new factories, though none had been destroyed in the war. Her industrial equipment is greater than before. She has restored her railroads to perfect condition. She has erected public buildings. She has made prodigious work of reconstructing her merchant marine. It is officially reported that forty German ships were built in the last quarter of 1922, and that Germany is the principal buyer of old English tonnage. Recently the Department of Commerce at Washington received word of a shortage of pianos in East Prussia. It was startled and asked for confirmation. It was true. The farmers were putting their money into pianos and fine furniture. Germans in their flight from the mark are spending their money as fast as they can get it for things they can keep and hoard. One hears of Germans buying eight or ten overcoats apiece.

What does this mean? The explanation is obvious when you get it. The German Government has printed and circulated one trillion paper marks in order to sink its own credit. The world saw and disbelieved. The world actually bought those marks, unable to imagine that the German Government would do this thing, and every cent the world has invested in marks is utterly lost. But the Germans knew what their government was doing, and why, and that each day the mark would be

136

worth less and less until its value was extinct. Therefore all this time the German people have had but one sovereign thought, which was to exchange marks for things as fast as possible. At the same time the German Government, to keep peace in the cities, did what it could to restrain the price of food. For that reason, of course, the farmers on selling their crops put their money into things like pianos and furniture and clothes, instead of putting it back into the soil. Thus all Germany has been buying and hoarding things, building factories, houses, ships and railways, to escape the consequences of the mark's fall and keep up the ghastly joke on the outlander. Agriculture at the same time has been stinted. Hence evidence of malnutrition and at the same time an accumulation of wealth in things, and all the while a propaganda for a food loan.

If propaganda be defined as a way of putting forth the liquid word with intent to affect the shape of public opinion, we have had much of it from abroad in these last few years. We run to meet successive waves of foreign speakers, writers and publicists, all at one time saying the same thing—now, that we must lend Europe the specific sum of $4 billion more; again, that we must cancel the debts; and again, the word cancellation having become taboo, that we must be just and generous and reasonable.

For a long time we were officially deaf to the European formula and to all the internal echoes and variations of it. The Government was. Then about the middle of December it seemed to take effect all at once. Suddenly there was an eruption of newspaper headlines. The Administration was coming to an end of its waiting aloof and was resolved to take Europe by the hand and lead her to restoration. The Washington correspondent of the *New York Tribune* went so far as to say, on the highest authority, that the Administration had a plan for putting normalcy into Europe, and that the "injection of the White House into the European situation could not possibly be averted, though every man, woman and child in the country were an irreconcilable."[8] British journalists here sent cables to the London newspapers, saying America was about to abandon her childish attitude of isolation, and American correspondents in London cabled that the news caused the flame of hope to burn brightly.

What had happened? Well, it isn't quite clear yet—not all of it; but apparently what had happened was that we had launched a propaganda upon ourselves. Our exports, especially exports of foodstuffs, had been falling somewhat, our surplus agricultural product was heavy, and on Capitol Hill was the farm bloc brooding ominously. Then the idea seems to have seized the Administration that if only the wretched turmoil in Europe could be settled and German reparations fixed, then Germany could borrow money, and the American farmer could sell his surplus grain abroad.

On Dec. 8 the President sent his annual message to Congress. In one paragraph the thought was adumbrated that if people would but sit around a table the world might be rid of its afflictions. On the following Tuesday occurred the regular biweekly meeting of the President with the press. On this occasion there were several questions about that thought in the message to Congress. He talked about how the state of the Pacific had been settled at the Washington Conference.[9] Why not a similar conference to settle the matter of German reparations?

Thus it began. The headlines grew wider and deeper. There was news on high authority—this time a member of the Cabinet who would not be named—that there would be starvation in Germany before spring for want of 80 million bushels of wheat unless German reparations were fixed so that Germany could borrow; news from London that a loan of $1.5 billion to Germany would be effected at once; news that the first feature of the American Government's plan was a commission of American experts to determine how much

Germany should pay; news that wheat was strong at Chicago on expectations of a large food loan to Germany; news that J.P. Morgan & Co. had not pledged their support to a loan of $1.5 billion to Germany, saying nothing could happen until the sum or reparations was reasonably fixed; Senator Capper[10] saying farmers were for almost anything because they need markets.

First and last, it was an amazing episode.

Into this do-something American atmosphere came the Chancellor of the British Exchequer[11] at the head of a commission to discuss what should be done about Great Britain's debt to the U.S. Treasury. The British Debt Commission was received at Washington by the American Debt Commission. The head of the American Debt Commission said how pleased we were to receive the distinguished visitors and nothing whatever about our side of the debt controversy. The British Chancellor of the Exchequer replied with a carefully prepared argument against payment of the debt according to the bond. Both compositions were delivered to the newspapers. So it was that in the first-page news the British case was stated and the American case was not.

The Chancellor of the Exchequer touched both the merits and economics of the debt. He touched the merits when he said: "The debt is not a debt for dollars sent to Europe; the money was all expended here, most of it for cotton, wheat, food products and munitions of war. Every cent used for the purchase of these goods was spent in America; American labor received the wages; American capitalists the profits; the United States Treasury the taxation imposed on those profits."

So far as it was true that the money was spent here, that has nothing to do with it. What we loaned was not money, but things. And the money that was needed to be circulated for the purpose of loaning things to Great Britain was raised by the sale of Liberty Bonds, of which more than $4 billion were on Great Britain's account alone. To pay the interest on these

139

Liberty Bonds—interest due from Great Britain—the American people have been taxing themselves $175 million a year.

He touched on the merits of the debt again when he said: "Now, seeing that the debt is a debt for goods supplied, it would be natural to ask, why not repay it with goods? Those goods were supplied in wartime at war prices. Prices have fallen so that thus to repay $4 billion Great Britain would have to send to America a far greater bulk of goods than she originally purchased."

One had thought the English would be the last people in the world to hold for scaling the principal of a debt up or down with fluctuations in prices.

On the economics of the debt he knowingly stirred all our bugaboos. He said: "The payment of our debt to you will impose upon us the necessity of levying heavy taxes to meet those payments... Further taxation would decrease the purchasing power of the British workingman and reduce our consumption of American products."

There go our foreign markets again!

He said: "The American farmer as well as the American workingman will feel the pinch." Food for the brooding farm bloc.

He said: "Would it be possible for America to accept payment in coal, steel, iron, manufactured cotton goods, and so forth, a method of repayment which would affect the employment of her people for years to come?"

This speaks to the fear, industriously cultivated among us, that we shall be ruined, that our factories will shut up, that our prosperity will wither, if we received from Great Britain $281 million worth of goods a year. That is all that is required of her to pay the interest in full and redeem the principal in 25 years. Annually, $281 million worth of goods to be received among 110 million people! That is $2.55 per capita per year.

We undertake to bear it.

Instead of telling the American farmer that the Government must settle things in Europe in order to sustain the foreign market for his surplus, the farm bloc ought to be telling him this: "Tranquillity in Europe will be a human blessing, though not for the reasons you think. Prepare yourself for the immediate effects. You will not like them. During the war and ever since our exports our exports of food to Europe have been abnormal. American agriculture has been supplying the difference between normal and subnormal food production in Europe. Russia is still out. But Russia presently will come back. Agriculture all over Europe is coming back. When Europe returns to normal she will be 95 percent self-sustaining in foodstuffs, as she was before, and American exports therefore will fall to what they were before the war. You are overproducing to meet the aftermath of a war demand that will tend to disappear no matter what we do. Therefore govern your work accordingly, and let your production down."

Those who fan the fear that we will lose the European market for manufactures must have forgotten what and where we are. Our foreign trade is nearly a quarter of all the foreign trade in the world. Great Britain has another quarter. When you think of it that way it is dazzling. A quarter of all the foreign trade in the world! But for all that, how much of our total industrial production is sold abroad? Less than 4 percent. The share to Europe is less than 1 percent.

Less than one-hundredth part of our industrial production sold to Europe! Yet we are to imagine that if anything happens to the European demand for our manufactured goods American industry will fall on its face.

Now, we are by way of overtaking the delusion that foreign trade is so vital to this country. One does not say foreign trade is unimportant. It is very important. It is infatuating. It is the highest way of mankind with the material things of life. But to us it is not vital. And in telling ourselves so much that it is vital, beginning really to believe it, we are about to forget that in the mysterious dispositions of human destiny there was allotted to us a portion of the globe unlike any other portion thereof—a place in the sun where 100, 200, 300 millions of people may live by themselves, to themselves, in perfect security, and be wholly self-sustaining. Could this have been by chance? Is it not wiser to believe the fact—ordained for purposes of that experiment with liberty in which we are engaged?

Isolate us as we are, cut us off entirely from foreign trade, and what would happen? We should have to do without some tropical fruits, get on without coffee, produce our own sugar from beets, which is rather hard work; find substitutes for rubber, and some new alloys in small quantities to put with our ores to get certain qualities of steel; use aluminum or something else in place of tin cans—and that would be about all. There might be a panic in Wall Street and a year or two of commercial readjustments. Well, we have panics and violent periodic readjustments as it goes.

Then we should begin to look around. We should very soon see that this portion of the earth needs yet an endless amount of work done upon it. There are deserts to be watered, swamps to be drained, rivers to be harnessed to wheels. There is the railroad system to be rebuilt. There is the gigantic task of converting coal into power. There is already the outline of a superhydroelectric project for which it will be difficult to find the capital.

And yet it is supposed that we must export capital in order to prosper; that to save and keep our foreign markets we must continue to give, forgive and lend our things away. This idea, besides, is intrinsically fallacious. Foreign trade does not necessarily follow capital. Proof is contained in our economic history. In the twenty years preceding the war our foreign trade increased faster than that of any other country, only Great Britain and Germany doing more; but we had no great loans abroad, no mercantile marine, no colonies. How did this happen? In a very simple way. We had a surplus of certain things that people wanted and they had things that we were willing to take in exchange. There is nothing else to foreign trade, rightly conducted. So it was and so it will be. They will continue to want our cotton and our copper, because they need them, and to offer us things in exchange—unless, of course, we prefer to go on lending our cotton and copper away, as we have been doing these last eight years. There is no end of that until we are weary of doing it.

Not at all is this a thesis for economic isolation as an American policy. It is only to show how absurd it is to say that we shall have to abandon a political way which is our unique and precious right and go forth in the world against our will for economic reasons. We may do as we please about it. And if we please not to participate in the distractions of European politics, even if we let Europe entirely alone, we are neither ruined nor impoverished.

"But the debts!" you say.

The British Chancellor of the Exchequer said: "Had it been possible to find in the world a nugget of gold worth $4 billion, we would have spared no sacrifice to secure it and we would have brought it with us; but unfortunately the limitations of Nature put such a simple method of payment out of the question."

And that is how all our European debtors are thinking of their debts. If only they could find a great nugget of gold! If only there was some way to pay debts without performing the equivalent in labor!

The first question—the only question in fact—is a debtor nation's will to pay. There is no saying how much it can pay. That is an x factor. The highest financial opinion is worthless. All high financial opinion said the war could not last beyond four months because people could not produce things fast enough to keep it going. Its requirements increased tenfold, and people kept it going for four years. What they could produce was amazing, beyond any estimate.

It is only a matter of how much they will do. Nobody has yet tried to pay. Germany has not tried. She is without any will at all to pay. It is notorious, as France says. But the measure of France's will to pay is that against the sum she owes the United States Treasury she has written down in her budget: "Political debt." This is literal.

The economic productive power of France is reduced by more than $500 million a year by her standing army. That would pay the interest on her debt to us about three times. Who shall say what they can pay?

We could afford to be more pleasant about it if, as so many people seem to think, all that had happened was that our European debtors borrowed and took hence $10 billion worth of goods and left their I.O.U.s in the United States Treasury. But in order to lend the Allied countries that $10 billion worth of goods the American Government first had to buy the goods. To buy them it had first to raise the money. What the American Government did was to sell Liberty Bonds. With the proceeds of those bonds it bought cotton, wheat, food products and war munitions and loaned them to Britain, France, Italy and the other Allied nations, who left their 5 percent I.O.U.s at the United States Treasury.

The I.O.U.s still lie there in the Treasury, and the $10 billion in Liberty Bonds are still outstanding. The interest due from the European borrowers was to have paid the interest on the Liberty Bonds. But if they do not pay, we still have to pay interest on the Liberty Bonds. So the American people are being taxed $425 million a year to pay the interest our foreign debtors do not pay. The American people have already been taxed more than $1.5 billion in that way. And if the interest on Great Britain's debt, or on any of the foreign debt, is made less than 4.25 percent a year, which is our interest on Liberty

144

Bonds, the difference will be a permanent addition to our taxes, because interest on Liberty Bonds cannot be reduced.

There were several efforts to bail out Germany in the 1920s. The crunch came in 1931 with the onset of worldwide depression, the failure of the Kreditanstalt Bank in Austria, and the falling dominoes of countries going off the gold standard.

'All of Europe May Crash'

From "On Saving Europe," *A Bubble that Broke the World, 1932*

From the *New York Times*, June 23, 1931: "Tremendous buying enthusiasm swept over the security and commodity markets of the world yesterday in response to week-end developments reflecting the favorable reception of President Hoover's proposal for a one-year moratorium on war debts and reparations. The world-wide advance in prices added billions of dollars to open market values, with stocks, bonds, grain, cotton, sugar, silver and lead in heavy demand. Pronounced strength developed in the German bond list, the gains ranging from 2 1/2 to 13 1/2 points. . . United States government bonds failed to participate in the move, all of them closing behind minus signs."

The last line fell obscurely at the end of a paragraph. And that was all the notice anyone bestowed upon the most significant fact of a delirious day, namely, the fact that everything in the world went up with the single exception of United States government bonds. And why was that? United States government bonds were telling why, and telling it loudly to such as would listen. This is what they were saying:

"Again this business of saving Europe with American credit! Do you ever count up what it has cost you already? It is becoming more and more costly; and, besides, you may not be saving Europe at all. You may be only inflating her. Better may turn out to be worse."

As it did. The worldwide rise in everything but United States government bonds was fictitious, a momentary delusion. Worse was to come.

Specifically, the Hoover debt holiday plan was to save Germany from financial collapse and so avert a disaster. The first cost to us was reckoned at $250 million.[12] That was the sum we should have to forgo on account of war debts owing by Great Britain, France, Belgium, Italy and others to the American Treasury. We could not propose simply that Germany should stop paying reparations for a year to her European creditors. That would have cost Great Britain, France, Belgium, Italy and others too much. They could not afford it. If they had to forgo reparations from Germany and still pay interest on their American war debts they would be hurt in their pockets. So what we proposed was that if Germany's European creditors would give her one year of grace on reparations, the United States would give them one year of grace on their war debt payments to the American Treasury.

Even so there were difficulties, because it would still cost Europe something to save Germany. France, Great Britain, Belgium and others had been collecting a little more than $400 million a year and paying the United States a little more than $250 million a year. After long and painful negotiations, the plan took effect. It cost us $250 million. Well, a little more. The Federal Reserve Bank in New York made a loan to the Reichsbank to keep it open. Say, then, it had cost us $300 million. Was it not cheap?

We thought we had done a grand thing. The diplomats of Europe were saying so, on typewritten slips, or in interviews, and the American correspondents were quoting them to us by cable. But the words of diplomats are purposefully suave. What people were really thinking and saying, even the diplomats, was very different. They were saying: "This is the beginning of the end of our hateful war debts to the U(ncle) S(hylock) Treasury."

Conservative British newspapers did play up to the official Downing Street tune. The popular papers were sarcastic.

French opinion was caustic. These Americans, always saying they wouldn't and didn't, now again blundering their hands into the affairs of Europe, not understanding them at all. Interfering without knowing what it is they interfered with. Using their power of credit to dictate terms between France and Germany. Why shouldn't they lend their credit as credit merely, in a financial way, and otherwise mind their own business? Besides, they were in bad manners, as usual, to propose that France should forgo German reparations for a year without having first consulted France about it.

Comment in Germany was brutal and a little exultant. The Americans were obliged to save Germany from bankruptcy in order to protect the $2.5 billion or more they had already loaned to her. It was to save themselves that they were saving her and saving Europe.

However, we still thought very well of ourselves. And looking at it unromantically, the solvency of Europe was a bargain at $300 million, if really we had saved it. But in a little while it appeared clearly that we hadn't. Within two weeks the whole of that $300 million credit had been swallowed up and Europe was saying to us:

"Now see what has happened! The Hoover plan was all right; the intention was good. Only it was inadequate in the first place, and then, unfortunately, the dilatory and public discussion of it has advertised Germany's condition to the whole world. Now Germany's private creditors are in a panic. American banks are calling their deposits out of German banks. The Germans themselves are in a flight from the mark. What are you going to do about it? If after this you let Germany go down, it had been better to have done nothing at all. And if you let Germany go down, all of Europe may crash."

So there had to be a second Hoover plan to save Europe. The second plan was that the American banks should stop calling their deposits out of Germany and relend her the money for a certain period, say, six months. That meant probably $600 million more American credit. The cost of saving Germany was suddenly multiplied by three. Nevertheless, it had to be done.

Yet who would say what it was worth to save Germany, first for her own sake and then for the sake of Europe? It was no longer a bargain; still, thinking of the enormous investment of American money in Germany, now all in jeopardy, it might be worth even a billion dollars—that is to say again, provided we had really saved the situation. But had we? No.

In a few days more it was clear that what all this American credit had bought was only a postponement of evil. The German crisis had still to be met in some radical manner, or else what would happen at the end of the Hoover holiday, or even before that, when the money perforce loaned by American banks for six months was due again? The only radical solution Germany can think of, naturally, is to get rid of reparations; then to borrow more American credit. And the only radical solution the rest of Europe can think of is to get their American war debts canceled.

But there had been hardly time to begin thinking of radical solutions before another crisis developed. There was an international run on the Bank of England for gold. Her gold began to give out. What could the Old Lady of Threadneedle Street do? What could save the credit of the Bank of England? Only American credit could do that. So the Bank of England came to New York and got a big loan from the Federal Reserve Bank.

American credit had twice saved Germany, once for herself and once for the sake of Europe, and now it had save the

Bank of England—all in less than three months. And the cost had been roughly a billion and a quarter.

Who still could say it had not been worth it?

But again the sigh of relief was interrupted. After all that, another crisis. Germany was not saved; she had been only floated on a raft of American credit. Europe as a whole was not saved because Germany wasn't. And for these reasons the Bank of England discovered immediately that the loan she had got from the Federal Reserve Bank was not enough. The Bank of England itself was not saved. She had underestimated the amount of saving required. What to do?

Everybody thought of the same thing at once, as if it were new—the same magic, the same miraculous fluid. More American credit.

But now certain new difficulties. One is that the Bank of England cannot borrow enough. Besides, going to New York again so soon with more I.O.U.'s in her hand will hurt her credit. The American bankers may lift their eyebrows. The next idea is that the British Government itself shall borrow American credit to save the Bank of England. The only weakness of this idea is that the Labour Government of Great Britain is not in good credit. It is a socialist government and year after year it has been closing the national account book in red ink. It spends so much money upon schemes of social benefit, particularly in a public wage to the unemployed, that it cannot balance its budget.

American bankers had been sounded out to see if they would mind. They had said: "Really, before expecting us to float a British loan you ought to do something about your books. They are too much talked about. Can't you economize, spend somewhat less on those meritorious social schemes and balance your budget? If you did that the talk about the red ink in your national account book would stop and it would be easy enough to float a British loan in America, or to give the British Treasury any amount of bank credit."

Whereupon the British decided to change their government, adopt a program of social economy and balance their budget. This had long been indicated as a necessary thing to do. The insolvency of the socialist Labour Government was hurting the credit of the pound sterling. Nevertheless, the disagreeable task of reducing public expenditures was postponed until the Bank of England had exhausted its power to borrow American credit on its I.O.U.'s. Then it became imperative for the British Treasury to put itself in good standing as a borrower.

When the news came from London that the British had changed their government and now were going to balance their budget, Wall Street bankers were already discussing a loan to Great Britain. "They reiterated their preparedness," said the *New York Times*, August 26, "to provide a substantial loan if the new government requires it." Further: "The amount, bankers said, should be as large as can be readily supplied by the banks of the country and the credit should run at least a year. A number of bankers believe Great Britain would benefit from a long-term loan and a few of them believe British credit is still strong enough to make a public offering possible even in the present depressed bond market."

The next day the news was that negotiations had been formally opened and on the third day it was announced that American bankers had loaned the British Treasury $200 million for a year.

But what was the popular reaction in England? They said Americans had used their power of credit to interfere in the politics of Great Britain, even to the point of demanding the overthrow of the Labour Government. That was the reaction. The *Daily Herald*, organ of the Labour Party, said: "Among the reasons Mr. MacDonald[13] advances for imposing new privations on the most unfortunate section of the nation is the 'pressure of public opinion abroad.' Whose opinion? Not that of the democracies of Europe or America, oppressed by unemployment and distress for similar reasons, but that of foreign bankers, who laid down to the British Government terms, including changes in the unemployment benefit scheme, upon which and alone upon which they were prepared to render financial aid to the Bank of England."

Which was to say, the Americans had no right to name the terms on which they would lend their money to save the Bank of England or to save the credit of the British Treasury. They ought to lend their money and mind their own business.

How do people arrive at this ground of unreason—the English people, who before us were the world's principal creditors with a creditor mentality?

It is not simply that political passions have distorted the facts. That is true. But the facts belong to finance and finance is in its own world. It knows neither the way to go on nor how to get back. Having raised international debt to a new order of magnitude, now it faces international insolvency of the same grand order, and it is appalled. It cannot manage the facts. The only solution it can think of is more European debt, more American credit. By itself it cannot create any more debt. If the resources of private credit are not quite exhausted, the credulity of the creditor is about to be. But there may be still some resource left in the public credit of Europe. Finance at this point accepts the mentality of the crowd in the street. Let government do it. Let all the European governments increase their debts who can, to save themselves and one another. This is literal.

By agency of international finance, Germany, in six or seven years, borrowed nearly $4 billion, two thirds of it from American lenders. It was much more than Germany could afford to borrow—that is, if she cared anything about her own solvency. Having procured this money, having exhausted every kind of German security that could be made to look like a bond, international finance came to the sequel and said: "Germany must have more credit, or else her whole financial structure will collapse, and if that happens international finance cannot answer for the consequences. They will be terrible. But Germany has no more security to offer. Therefore international finance cannot float another loan. But if Germany's creditors will collectively guarantee a German bond issue, international finance can float that."

Try going on from there. Suppose Germany's European creditors, namely, Great Britain, France, Italy, Belgium and others should guarantee a German bond issued for more American credit. When that credit was exhausted, what would happen? Perhaps then, in order to go on lending American credit to Europe, we should have to guarantee our own loans. And what better security could you ask? An American loan to Europe guaranteed by Americans!

Well, what is so very strange about that idea? All the American war loans and post-armistice loans to Europe were guaranteed by the United States Government. It borrowed the money on Liberty Bonds and guaranteed them. If Europe does not pay this debt the American Government will. It cannot be wiped out or canceled or reduced. It can only be transferred from the European taxpayer to the American taxpayer.

If the American lender is not a menace to the financial sanity of the Old World, the least definition of him would be to say he is to Europe a fabulous enigma.

Critical European economists say we are the worst lenders in the world, because we lend impulsively, in a reckless, emotional manner, not systematically. That is true. It is true that as lenders, simply so regarded, we are incomprehensible to ourselves and to others. Beyond all economic or financial considerations there is pressing upon us continually that strange sense of obligation to save Europe.

It seized us deeply during the war. It carried us into the war. We were going to save Europe from Germany, the German people from the Hohenzollerns, little nations from big ones, all the people of Europe from the curse of war forever. There were other motives, to be sure. We had money on the side of the Allies, though by such measures as we now use it was very little. Our sympathies went to the Allies. We hated the way the Germans made war. Some of us may have been a little afraid of a German Europe. Allied propaganda to get us in had its great effect. Yet for all this we should never have gone in without the emotional thought images that made a crusade of it.

A war to end war. Where? In Europe. A war to make the world safe for democracy. Where was democracy supposed to be in danger? In Europe. A war to liberate oppressed nationalities. Where? In Europe. Not a war against the Germans— we had no quarrel with the German people—but a war to deliver them from a tyranny of their own bad warlords. And from no realistic point of view was any of this our business.

The allied nations were not interested in our thought images, or, if at all, in one only because it worried them, and that was the one about saving the weak from the strong, otherwise, the right of self-determination for little people. The Allies did not care what our reasons were. We could be as romantic as we liked, only so we came in on their side, for unless we did the war was lost. They were not themselves fighting to make the world safe for democracy, nor to end war forever, nor to deliver the German people, nor to put destiny in the hands of the little people; they were fighting to beat Germany, and with American assistance they did beat her. None of the things we thought we were fighting for came out. What survived was a continuing sense of obligation to save Europe.

Our own exertions in a war we had been much better off to stay out of cost us $25 billion. Then, in addition to that, we loaned out of the United States Treasury more than $10 billion to our own associates. Lending to Europe out of the United States Treasury ended with the post-armistice loans. Then private lending began—lending by American banks and

153

American investors. Counting our own direct war expenditures, the war loans, the post-armistice loans, and the private lending since, Europe has cost us more than $40 billion in less than fifteen years. That sum would have represented a fifth of our total national wealth in the year 1914.

Cast out the cost of our own war exertions. Pass the war loans to the Allies out of the proceeds of Liberty Bonds. Say that we were morally obliged to make them, whether anything should ever come back or not. Pass also the post-armistice loans out of the United States Treasury, which were for cleaning up the wreck in Europe. These constitute the war debts for which we are now hated in Europe and which no doubt will turn out to be worth very little. If the United States Treasury went to Wall Street to sell the long-term bonds it took from the Allies in place of their promissory notes, it would be lucky to get twenty cents on the dollar for them.

So consider only the private debt, delivered to Europe since the war by American banks and American investors. All the terms were financial. The character of finance is selfish. Therefore, as to this private debt, representing $5 billion or $6 billion of American credit poured into Europe during the past eight years, it is permitted to ask: What have we gained thereby?

Not the friendship or good will of Europe. On the contrary, we have raised against us an ugly debtor mentality. This, you may say, is inevitable in the shape of human nature; creditors must expect it and allow for it. But what gives it a sinister political importance is the prejudiced manner in which it is exploited, not only by the press and the politicians, but by responsible statesmen, by finance ministers who cannot balance their budgets, by governments when it is necessary to increase taxes.

Germany tells her people if they did not have to pay reparations—called tribute—to the once-allied nations, German wages would go up, German taxes would come down, German poverty would vanish, the German sun would rise.

The once-allied nations say to Germany they are sorry; if they did not have to pay their war debts to the United States Treasury they could forgo reparations, or in any case a great part of them, perhaps as much as two-thirds. Yet all the time they keep saying to their own people that their troubles are multiplied by the necessity to remit enormous sums to the United States Treasury. That they collect these sums first from Germany is not emphasized. And the fact that so far there has been no payment of either reparations or war debts but with the aid of American credit does not interest them at all.

American loans to Germany have enabled her to pay reparations. Out of reparations from Germany the others make their annual payments on their war debts to the American Government. Anything we have got back from Europe was our own money, the worse for wear, and very little of that. But if you say this to a European, even to one who knows, he is offended. Very few of them do know, as a matter of fact; it is easier to believe what they hear from those who exploit the debtor mentality.

For a long time it was supposed that European feeling against America as the Shylock nation was owing to the nature of the debt—that it was a war debt and had a public character. Certainly there would be no such unreasonable feeling against a debt owing to private creditors. So we said, and saying it we continued to lend American credit in Europe until the weight of the private debt exceeded that of the war debt. Owing to its sheer magnitude this private debt now begins to assume a public character, and as it does there begins to rise against it the same excitable popular feeling. Why are Americans so rich? Where do they get all this credit? Do they mean to enslave the world with their gold?

This is the sequel international finance does not foresee. When it comes suddenly to the end of its own resources, as it did in 1931, it must call on governments to interfere; after that all talk of keeping finance free of politics is sheer nonsense.

The real crisis in Germany last summer came after all nations had been relieved of war debts for one year, under the first Hoover plan. It was concerning the solvency of Germany in respect to her debt to private creditors that a seven-power conference of prime ministers was held in London in July. There the United States was represented by the Secretary of State and the Secretary of the Treasury,[14] and there came forth the second Hoover plan, to save Germany from having to default on her debt to private creditors. The situation had got beyond the control of international finance; therefore, governments were obliged to interfere.

Again, when the British had to change their government in order to borrow American credit to save the Bank of England, a financial transaction with private creditors assumed a public character. The British Government borrowed from American bankers. Because the American bankers had stipulated for public expenditure to be reduced and for the British budget to be balanced, it was possible, even plausible, for the Labour Party to say the Americans had exerted their colossal money power to destroy the Labour Government of Great Britain; and there are hundreds of thousands of unemployed in England who will think American bankers responsible for their diminished weekly dole.

Our loans to Europe are of all kinds. They represent borrowing by European governments from the American Government, borrowing by private organizations in Europe from private American lenders, and borrowing by European governments, states and municipalities from private American creditors. Less and less do these distinctions matter, because more and more the character of an American loan is merely that particular aspect of one great body of debt. The political implications of it simply as debt take us unawares.

In the September 1931 number of the *Revue des Deux Mondes,* M. Henri Bérenger, formerly French ambassador to the United States and co-author of the Mellon-Bérenger war-debt refunding agreement between France and the American Government, has an essay in the fine style of French logic on what has happened to the foreign policy of these Americans. For 145 years they founded their foreign policy on Washington's farewell address to the American Congress. The words were few. No foreign entanglements. Woodrow Wilson was the first president to preach another doctrine, and the Americans rejected both him and his doctrine, and thereafter they sent only official observers to sit at the councils of Europe. "Then," says M. Bérenger, "President Hoover issues his messages to the world and sends his Secretary of the Treasury and his Secretary of State to negotiate with European ministers... What has taken place on the other side of the Atlantic to make such derogation of the Washington doctrine possible, even popular?"

He answers his own question, saying: "For seven years American bankers have been engaged in entangling the United States with Europe... Indeed, the network of steel and gold that America has cast upon Europe has been so powerful that it has become jammed of its own weight. A crash in Berlin is immediately felt in Washington and every panic in Frankfurt is felt in Wall Street. When the crisis becomes worse and extends itself to the City of London the United States is so entangled that it is in danger of being strangled."

The French see it. In less than ten years finance has accomplished a fact the idea of which had been rejected by the American people for a century and a half, namely, the fact of foreign entanglement.

Since our lending to Europe bears us no friendship, only more and more dislike, and since it has caught us in a net of foreign entanglements contrary to our native wisdom, the question remains unanswered. What do we get out of it?

Now the voice of foreign commerce, saying: "But our lending abroad did increase our export trade. Our loans to Europe enabled her to buy from us great quantities of goods that otherwise she had been unable to buy. This kept our factories going, it kept our own labor employed."

And it is so, it did for a while. There is probably no point beyond which your export trade cannot be further inflated so long as you lend people the money with which to buy your goods. But if it is good business when, having loaned your foreign customers the money to buy with, the goods are no sooner gone than you begin to wonder if you will get anything back, unless again you lend them the money they pay you with or forgive what they already owe—if that is business at all, then common sense is daftness and international finance has itself the secret of wisdom.

Another voice is heard, saying: "But remember, this modern world is all one place. No nation may enjoy separate prosperity, not even this one. A war-haggard Europe is properly the concern of a country that had resources to spare... That was reason enough for putting American credit at the command of Europe. Besides that it was our duty to do it, we should have been intelligent to do it on the ground of enlightened selfishness."

This high and excellent thought belongs to a harmony the world is not ready to play. There is first the probability that it will be embraced from opposite sides differently, by the lenders with one enthusiasm and by the borrowers with another, and that the transactions between them will not be governed by the simple rules of prudence, judgment and moral responsibility. When, moreover, you talk of lending as a duty, what do you mean? And how afterward shall you treat the contract? There is the further danger that the thought will be degraded to the saying that a rich nation, only because it is richer than others, is obliged to disperse its surplus among the envious and less fortunate. That idea, indeed, has been asserted by many European doctors of political economy, who either do not see or care not that international borrowing tends thereby to become reckless and irresponsible, and is soon tinged with the ancient thought of plunder.

After World War II, America treated its ex-allies even more generously. Garrett didn't approve.

A Formerly Capitalist People

From "Review and Comment," *American Affairs,* January 1948

The words American capitalism evoke an image that now is extensively unbeloved in a wretched and envious world. It is a name we have. Is it a fact or is it a myth? That is to ask, are we a capitalist people? The answer is not in what we think or say, nor in what the world thinks; what we do is evidence. Imagine a nation in every way like this one, including the sentiment, except only that its economic philosophy is definite and uncompromising. It is a capitalist nation, and everybody expects it to behave in that character. How would it now behave? What would it be saying to Europe?

It would be saying to Europe: "You need these three things and these only—food to eat while you are hungry, a supply of raw materials on which to act with your labor, and some new machines to improve your industrial equipment. As for food, we have a surplus and you are welcome to it. We have shared our food with the world before and we know how. We will not only send it; we will distribute it by the hand of the Red Cross or maybe through our Quakers, who, as you have reason to know, do a very good job of it. If you are humiliated to dip your spoon into the American bowl, we are sorry but that cannot be helped.

"As for raw materials, you may obtain these by the familiar device of commercial loans, the use of which you know as

159

well as we do. For new machines you need capital loans. We have a surplus of capital and you are welcome to borrow it. Our people will provide it and our bankers will lend it to you on terms that are customary. That is to say, we give you free access to the American money market both for commercial loans and for new capital, and we do this in consideration of your very evident need, notwithstanding the fact that only a few years ago we passed a law closing the American money market to any European government that was in default on its debts to the United States Treasury. Those repudiated debts are now forgotten and we say no more about them."

That would be all. It would not be necessary to say that among borrowers we should prefer free enterprise nations over those pursuing a socialist policy. That problem would take care of itself. The British steel people, for example, wanting an American loan, might be told that the rate of interest would be 15 percent. If they said, "But that is prohibitive," the American bankers would say: "The risk is high. After you have got your dollars the British Government may nationalize your industry and offer to pay back our money with blocked sterling." If to this the British steel people answered, "But we hear you are going to lend capital to the Belgian steel people at 4 percent," the American bankers would say, "That is true. It is a better risk. We think American dollars will be safer in Belgium." And if the British steel people said, "But this means that the British steel industry will be transferred to Belgium," the American bankers would need only to say, "That is something for the English people to think about."

Only twenty-five years ago it would have been the natural behavior of a capitalist people, perfectly understood and giving no political offense whatever. The British especially would have understood it, because they handled their own capital that way. And after all, what more could the world expect of a capitalist nation than food without price and access to its money market for loans?

160

We shall not behave like that. Seriously to suggest it is to give offense. Therefore, this paragraph would be entirely fanciful but for the purpose, which was to stalk the answer to the question proposed: Are we a capitalist people? If you do not see the answer, then perhaps it got away; or, it may be that you are looking at it and do not see it, because it is endowed with so much protective coloring.

CHAPTER SIX NOTES:

1 Gov.-Gen. Dwight Davis, founder of the Davis Cup in tennis.

2 Maj.-Gen. Leonard Wood, 1860-1927, participated in the last campaign against Geronimo, commanded the Rough Riders in the Spanish American War, was physician to President William McKinley and ended his career as Philippine governor-general, 1921-1927.

3 *The Philippines: A Treasure and a Problem* (1926). Nicholas Roosevelt was a nephew of Theodore Roosevelt.

4 Jericho is where Jesus stopped and gave sight back to the blind man.

5 Shylock is the Jewish moneylender in Shakespeare's *The Merchant of Venice* who demands a pound of flesh in repayment of a debt.

6 Joe Robinson, 1872-1937, Democrat of Arkansas, was senator from 1913 until his death, serving as minority leader 1923-1932 and majority leader 1933-1937.

7 Values are in gold dollars. For 2008 dollars, multiply by about 16.5..

8 The irreconcilables were the senators who were determined to vote against the Treaty of Versailles even if it was offered with reservations (which it wasn't).

9 The president referred to here is Warren Harding. At the Washington Conference the United States, Britain and Japan signed a treaty limiting capital ships of their navies to a fixed number in the ratio, respectively, of 5:5:3. Japan withdrew from the treaty in the mid-1930s.

10 Arthur Capper, 1865-1951, Republican of Kansas, was senator 1919-1948. He was publisher of the *Topeka Daily Capital* and *Capper's Farmer*.

11 Stanley Baldwin, a Conservative, was Chancellor of the Exchequer Oct. 1922-Aug. 1923.

12 $3.6 billion in 2008 dollars. To translate, multiply the 1931 dollars by 14.5.

13 James Ramsay MacDonald (1866-1937) was prime minister in Britain's first two Labour governments, in 1924 and 1929-31. In the 1931 gold-payments crisis, MacDonald agreed to form a coalition with the Conservatives and Liberals and accept the cut in social benefits the American bankers demanded, whereupon the Labour Party expelled him.

14 The Secretary of State was Henry Stimson, 1867-1950, who had been Secretary of War under Taft and would be again under Roosevelt, 1940-1945. The Secretary of the Treasury was Andrew W. Mellon, 1855-1937, who held that post under Presidents Harding, Coolidge and Hoover, 1921-1932.

Chapter Seven
WAR

Benito Mussolini made the argument that in a world of haves and have-nots, war was inevitable. That was the old idea of war for economic gain, which Garrett believed had been shattered in World War I. In the Saturday Evening Post of August 11, 1928, in "What Has Happened to War," he had written, "Nothing in the form of portable wealth could begin to pay the cost of modern conquest."

A decade later, war came anyway, and the old arguments came back about war for markets, war for profit, and war for plunder. Garrett stated his arguments again.

War Has Lost Its Pocket
From "War Has Lost Its Pocket," the *Saturday Evening Post,* January 13, 1940

O nly a little while ago we were by way of passing a law to take the profit out of war. But there was already such a law. We did not pass it. No parliament nor any congress of nations had passed it. With no celebration it had passed itself. And if it has not yet established itself in world intelligence, it is because, firstly, it took place as a fact not all at once, but gradually, so that you cannot make a stroke through time or touch a place and say it was then and there the economic motive for war became bankrupt in principle; and because,

163

secondly, the immemorial idea of conquest deeply inheres in the human race.

Certainly the President was unaware of it when he was saying in his Chautauqua speech, in 1936: "If war should break out again in another continent, let us not blink the fact that we could find in this country thousands of Americans who, seeking immediate riches—fool's gold—would attempt to break down or evade our neutrality. They would tell you— and, unfortunately, their views would get wide publicity—that if they could produce and ship this and that and the other article to the belligerent nations, the unemployed of America would all find work..."

Three years later, the war on another continent did come. Then two unpredictable things happened. One was that in his message to Congress for lifting the arms embargo, it was the President himself who spoke of the greater profit from selling the finished implements of war, instead of the raw materials only. He said: "From a purely material point of view, what is the advantage to us of sending all manner of articles across the ocean when we could give employment to thousands by doing it here?"

The other was that business nailed on its lintel these words: "American industry hates war!"

The National Association of Manufacturers said: "No sensible person believes that profits can come out of the wreckage of human life and economic dislocation." The United States Chamber of Commerce said: "We wish no profit advantage." In all the McGraw-Hill industrial and business publications appeared a message beginning: "Business stands against war. Let us take a clear-eyed look at this thing we call war. War is a political tool for domination or suppression, a device of futility." Such was the voice of business, big and little; and it was raised not only against war as a moral evil but against a war boom and war profits as economic evils, even in a neutral country. In this position, no two divisions of business were more positive than the steel and chemical industries, whence come guns and explosives.

Nothing that was believed of business, as to its foresight, wisdom and character, could have prepared any expectation of this radical event. The cynical opinion of it was that the role of a supplier to a war in Europe was an answer to faith and prayer. A neutral and distant geographical position, a surplus of raw materials, a surplus of industrial capacity, a surplus of labor, and a law to save business from its own folly, saying the war customers must come themselves and get the stuff and pay cash down on the barrel head at the dock. The profit motive could ask for nothing more. But instead of the fools' rush that had been predicted, there was a violent contrary reaction.

American business represents perhaps the most powerful economic machine in the world, and it makes this original declaration—that it has neither heart nor stomach for war profits. Such a thing has never occurred, neither here nor anywhere else. Twenty years ago it was unimaginable.

What does it mean?

Several answers are current in the market place. Among forty-one directors of the United States Chamber of Commerce, for example, thirty-six have been in the trenches. They remember what war is like, and they are fearful that a material stake in the outcome might tend to involve this country as a belligerent. Secondly, business remembers the last war boom and the agonies of deflation. Thirdly is the dread of the Mobilization Day Plan, under which the Government would lay its hands on all business, with the possibility that it might never take them off.

These are reasons, no doubt, and yet they bear hardly more than their own weight. What is significant is not the attitude of American business toward war as it might involve this country. That could have been taken for granted. The thing to be accounted for is the adverse judgment pronounced upon war profits as such, even though it should be guaranteed that the country should stay neutral and not itself become involved.

There is, of course, the moral aversion. War profits are stained with blood. But that is an emotional consideration, not rational, and give it what weight you will, it is still not enough.

What remains to be found is an adequate reason. And that reason would be that American business, for the first time, and by an intuition of its own not yet entirely rationalized, has arrived at the truth that war as an instrument of economic policy is obsolete. If that is so, it follows as a fact that there is no profit in war, and a new way of thinking begins.

This truth, now to be affirmed, is not one of the immortal verities, like a moral truth, nor is it in any way a consequence of civilization. It is an economic truth, belonging to our time and to the modern environment with which science, invention, technology and mechanical power have surrounded life.

When Joshua slew his thirty-one kings and burnt their cities with fire "and all that was therein: only the silver, and the gold, and the vessels of brass and iron, they put into the treasury of the house of the Lord;" when the Greeks were swarming in the Mediterranean world to look for well-timbered and well-watered land; when Caesar was enslaving his million wild Gauls; when tribute from the conquered provinces was enough to enable Rome to provide bread and circuses and abolish taxation at home—then and for two thousand years more, conquest was a rational enterprise. War could be made to pay.

It was so down to the year 1870, when Bismarck maneuvered France into a war, laid siege to Paris and won the game. The Germans went home with Alsace, part of Lorraine and five billion francs in gold out of the French stocking. But that was a fluke, and may be the last pure gain on the gaming table of war. Why? Because, thanks again to science, invention and mechanism, the cost of war is too great. The cost of taking Paris today would be enormously more than any sum of tribute the French could be made to pay, just as the cost of stopping the Germans twenty-five years ago was so great that the Allies never could get it back in German reparations. It was impossible.

What were the economic objects of conquest? In probable historic sequence they would be land, slaves, treasure, tribute and trade. What has happened to them, one by one, is that either the necessity has disappeared or that the object has passed beyond the reach of conquest because the meaning and character of wealth have changed.

In land you have the first and clearest example of a necessity that has vanished. When nine-tenths of man's labor had to be laid upon the land merely to clothe and feed himself, and even then there was never plenty; when tillage was for subsistence primarily and not for profit, then fertile land was a matter of life and death.

Now hardly one-quarter of man's labor is required on the soil to produce plenty. In the whole world there is a surplus of agricultural produce, and it is so great that on three continents agriculture is ill-rewarded at the natural price, and governments either subsidize it or protect it with tariffs. This is not a temporary condition. Whereas the productivity of the soil and the labor laid upon it has been increased already two or three fold, there is new knowledge in the field of agrobiology to increase it many-fold more. The amount of human life that may be sustained on a given area of land is, in fact, an unknown quantity. It follows that land is not a rational object of conquest for two reasons—namely, first, that for an industrial nation it is cheaper to buy agricultural commodities than to produce them, and, secondly, that the productivity of the land it already possesses may be wonderfully increased.

Fear of famine, on the western side of the world, at least, has been banished. Yet remember, this has occurred only in our time, whereas land hunger is from the oldest fear memory in the tissues of the human race—the memory of scarcity.

If you look, you will see this again and again—that the facts of human behavior, political behavior especially, contradict the facts of modern existence. Change in the vital conditions has been sudden, eruptive, and, so far as we know, causeless—who can say what caused the machine?—whereas habits of thinking and feeling change slowly.

Slavery was an institution older than written history. The moral sense of mankind did not destroy it; the machine did that. Yet the machine is new. It has neither a tradition nor any way of accounting for itself. Each day it is new again. It destroyed the economic value of slavery because it is cheaper than slaves. In the time of Cato, a fair price for a farm slave was $250. Which will you have—a tractor or four slaves? There was no original necessity for the machine. Civilization might have continued on forever without it. Now life is more dependent upon machines than it ever was upon slaves. In one century and a half the population of the world has more than doubled, all owing to the machine. Abolish the machine and half the human life in the earth would perish.

Well, then, why is the machine not a rational object of conquest? Why not capture the machine instead of the slave?

The French had that thought when, in 1923, because reparations payments were not forthcoming from the Germans, they occupied the Ruhr Valley. That was the very heart of industrial Germany. The machines were there. Along with the troops the French sent engineers and technicians. The troops were to command obedience; the engineers and technicians were to supervise the Germans at work.

I was there. From the hotel in Essen, which had been staffed with French cooks and French servants because they were all afraid to touch German food, three army officers and an engineer took me in a French motorcar to a water tower commanding a panoramic view. They spread out a map on which the industrial plants were marked. Over there was Stinnes, there was Thyssen, there was Krupp. Then we rushed off to visit them. Each plant was surrounded by a high brick wall; and each time we came to a gate, there was a lone German watchman, unarmed, his arm upraised, rotating his palm against us. That was enough. The Frenchmen dared not pass him. Why not? They could call their troops; they could knock down the walls. Yes; but they knew that at a signal a few Germans could wreck the machines, and it would take them only five minutes to do it.

The machine may be trusted only to willing hands.

The Germans now have captured the machines of Czechoslovakia and Poland. But who will work them? If the Czechs and Poles cannot be trusted to do it, or refuse, then they may be exterminated. That is possible. Only, mark it, each Czech or Pole who is exterminated is one customer less for the products of German machines, whereas it had been Germany's bitter complaint that her economy was in want of customers. The importance of this fact will become more apparent under the head of trade as an economic object of conquest.

We are coming to that. But first consider the change that has taken place in the nature of wealth.

I once made the acquaintance of a retired bank burglar who was chronically indignant at the dishonesty of bank figures. He knew that I wrote about banking in a serious way, and for a while he could not decide whether to blame my intelligence or my morals. One day he took from his pocket a carefully preserved piece of newspaper, the published financial state-ment of a suburban bank. Pointing to total assets, which is all that he understood of it, he said: "Look. That's what they tell the people they've got. Every bank does. They are lying. I know, because I examined that particular bank myself, and it wasn't there. You'd be surprised. I've seen more money in a faro bank."

I could not make him understand that the wealth of a bank is not in gold and currency, but in book entries, in bundles of I.O.U.s, in a stream of people arriving and departing, some to deposit money, some to receive, some to pay interest and some to borrow. What do the borrowers do with the money? One puts it into a machine, promising to pay it back with interest. He cannot pay but from the sale of the machine's product. The product, provided it satisfies a human want and people are ready to buy it, is truly wealth. The machine itself is not. It is but the means to wealth. All the wonderful and costly machines of the motor industry would be utterly worthless if there were not millions of people to buy new motorcars each year.

Nor is gold wealth, except in ornaments that satisfy an esthetic desire. Monetary gold is not wealth. The only reason we regard it as such is that people cannot trust one another not to counterfeit and debase their paper money. The case of a nation trading with her neighbors is that if her word is not good and her trade is out of balance, she will be unable to keep a gold reserve; whereas if her word is good and her trade is in balance, she will not need any gold, or hardly any. The gold the Germans have seized from Austria, Czechoslovakia and Poland is of little importance, except in a war economy. All the gold in the world would not solve Germany's peace-time economic problems. She could only spend it and consume what she bought, instead of producing and exchanging real wealth in a way to make herself and the whole world richer. When the gold was gone, she would be worse off than before.

Yet one hears the argument that Germany, being obliged to buy the raw materials required by her industry, first was drained of gold by reparations payments to the Allies, and then, having only the products of her technical skill to exchange for raw materials, the world turned against her goods, wherefore she could not buy because she could not sell, her exchange position was ruined, and she was forced to go to war in order to possess herself of raw materials.

Never was Germany denied access to raw materials at the world price—the same as was paid by everyone else. It is not true that she was drained of gold. Twice the world lent her gold to set up a new currency. It is not true that reparations drained her. She did not pay them. She borrowed the money to pay them, principally from us, and then defaulted. It is true that she has to buy raw materials and that what she has to buy them with is her technical skill in the form of manufactured goods; but that is true also of Belgium, for example. There were no more barriers in the world against German goods than against Belgian goods until, in this country, we raised tariffs against Germany to compensate for the subsidies she gave her own exporters, with a political motive, and this we thought unfair.

What Germany did was to use the proceeds of everything she could sell to build a war machine, and that is what ruined her exchange position. If you buy raw materials to make a machine, you can sell either the machine or its products, and the whole world is thereby richer; but if you buy raw materials to make implements of war, intending to use them yourself, as Germany did, these you cannot sell, and your buying power declines. Having pursued that policy, a nation finds itself in an impossible dilemma. In no case can the war implements be converted back into things that satisfy human wants. You can convert food into guns, by doing without butter and having armaments instead, but you cannot convert the guns back into butter. So, therefore, that nation must make a desperate choice between two evils. One is to suffer an immediate economic disaster from demobilization, which will entail unemployment and then years of hard work and privation until new wealth can be created; the other is to release the war machine on its destructive and profitless errand.

There was, it is true, a high emotional barrier against German goods. That was the boycott, in retaliation for her treatment of the Jews, and it did great harm to German trade. There the cause was not economic; the consequences were. And from this you come to a kind of wealth, imponderable and yet very important, that cannot be bought or sold.

Since the great wealth of the modern world consists not in things that can be seized and dragged home, but in the continuity of process and exchange, in debits and credits, in the faith of contract, in mass production as a means and mass consumption as the end, none of which may be commanded by force, all of which are beyond the reach of conquest, it follows that the good will of neighbors is itself a priceless commodity. It has been cultivated more or less; never has it been conquered.

But the toughest of all surviving delusions are those concerning trade as an object of conquest—ideas such as economic empire, colonies to exploit, preferential markets, pathways of one's own to the sources of raw material and then to the customer.

One must allow that if these ideas now are obsolete, that was not always to be said of them. Not long ago, they were valid enough. They were valid for Great Britain while she was founding her empire. What happened to them was that the world passed from an economy of scarcity to an economy of plenty; and that has taken place within one lifetime.

It may be strange that one of the visions of a world of wealth beyond conquest occurred in Germany. I was there during the second year of the World War. The man I most wanted to see was Walter Rathenau, because he was the economic dictator, with absolute power over physical resources. My errand was to find out, if I could, whether it was true that Germany's material means to war were about to be exhausted. Those who might have performed an introduction were discouraging. They said I might as well be wanting to see the

Kaiser. So I sent a note around to him, and the answer was that I might come in the next morning at ten, for half an hour.

It was winter. Snow was falling. He was alone in his office and the temperature was uncomfortably low. We stood at the window looking out, and that made it seem warmer inside. I had expected to meet an industrialist, for he was head of the celebrated German electric industry founded by his father. Or I had expected to meet a great administrator, which he was. I knew also that he was an engineer and a chemist. But his faculties exceeded all of that. He was statesman, philosopher, thinker, seer of forms that have not yet arrived—one of the rare imaginative minds of his time.

I do not recall how it was that the conversation took a certain turn. Lunch was forgotten. At dark, the snow still falling, as it may in Berlin all day long without leaving its coat, we were yet at the window.

What had we been talking about? Not the war. I remember that as we went on, the war seemed a thing misplaced in time, meaningless in itself. Whether Germany's resources would permit her to go on for a month, a year, two years—what difference did it make? Sometime it would end, and then the problem would be what it was before. How shall competitive people live together in the world, no insulating partitions of space, solitude or silence between them? Afterward he put some of it down in a book entitled, *In Days to Come.*

Here was a man bending the physical power of Germany to the breaking point in order to wage a nationalistic war, because that was his job, and at the same time dreaming the outlines of an international world. Not a world without nations in it. Not anything like a universal utopia. No, nor a socialistic world. But a symbiotic, or a living-together world, in which those having special traits of mind and hand should produce certain things for all, and exchange them for unlike things produced by others in the same way, which would be trade on a basis of mutual and equal satisfaction. Trade of that kind would save so much in the cost of senseless competition, the waste of duplication and, most of all, the cost of war and armaments, that in time to come the human race might be truly and responsibly rich.

He saw, perhaps, the luminous phantom of it only. There would need to be a change in the philosophy of government, and he had not thought that problem through. Nevertheless, a moment of vision in the chasm of that war becomes a movement of thought in the chasm of this one, and now the American Secretary of State and the British Prime Minister[1] are talking of a world of "full trade," beyond aggression. It is the same theme.

While the World War lasted, Rathenau's genius for administration made him indispensable to his country. Afterward, representing her in foreign affairs, his dream became a liability. It was not a German dream. The German instinct turned against him, and in 1922 he was assassinated.[2] How inevitable that was, then or later, is now apparent. The German sense of destiny is to be, not a people in the world but a world people; the German idea of trade is to conquer it by force. Hence Hitler.

So now we speak of trade. It is the last defense of war pretending to be an economic enterprise.

Consider, first, how all ideas of trade as a rational object of conquest imply one thing—namely, the power to take advantage, so that in the exchange of goods you will receive more than you give, else there is no profit in it. Trade in that character was a vast improvement over piracy and pillage, yet thanks for this much more to common sense than to morals. The weakness of pillage is that it was not feasible as a continuous business. Once you had taken what people had, you were obliged to wait until they created more of what you wanted, besides having discouraged them from doing it. But if you could swap glass beads for gold and ivory, that was much better, since it entailed no risk, did not dry up the source, and

174

saved you the cost of a fighting force with which you would have to share the loot.

Long after international trade had become highly civilized, very complex, and inseparable from the well-being of the world, it still retained more or less of that character. It was implicit in the mercantile doctrine of England down to the time of Adam Smith—the doctrine that in order to profit by foreign trade, a nation must sell more than it buys and accumulate the difference in gold. And even until now it has been implicit in the scheme of economic empire, colonies and colonial markets.

That principle of trade would work for a while. It worked best for England when she was the one great industrial nation. There might be two or three great industrial nations, exchanging the products of their machines and their high-caste labor for the food and raw materials produced by drudge and peasant labor, and still there would be profit in it. But the machine was uncontrollable. It got loose and went migrating all over the earth. And when it was—as I have heard a British lord say—that many countries had come to have industries to which they were not entitled, each one wanting to have a favorable balance of trade, the old principle was bound to break down. Everybody could not have a favorable balance of trade, for where would it come from?

It is the machine again. Industry had invented it for its own benefit and for a long time confined it, leaving food and raw materials to be produced by manual labor. Not until the machine began to act upon the production of food and raw materials did the world begin to change from an economy of scarcity to an economy of plenty. This was the incomparable event in the life of the race, since the Expulsion and Curse, and our intelligence has not yet been able to assimilate it. The word "surplus" appeared, not to mean blessing, but, in absurd contradiction to common sense, to mean economic disaster, panic and unemployment. The further absurdity is that with some glimpse of the right way, people all with one voice cry, "Trade, more trade!" and at the same time put up barriers against one another's trade.

There was a phrase above: "Mass production as a means and mass consumption as the end." The key is there. A problem that had been always the first economic anxiety of man has disappeared—how to produce enough. A problem hitherto unknown presents itself—how to consume what we produce.

That seems a simple statement. But what are its implications? It means that it no longer pays to exploit your customer or your colony for all the immediate profit it will yield, for if you do, you limit the power of consumption, whereas how to increase it is your real problem; and if you do not increase it, your profit will be limited and may altogether fail.

It means that the motive to possess customers, markets and colonies, in order to exploit them, is unsound economically and will in the end defeat itself.

And it means that economic empire, founded upon the ancient right of the strong to exploit the labor of the weak, has more past than future.

Within a domestic economy it means that the cost of satisfactions must tend to fall and the wages of labor must tend to rise, for unless it does, the fruits of mass production cannot be consumed. What is true of a domestic economy is true also of a world economy. The great object of trade, therefore, must be to raise the standard of living in the whole world, not to enrich a few nations. Always trade has had that effect, whether intending it or not; never has it been rationally conscious of that object, as now it must begin to be in order to save itself.

Beyond the thought of markets and colonies of their own to be exploited, those nations called the "have-nots," Germany foremost, keep saying they must possess their own sources of raw material in order to compete with the "haves," meaning especially Great Britain. They make an outcry of it, and it is specious. For metals, fibers, rubber, fuel and all basic commodities, there is a world market and a world price; in time of peace, raw materials flow freely to meet any demand as by gravity of price. Moreover, those who produce them are more anxious to sell them than any industrial nation is to buy them, and generally those who produce raw materials have a standard of living below that of the industrial life. Formerly, in the pioneer time of development, when the supply was inconstant or inadequate, it was well for an industrial nation to invest its capital in sources of raw material. But there is no longer any advantage in it; on the contrary, it may entail additional risk. Only in time of war is it important for a nation to possess its own raw materials. But by that fact the argument is turned upside down. A nation does not go to war to acquire raw materials for purposes of trade, seeing that in time of peace it is cheaper to buy them than to produce them. It is the other way. It was control of raw materials in order to go to war.[3]

But go on with it. Suppose Germany by force should get possession at the source of all the raw materials her industry needs. What will she do with them? She will convert them, of course, into manufactured goods. Then where will she sell the goods? What customers will she have that she did not have before? If the answer is that she must go on to conquer new markets for German goods, that means she must take them from her rivals, from England perhaps. But she cannot do that without hurting the economic position of England, and she cannot hurt the economic position of England without hurting her own, because in time of peace England had been her best customer. Therefore, what she will gain on the one hand she will partly or wholly lose on the other, for the web of trade now is such that rivals are one another's customers.

Twenty-five years ago, Germany was saying the same thing. She had come late to the feast and the world was all taken up. She had no place in the sun, nowhere to trade, no room at all. She was squeezed in an iron band and was obliged to break it by force. Such was her propaganda. Now turn to her figures of foreign trade. In the twelve years preceding the World War, she stood second only to Great Britain. Her share of the total foreign trade of the world was 14 per cent; Great Britain's share was 19 per cent. For ten years, Germany's share had been rising; Great Britain's had been falling. And in the year 1913, Germany's best customer was Great Britain, buying twice as much from Germany as Germany bought from her.

With no economic empire, Germany was already the most powerful industrial nation in Europe, and on the way to becoming the foremost nation in the world in trade. She was ahead of the United States and was overtaking England. Her exertions in foreign trade were prodigious; she sacrificed her domestic economy for the sake of it. Yet she was not thinking of foreign trade as a way of increasing the wealth of the world, nor of her own primarily. The motive was political. She regarded foreign trade as a means to Weltmacht, or world power. That was what she wanted most. Going to war for it, she lost it, and together with it, her eminence in world trade.

So also with Japan. A balance sheet of her career of conquest would be a strange and sorry thing to look at. What does she want in China? Trade, she says, and raw materials. The cost of taking the raw materials by force, over what it would have cost to buy them, has already devoured the profits of fifty years' trade; besides that, in doing it she has wrecked the economic life of China and killed her own customers by the hundreds of thousands.

Lying deep in the original contradiction, wherein the race hath both iniquity and grandeur in it by mixture, there are too many reasons for war—revenge, fear, honor, lust for power, delusions of racial and national aggrandizement, ideas of freedom and justice. But now and for the first time the economic-profit motive is not among them. It is as if in the blind mag-

178

nificence of his material achievements man had created a defense against himself, better founded upon self-interest than upon generosity, without knowing what he did or how, or that it would ever happen.

For now it is to be perceived that your enemy is also your customer. That was the problem that presented itself at the end of the World War. A strong Germany, restored by the aid of her trade rivals, would probably fight again; on the other hand, a weak Germany would be a poor customer.

War is no longer battle. It is a total thing. Once it starts, it cannot stop until one people has its foot on the other's neck. Then what will you do? The cost of this victory is greater than any sum of tribute that can be collected. You cannot kill a people, neither could you afford to do it if you would. Therefore, all you can do is to help your enemy up, dust him off, straighten his tie and put money in his pocket in order to begin trading with him again.

Garrett was against picking a fight with Hitler, which he thought Roosevelt was trying to do, but he was for a strong defense and for facing the realities of war head-on. He was for taxes, rationing, controls and conscription—for the duration and not a minute more. Here, in an editorial before Pearl Harbor, he states the case for taxes and controls.

Terrific Taxation

"Fifty Billions Wild," *Saturday Evening Post* editorial, September 13, 1941

Women mobbing the silk-stocking counters and a crockery factory that employs 2,000 people shutting down for want of a carload of borax were as the sudden, fantastic little winds that run ahead. What is threatening is extreme economic disorder.

To understand what is happening, you need no economic theory. The less of that the better, and much less to begin with would have been better still.

Think of the total possible output of all possible things as one pile. How is it divided around? Normally, in what we call a money economy, it is divided by price. Each thing in the pile has a price. If it happens that there is not enough of one kind of thing to go around, the price goes up, with two effects: First, at the higher price fewer people can afford to buy it, which lessens the demand; second, the supply will tend to increase because as the price goes up, the profit rises, and more people will employ themselves and their capital to produce it.

Now comes war, or before war a national-defense emergency, and the pile has to be divided first with the Government. That division is arbitrary. Price has nothing to do with it. With or without price, the Government will take what it has to have.

What is left when the Government is through taking is the people's pile, and that has still to be divided around. But in these altered circumstances, how shall it be divided around?

If the case is that the people's pile is less than the people want and less than they can afford to buy because their hands are full of money and there is more money than things, then you cannot leave it to price to divide the pile. If you do leave it to price, people will bid against one another for the things that are scarce and prices will rise uncontrollably, and the higher prices will not in the natural way tend to increase the supply because all the reserve power of the country will be demanded by the Government for its unlimited armament program—and so you come at once to the disaster of inflation.

In this situation, the first thing the Government thinks of is to control and fix prices. But when, by law or edict, the Government has commanded prices to stand still, there is still the people's pile, to be divided around. How? It cannot divide itself. To divide by price now is both impossible and forbidden. The function of prices has been suspended. How else shall the pile be divided?

Take it as to automobiles. The output in going to be reduced, maybe as much as one half, in order to release more materials for the defense program. If you cut the supply of automobiles by half and do nothing to control or limit the demand, what is going to happen? You will have two buyers for each automobile; two buyers with equal rights, and each one forbidden to pay more than the other. How shall it be decided between them? Which one shall have the automobile?

Obviously, demand must be limited or controlled. There are only three ways to do that—namely, one, raise the price to a point at which people can afford to buy only half as many automobiles as before; two, let the price stand, but tax the automobile to the point at which people can afford to buy only half as many as before; or, three, ration the automobile.

The motorcar industry did the only thing it could do. It started to raise the price. The Government said no to that. It said no to it because it might increase the profits of the motorcar industry. But having said no, the Government did nothing more about it. So what will happen nobody knows. The Government does not know. What is true of automobiles is true of every other thing that is going to be scarce. For months the OPM and the OEM and the OPACS have been talking about scarcity and doing nothing about it because they had not the authority. Therefore people have been grabbing at the pile. Vast quantities of things have vanished into big and little hoards. Every purchasing agent in the country has been over-buying because every other one was doing it. Worse than all, the Government itself has been grabbing, for fear the people would grab too much.

In the beginning, the Government fondly believed that a little inflation would be not a bad thing, touching especially wages and farm prices, and running until there was full employment. Now suddenly it sees the danger and is alarmed. Inflation has ramified itself in the soil, like a mighty weed running underground.

It must be stopped. To stop it, Government will have to control and administer prices. That is clear. But when that is done, demand must be limited and controlled, by terrific taxation properly designed for that purpose or by a system of license and ration, or a combination of both. And until the Government faces this simple problem and acts upon it in a comprehensive and fearless manner, there will be increasing economic confusion, tending toward chaos, with possibilities of ultimate disaster.

Government did control and administer prices. It shut down production of private cars a few weeks after the attack on Pearl Harbor.

In June 1950 war broke out in Korea, and government began reimposing wartime economic controls. Here, in the final issue of American Affairs, Garrett reflects on the need for, and the peril of, controls for war.

The Law of Controls
From "Comment," *American Affairs*, October 1950

The bitterness of the dispute about controls for mobilization or war has been sign and measure of the change that has taken place in the state of feeling between government and people since World War I. Nobody then had any fear of controls; everybody accepted them in good part, reserving only the human right to grumble. Nor is it now controls that people dread. It is something very much deeper. What it is may be understood when you set in contrast two postwar messages from the President of the United States. On December 3, 1918, President Wilson said to Congress:

Our people do not want to be coached and led. They know their own business, are quick and resourceful at every readjustment, definite in purpose and self-reliant in action. Any leading strings we might seek to put them in would become hopelessly tangled because they would pay no attention to them and go their own way.

While the war lasted we set up many agencies by which to direct the industries of the country in the services it was necessary for them to render. But the moment we knew the Armistice had been signed, we took the harness off. Raw materials, on which the government had kept its hands in fear there should not be enough for the industries that supplied the armies, have been released and put on the general market again.

It is surprising how fast the process of a return to peace footing has moved in these weeks since the fighting stopped. It promises to outrun any inquiry that may be instituted and any aid that may be offered. It will not be easy to direct it any better than it will direct itself.

On September 6, 1945, President Truman said to Congress:

I urge that the Congress do not adopt a resolution proclaiming the termination of the war. Such a resolution would automatically cause the death of many war powers and wartime agencies before we are ready; it would cause great confusion and chaos in the government.

It is the policy of this Administration not to exercise wartime powers beyond the point at which it is necessary to exercise them.

We should be prepared to undertake a great program of public works not only to improve the physical plant of the United States, but to provide employment to great masses of our citizens when private industry cannot do so.

It am directing the executive agencies to give full weight to the foreign requirements in determining the need for maintaining domestic and export controls and priorities.

There is the change. In World War I, people said: "We impose these controls upon ourselves through the instrumentalities of popular government, for the duration of the war only. When the war has been won, we will cast them off." It never occurred to them that the government would resist the idea, and it didn't. With the signing of the Armistice the whole wartime bureaucracy collapsed, as it was expected to do. The dollar-a-year men put on their hats, slammed their doors and went back to business. The railroads were returned to their owners. In a little while the economy was as free, or almost as free, as it was before.

But what people now fear is a very different sequel. They have seen what can happen. During the depression they accepted controls again and Congress surrendered vast powers to the President, including control of the public purse—and all of this at first was supposed to be for the duration of the emergency only. But the laws that were passed in the name of the emergency brought to pass, and were intended to effect, a revolution in the meaning and uses of government. The foundations of the Welfare State were laid.

Came then the mobilization for defense and after that World War II. But even during this war the doctrine of a planned economy for peacetime was systematically developed, so that when the war ended there was a blueprint for a further extension of the power and authority of executive government over the entire economy, touching everywhere the lives of the people. In all of executive government, after seven years of the New Deal and five years of war, there was no thought of taking the harness off, as President Wilson said, nor of leaving the economy to direct itself. The planners had it.

It is no longer possible for the people to feel, "These are controls we impose upon ourselves for the duration of the war." What they feel is that government imposes them and what they fear is that the road back will be forgotten.

And all the more pity that is. We know in time of crisis controls are necessary. We also know that neither total war nor total mobilization can be managed within the framework of a free economy, and we might have learned, if we haven't, that neither can it be bought within the limitations of peacetime finance. The will to survive must in the end overthrow all conventions.

Imagine then to begin with a free economy in which the free market is the controlling mechanism, and all goods are rationed among the consumers by the price, so that according to the price, some buy more, some less, some do without. Now suddenly introduce one consumer whose wants are preemptory and insatiable, to whom price is no object and who in any case will take what he cannot buy. That consumer is total war. What he represents is unlimited compulsory consumption. What then happens to the postulates of your free economy? Certainly nobody will deny that in time of crisis scarce commodities will have to be divided between this one consumer and the civilians by some plan of allocation or priority. That means rationing by edict. You cannot say a free market mechanism any longer governs the economy. Necessity governs it.

Thirdly, the time factor is changed. Your war consumer cannot wait. A battle may be lost, and it may be the last battle for all you know. This is ignored by the extremists who say: "Nevertheless leave it to the free market and it will work like this: the demand for war goods will cause the price of those goods to rise faster than anything else and the production of them will be increased accordingly by natural incentive." True, it would work that way, given time. But with the steel mills already working at top capacity, how long would it take for a rise of 10% or 20% in the price of steel to bring about an increase in the production of steel? While waiting for new steel mills to be built we might lose the war.

Knowing that the horror of total war is riding on the wheel of chance, and that if it starts it will start suddenly, it behooves a rational people to enact beforehand a complete law of controls, any or all of which may be invoked immediately with no further debate in Congress about it. After that the only question from day to day would be: How much mobilization?

It sounds so simple. And it would have been simple if people had not learned how much easier it is for an anaconda government to swallow power than to regurgitate it.

1 Cordell Hull, 1871-1955 was Secretary of State and the most prominent free trader in the Roosevelt administration, Neville Chamberlain, 1869-1940, was the British Prime Minister.

2 Walter Rathenau, 1867-1922, was minister of reconstruction after World War I and became foreign minister in 1922. He negotiated the Treaty of Rapallo with the Soviet Union in 1922, canceling war debts and claims, recognizing the Soviet government, opening up trade and, in a secret provision, allowing Germany to test in the U.S.S.R. weapons forbidden by the Treaty of Versailles. Rathenau was negotiating a reparations treaty with the Allies when he was assassinated by anti-Semites. A Jew, he was accused posthumously by the Nazis of sabotaging Germany's war effort. He is honored by Liberal International, the world association of liberal parties.

   In 1916, in the penultimate paragraph in his ten-part series in the *New York Times*, Garrett quoted Rathenau without naming him. After exploring the possible ideas for peace, and saying that none appeared likely, Garrett opined, "You get the feeling in Europe that people are mad." And then he wrote: "He who might be called the economic dictator of Europe says calmly: 'Isn't it nonsense? Can you imagine what it is all about? I can't. It seems to me to be the most terrible nonsense. But I see no way out of it.' And he goes on cruelly bending the industrial energies of Germany to the uses of war. That is his job."

3 In "Socialism in the Red," in the *Saturday Evening Post* of June 16, 1934, Garrett wrote: "If international trade was a source of war in private hands for private profit, what will it be when it is for national profit in the hands of armed and sovereign states?"

Chapter Eight
A NEW PROPRIETOR

Garrett wrote that in the 19th century, "railways were made in hope, rejoicing and sheer abandon of willful energy." By 1910 railroad rates were regulated, and in 1917 the government seized the railroads for the duration of the war. In 1920 they were returned but with a federal right to mediate labor disputes. In 1926 came the Railway Labor Act, which was strengthened under the New Deal. Here is what it did.

Peace on the Rails
From "Peace on the Rails," the *Saturday Evening Post,* September 9, 1939

It is an article of current opinion that between the railroads and labor there exists a model peace; and since there is nowhere else much peace to boast of, people are asking, "Why can't industrial relations generally be settled in that same design?"

Our sickest elephant is the railroad industry. It is physically and visibly shrinking at the rate of 2,000 miles a year, besides what else is taking place inside for want of vitamin P.

Nearly one-third of the total railroad mileage of the country is in the hands of trustees and courts, under certificate of illness, to avoid the sheriff. The Congress holds hearing without end and passes the ever-longer law, the Interstate

Commerce Commission is lost in the abyss of statistical knowledge, and this year the high schools are debating the plight of the railroads: Shall the Government take them over?

The relation of all this to the peace is mural. What we want to know about the peace is whether it is a natural peace or a peace of appeasement, a free or a boughten peace, and how it works. It is a curious fact that we know very little about it.

The public takes it for granted as something that seems to be working, thinking about it only when it happens to be reminded that there has not been a serious railroad strike for a long time.

The Government takes it with pride of authorship. Whatever else it may have done to the railroads during fifty years of regulation and control, it may say it has brought this peace to pass.

How, then, do the railway unions take it? They take it extremely well, and this is so for the reason, first, that it perfects and implements their monopoly.

In the hands of a labor union or in the hands of a wicked capitalistic trust, there is one principal use of monopoly, and that is to control the price. With unemployment among railway workers increasing at a terrific rate—200,000 men laid off in one year—and with the decline of the railroad machine become a matter of public anxiety, even from the point of view of national defense, the price of railway labor has been raised to its highest point. The advantage of monopoly is that you can buck a falling market in that manner, raising the price as the demand falls.

The fact is that the actual number of railway workers has been for a long time falling, owing partly to operating efficiency generally. Nevertheless the total payroll has all the time been rising.

In 1916 the total number of railroad employees was 1.6 million; in 1938 it was only 900,000. The average pay per worker had more than doubled. Most of the increase in the average pay per worker was from a rise in wage rates; the rest of it, to a very large extent, represents the fattening of the payroll by imaginary work. The meaning of that will be explained later.

After the general wage increase of 1937, a union magazine calculated that since 1933 the employees had succeeded in raising payroll expenses by $452 million a year. The railroad statisticians make it somewhat less, $389 million a year. One more figure. The gross earnings of the railroads in 1938, compared with the low point of the depression, showed an increase of $424 million. By its own calculation, labor got a little more than all of it; by the calculation of the railroad statisticians, it got only 92 percent of it.

You can see it has been a very profitable peace, not for railway labor in the whole, but for the surviving number possessing prior right to employment under the rules of seniority; and now these are moving for a six-hour day.

Secondly, what endears the peace to the labor unions is an element of intense psychic satisfaction.

In the days of happy ruggedness, the boss could say, "Casey, you're fired. Go get your time and be damned sudden about it." It may have been that Casey had forgotten to lock a switch, or that he damaged a piece of property, or that he was caught in the tool shanty with a can of beer; it may have been only that the boss did not like his shoes or the way he walked in them. Whatever it was, and the boss having said it, Casey was certainly fired.

All that is changed. Now, if the boss must do it, it behooves him to do it gently, and say "Mr. Casey," because Casey will take it to court where the judge will be five Caseys of his own choosing and five of what he would call shirts, representing the railroads; and the chances are two to one that he will return with an order saying that he shall be reinstated in his job, with full pay for the time he was off, his seniority rights unimpaired, as if nothing had happened. And thereafter, when he comes near the boss, he may give him the dirty whistle.

What is this court and how does it work?

To find out what it is, we have to take up the law—the law of peace, called the Railway Labor Act, passed in 1926 and amended, New Deal wise, in 1934. It is a clumsy law, new writing over old, and falls into two parts—one for the major purpose and one for the minor purpose.

The major purpose is to keep the general peace, which is liable to be broken only by premeditated disputes over basic wage rates, hours and working conditions. To act upon disputes of this character the law creates a National Mediation Board. It intervenes first with an offer to mediate; if that fails, it must try to persuade both sides to accept binding arbitration; if that is declined by either side, then the President may appoint an emergency board to investigate and report.

That is all. There the law stops. So far as the law goes, nobody has any power to oblige the peace.

The minor purpose of the law is to keep the peace in particular cases, such as the firing of Casey. To act upon grievance cases the law created the court of labor justice, called the National Railroad Adjustment Board, and seated it in Chicago.

The membership is exactly balanced. The labor unions choose and pay and control one half; the railroads choose and pay and control the other half. The labor members vote for labor and the railroad members vote for the railroads, and justice stops on a dead center.

The law imagined that this might happen and provided that in case of deadlock they should call in a referee. But it happens that they deadlock on the referee. The law imagined that, too, and said that in that case the National Mediation Board at Washington should send a referee. That suits the labor members perfectly. So long as the Government is prolabor, the National Mediation Board will send a liberal referee.

It is a nice job, paying $75 a day and expenses, and, of course, the referee is anxious to please, so that he may be called again. If he turns out to be not liberal enough, the labor members can make it so unpleasant for him that he will retire, or so disagreeable for the National Mediation Board that it will never send him again. One referee, and a liberal who had thought of himself as a friend of labor, walked out in anger and resigned, saying in his letter to the National Mediation Board that the "abuse and obstructive tactics of the labor members" made it impossible for him to "continue to submit to an attitude which is lacking in ordinary decency as well as in a sense of justice." That was what the labor members wanted. They got another referee, more to their liking.

From a judicial point of view it is a fantastic court. The petitioner is always labor—that is to say, Casey, although he himself never appears. His case is presented by a committee in writing, and the railroad, being notified, sends counsel to rebut it. No witnesses are called, no oaths are administered, of the oral arguments there is no transcript permitted. In the deadlocked cases, the referee, to whom the railroad vernacular is a strange tongue, must decide between two conflicting statements of fact, both of which may be prejudiced; and, moreover, it may be that the case before him is a guinea pig, seeming to involve only one day's pay for Casey, because somebody else performed and was paid for work that he says he should have been called upon to do. But if that claim is sustained, the precedent may apply immediately to thousands of fictitious days exactly like that one, and nobody knows how much it will cost the railroads. The railroads themselves do not know until the claims come in.

Another peculiarity about this court is that it works in a sealed atmosphere. Publicity is taboo. The labor members object. A few weeks ago four newspaper reporters unexpectedly appeared and sat down. Such a thing had never happened before. The labor members recessed themselves to think it over. They said, first, it was unfair because no newspaper reporter could be expected to understand what he heard there; second, it was unfair because these reporters represented papers that were unfriendly to labor; and, third, they said it must be a conspiracy on the part of the railroads to bring publicity on the work of the court. And then they threatened that if the railroads continued on this line, the labor organizations would retaliate. How? By changing their policy of cooperation to one of opposition and thereafter standing against the railroads at Washington. Meanwhile, so long as the reporters were there, they would instruct those presenting cases for labor to make no oral statements and answer no questions. A curious kind of strike. Half the court and all the petitioners on a silence strike against publicity.

It may occur to you that we have been using a wrong word. This is not a court. It is a new kind of instrumentality for which we have not found the suitable name.

The answer to that is in the law. The law says this is a court above all other courts. Its decisions are final and there is no appeal. The only way to go from the National Railroad Adjustment Board to a court of law is a way left open to labor, and labor will not take it. The law says that where an award calls for a payment of money and the railroad refuses to pay the money, then labor may go to a court to enforce its claim. You may suppose, therefore, that in order to reach a court with an award it thinks unfair, a railroad has only to refuse to pay and get itself sued. But the labor unions are too smart. They will not sue for the money. Instead they will say to the railroad, "If you do not pay, we shall be obliged to use our economic strength," meaning they will strike. That would put the railroad in the bad position of courting a strike sooner than to pay a lawful award.

Before coming to the cases and awards, there is something to be said of the book of rules. In the beginning there was a bulletin board. All the rules were posted there, and whether you liked them or not, if you broke them you were fired. The operations of a railroad became more complex, the rules multiplied, and many of them were complained of by the men. In time they were reduced to written agreements, subject to change only by consent, signed on one side by the management and on the other by the men, acting as a union. In the course of a hundred years, the book of rules became a bible of complete experience, intelligible only to railroad people. There were rules of conduct, rules of discipline, rules of what to do when the train stopped on the main line, how to stand at an open switch, who was responsible for the flag. These rules were written not by lawyers but by foremen, superintendents and managers—by railroad men for railroad men. Each railroad had its own book, and when there was a dispute, the matter could be settled on the spot by understanding, not by legal interpretation.

What the National Railroad Adjustment Board undertakes to do is to make one legal book of rules for the whole country. Thus it is interpreting, and rewriting, all those thousands of rules that have hitherto been construed to mean what they were understood to mean by the men who made and agreed to them.

Every case that comes before the board is a claim against the railroad; and the claims are, in general, of two kinds.

One is the claim of Casey fired. He demands to be reinstated, with pay for lost time, on the ground that he was unfairly fired. These come under the file head of discipline cases.

The other kind of claim is a claim for money.

The discipline cases fall under two heads. Under the first head are the Rule G cases; under the second head are all others.

The first, the strictest, the unarguable rule in the whole book is Rule G. It forbids the use of intoxicants under pain of immediate dismissal. What can happen on a railroad from one

instant of dimness of faculties is so terrible that violations of
Rule G by long tradition are unforgivable, or have been hitherto. But the National Railroad Adjustment Board now con-
strues Rule G in a liberal manner.

The cases that follow are taken directly from the record,
omitting the name of the person and of the railroad. The name
of the person shall be Casey.

Award 1757. Casey is employed in the switchyard. He was
drunk. There seems to be no doubt of it. He was arrested in a
public street for drunken driving, having sideswiped a police
car; in police court he pleaded guilty, was fined twenty-five
dollars and was forbidden to drive a motor vehicle in the state
for a year. Hearing this the railroad fired him. His committee
comes now before the board demanding that he be reinstated,
with full pay for the two years that have elapsed. The board is
deadlocked on it, the labor members voting for Casey and the
railroad members against him. The referee votes with the
labor members, and the finding is that, "While the conduct of
this employee may have been censurable on purely moral
grounds, and while it may have detracted from his usefulness
as a yard employee, the carrier did not establish as a fact that
his conduct so far impaired his usefulness or competency that
it was justified in permanently separating him from the service." Casey is reinstated.

Award 3612. Casey is now a brakeman and conductor
extra, but in the same kind of trouble. The railroad has fired
him on evidence that he was arrested on the highway for bad
driving, examined by a doctor who said he was drunk,
arraigned in the county court and fined $200. The referee
finds that because he was off duty at the time there was no
violation of Rule G. Casey is reinstated with pay for lost time.

Award 3617. This time Casey is one of a crew that gets
into trouble on duty. When the crew reported after lunch, the
yardmaster thought something was wrong. He called the train-
master, who called the doctor, and the doctor said only that the

engineer and fireman were fit for duty; the others, he said, had all been drinking, and they were tried on that charge and fired. On the claim for reinstatement the board deadlocked, as usual, and the referee, finding with the labor members, said: "Considering the gravity of the consequences, the evidence in this case is considered insufficient." Casey is reinstated.

And so you may go on through the Rule G cases until it occurs to you to pause and calculate the batting average. You find that on forty-three appeals Casey has lost eleven and won thirty-two. And then you come to—

Award 3512. This time Casey is an engineer. One afternoon when he came for his engine, the roundhouse foreman thought he was not in a condition to take it out, and so notified the yardmaster, who called the company doctor. The doctor said he was under the influence of intoxicants and he was fired.

When he came before the board for an order to be reinstated, his defense was that he had had only one bottle of beer; all the rest of it was from aspirin tablets and cough syrup. The board by habit was deadlocked again. A referee sat on it, and the finding was this: "It is admitted that there was a mild Rule G violation, but the evidence does not warrant the conviction that the condition of incapacity indicated was intoxication, and the circumstances rather negative it." And the award was this: "Claimant to be reinstated, seniority unimpaired, with pay for half the time lost."

Here we leave Casey. He was found to be half wrong that time, but the railroad was found to be half wrong, too, and these two halves of wrongness make his job whole again. This is the award that is referred to among railroad men when they speak of the "half-drunk, half-pay case."

Nearly all the other discipline cases arise from rules that guard the safety of operations. The usual case is that the employee has been charged with dereliction, tried according to the rules, convicted upon evidence and dismissed by the railroad. Then his committee comes before the board with a demand that he be reinstated. In each case that will be mentioned —and these are but a few out of many—it was the referee that enabled the board to decide in favor of the claimant.

On a large Eastern railroad a conductor and brakeman had been dismissed under a charge of bad flagging.

The rules about flagging are very strict. The defense in this case was that flagging on that division had become somewhat lax; the management, to correct it, had ordered an observation to be made unawares to the men, and only these two had had the bad luck to get caught. The board reinstated them, with full seniority rights, but without pay for lost time.

On a Western road there had been a series of collisions, five bad ones in two years, and the management decided that leniency was a weakness. The next engineer who had a collision was tried, found guilty of breaking the rule that would have prevented the accident, and was fired. The facts were not disputed. The board conceded that the engineer was in error. Yet it thought the discipline excessive and ordered him to be reinstated, with no pay for lost time.

On the same road another engineer on a straight track collided with a train twelve car lengths beyond the switch where he should have headed in; and he was fired. The board found that he was to blame. The facts were indisputable. Yet because the damage was not very great, it thought the discipline too severe and ordered him to be reinstated.

On an Eastern road a conductor was dismissed. The charge was that he had brought his train out on the main line without proper flag protection. An extra came along and hit him. The railroad produced a record showing that he had often been reprimanded for violating orders, that he had been charged before for improper flagging, and that he had let his flagman sit on the ballast just behind the caboose, instead of sending him back to where he ought to be. The board reinstated him, but without pay for lost time.

Here you have the operating officials of the railroad saying that a certain man is dangerous and a referee saying he isn't who was never in the operating department of a railroad, who never saw the man and who could know really very little about it. Or does he say the man is not dangerous? No. He says only that he shall be reinstated.

On a Southwestern road there was arranged a surprise test, under official supervision. Torpedoes had been placed on the track ahead. It was a passenger train. The engineer brought the train to a stop and whistled out with the flagman, who went back with the flag, all according to the rules; but when the flagman was whistled in, he forgot to leave any torpedoes behind him, as the rule requires. The defense of him before the board was that it was a surprise test, wherefore there had been no danger, and that, besides, it had happened on a piece of track where the seeing was clear for three miles. The railroad represented in vain that only a short time before on that same division two passenger trains had collided in the middle of a ten-mile tangent. The brakeman was reinstated.

You may wonder what is happening to morale and discipline in the operating department of a railroad. Well, it seems that what has so far saved discipline from a very serious collapse is a fine, surviving gang spirit in the rank and file of men. Pride of craftsmanship more than one hundred years old does not go to pieces all at once.

But the National Railroad Adjustment Board's important work, after all, is to put fat on the payroll. Here the word "fat" is used in a very old sense, to mean pay for work you do not do. The amount of it in the payroll is all the more amazing in view of the lean condition of the industry. You would hardly believe it could be fried out.

Taking it from the annual wage bulletin of the Interstate Commerce Commission, the record for 1938 is that "time paid for, but not worked," amounted to 17,357,174 days, and for these the railroad paid wages of more than $120 million.

There are five unions that touch the trains, and, in moving the trains, they touch one another in a thousand jealous ways. Each one has its own agreement with the railroad. If a man does with his left hand a thing that by the rules should have been done by another with the right hand, his status changes and he is entitled to another rate of pay, or an extra day's pay; or it may be an act of infringement, in which case the man who should have done it must be paid also as if he had done it. For example, if a passenger brakeman minds a string of empty cars from the station to the coach yard half a mile distant, he becomes a conductor, entitled to conductor's pay; or he may regard himself as a trainman required to do yard service in place of a yard switchman, and besides his day's pay as a passenger-train brakeman, he is entitled to another day's pay as a yardman; and then a yardman may say that it was his work and claim an extra day's pay because he was not called upon to do it. They put in these claims, the railroad denies them, and then a committee takes them before the Railroad Adjustment Board.

The best way to make the facts clear will be to stalk some of those seventeen million days that are paid for but not worked, a few at a time.

On the Rock Island, at Shawnee, Oklahoma, the yard switchmen do not work on Sunday because there is no regular work to do. One Sunday a special CCC train[1] on its way to Texas stopped there to change road crews, and the outbound crew changed the caboose. The three members of the six-day yard crew, who were not there, all claimed a full day's extra pay, on the ground that they should have been there to change the caboose. The National Railroad Adjustment Board gave it to them.

On the B&O, a freight train arrived at the Riker, Pennsylvania, yard in the rain. That was the end of its run. The yardmaster told the crew where to leave the train. Seeing that the train was going to pass the caboose track, one of the brake-

200

men asked the engineer please to kick the caboose off there because he and the other brakemen lived in the caboose and were anxious to dry their clothes and get some supper. There were no orders from either the conductor or the yardmaster. It was such a thing as men do for one another, it took only two or three minutes, and the engineer did it for the comfort of the brakemen. But the fireman on that engine put in a claim for a full extra day's pay at yard rates, and the National Railroad Adjustment Board gave it to him on the ground that he had been "required" to perform a yard service.

On the B&O at East Salamanca, New York, a yard crew at the end of a day made up a train and went home. Came then the inspector and found two bad-order cars in the train. When the train crew arrived to take the train, they were asked to switch the two cripples out. For doing this, the conductor, brakeman, engineer and fireman, each in addition to his regular pay, put in a claim for an extra day's pay at yard rates, and the National Railroad Adjustment Board awarded them the money on the ground that someone ought to have known about the bad-order cars before the yard crew went home. It cost the railroad four extra days' pay to get two crippled cars switched out of a train.

These are customary cases. They go on and on.

In the next phase, the yard question assumes enormous proportions.

The railroad yard is a place where trains are broken up and re-formed. A long time ago, train crews did all the switching. As the work of switching increased, yard work came to be separately organized. Engines were built purposely for it and men were regularly assigned to it. Naturally, a distinction arose between yard crews and road crews. Then it became convenient to have separate agreements for the two kinds of work.

A railroad's agreement with its yardmen covered yard work only, but its agreement with the train crew had to cover switching, too, because a train crew would always have to do switching along the line and also in a yard when the yard crew was not on duty. In a big yard the yard crews work three eight-hour shifts, and there the train crews, by agreement, do no switching at all; in a little yard there may be only one eight-hour shift of the yard crew. But whenever a train crew does switching work, it is paid for switching work in addition to regular pay for train work.

The need for yards is continually changing. Sometimes the traffic goes away, or with faster trains the need for an intermediate yard may disappear. Hitherto it has been the right of a railroad to reduce the yard-crew service as it might see fit, or to discontinue it entirely when the traffic no longer justified it; in which case the train crews were required to do the switching at the pay agreed upon for switching work, added to their pay for train work.

But now the National Railroad Adjustment Board, going on from such cases as have been cited, arrives at this astonishing question:

Having once established a yard with regular yard-crew service, has the railroad a right ever to reduce or discontinue that service?

In a series of decisions from which there is no appeal, it has answered its own question by saying to the railroads, in effect: "You may reduce or discontinue yard service if you will, but if you do it you will have to go on paying the yard crews as if they were performing the work, besides at the same time paying your train crews a double wage—that is to say, a wage for the switching work they actually do, then a penalty wage at full yard-time rates because they are required to do work that the yard crews ought to be doing."

More than this, it has decided that where a railroad has already reduced or discontinued yard-crew service at a regularly established yard, it must go back and pay these double-penalty wages for imaginary work performed in imaginary time by nobody at all, over a period of years.

At Haileyville, Oklahoma, as traffic declined, the Rock Island Railroad reduced its yard service to one switch engine and one crew, working from six in the morning until two in the afternoon, so that in all other hours the train crew had to do their own switching, paid at switching-work rates. After a time the unions put in a claim—follow it here—a claim for an extra day's pay at yard rates, to be paid to all train crews for each time they had done any switching in the Haileyville yard, although they had already been paid for every hour and minute actually worked in switching, and then an extra day's pay to the yard crew for each time a train crew had done any switching. The National Railroad Adjustment Board allowed the unions' claims and the money had to be paid.

How did the board arrive at that decision? Mainly by a definition of the word "seniority." This is an old and well-understood word. The dictionaries define it as one's place in the line of service. A senior must be considered before his junior to fill the next most preferred job in the line of service; if the number of jobs is reduced, the seniors will keep theirs and the juniors will go. Always the word had been so construed in the railroads' agreements with labor.

Now the National Railroad Adjustment Board redefines seniority as "a preferential right to perform certain classes of work in exclusion of all others not holding such seniority in that service. Once established, it cannot be arbitrarily destroyed."

Under that definition, the board holds that once a railroad has established a yard, the yardmen acquire the exclusive right to do all the switching that shall ever be done there, and that it is a right that cannot be taken away from them. If the railroad requires others to do the switching in that yard, it must pay double wages to those who do it and full wages to the yardmen as if they had done it.

This same railroad, in another place, was ordered to pay punitive wages to yard crews it no longer employed. It was difficult to find them. One was a postmaster, one was farming, one had gone to California and one was in jail.

On one railroad, such an award for work not performed was retroactive over a period of more than three years. When the men could not be identified, the railroad said to the chairman of the local union, "Here, you take the money and divide it around as you like," which was done.

There are a long line of these cases. The principle is established and there is no appeal. One result is that the railroads are continuing to operate obsolete yards, and thus large capital expenditures for bigger locomotives to make faster and longer train runs, purposely to reduce costs, are defeated.

Two ideas now control railway labor. One is to make work and defend jobs in a shrinking industry; the other is that those who by right of seniority survive are entitled to all they can get. These are the ideas that are common to organized labor. If the railway labor organizations have pushed them far, it is because they can.

That the behavior of railroad labor should be monopolistic is natural. How do human beings behave who possess monopoly?

That it should resist both change and necessity tending to produce more unemployment is not natural.

Where it is charging more than the traffic will bear, it is stupid and hurting itself, for that is a condition that cannot last. There are branch lines, for example, where, with shrunken and special trains running under full-crew laws, the labor cost is more than the total gross revenue. That cannot long continue.

But these are further questions. The immediate subject is the model peace and harmony that is said to exist between the railroads and labor.

And there it is.

204

Wage and price controls ended after World War II, and in early 1946 the steelworkers, electrical workers, coal miners and railroad workers went out on strike. When owners of the coal mines refused to accept the United Mine Workers' demand for a welfare and retirement fund, President Truman seized the mines by executive order under authority of the War Labor Disputes Act and agreed to the miners' demands.

An Act of Seizure

From "Review and Comment," *American Affairs,* July 1946

By an act of seizure to end a strike the government now is in possession of the soft coal mines. Having nothing to lose but the taxpayers' money, the government is an easy and generous boss. To induce the miners to return to work it made a better bargain with them than the private boss was willing to make. And so, as it always is at first, the miners are better off. Have they lost anything? Is this benefit of government without price? Suppose now they should want to strike. Are they free to do it? If they refused to mine the coal on the government's terms they would be striking against the government. Note how the language changes. Formerly if the miners refused to mine coal one could say, when it became very serious, that they were striking *against society*, but even that was an intellectual abstraction. Most people thought of it simply as an economic struggle in which the consumer was getting hurt, and public opinion turning strongly one way or the other would presently end it, because neither side could afford to go too far. But now when the same kind of struggle reaches a certain point the President announces that it begins to assume the character of a strike *against the government*, and that is a very different thing. Thus little by little we become accustomed first to the words and semantic tones and then to the experimental acts of authoritarian government, commanding obedience. For another while we get our coal and our weekend trips to the seashore—and almost unawares we also get the habit of saying, "Let the government do it."

Regard the strike of the coal miners in perspective. Long before the situation had become critical it was evident that the principle of collective bargaining had broken down. Why? Because the government had set the pattern of direct intervention in economic disputes. It was equally evident that the government's own substitute for collective bargaining had broken down. That was fact finding. Everybody knew that when the crisis came the government would take over the mines. It was necessary beforehand, however, to make John L. Lewis[2] the image of reckless labor leadership drunk with power. What were the three simple facts? First, the miners broke no law. Second, they broke no contract. Third, they committed no violence.

Certainly no thoughtful person could look at these facts without being upon notice that the book had not opened there. It opened, in fact, eleven years ago when the revolution passed a law deliberately intended to foreshorten the economic power of one class and to increase the power of another.[3] Besides granting organized labor a monopolistic power—the power to say who should and should not work and on what terms—the law conferred upon it the privileges and immunities necessary to implement the monopoly, such as complete immunity from the antitrust laws and from the laws against extortion and conspiracy, in so far as acts of extortion and conspiracy might be connected with a labor dispute. Now, what will any class do with a grant of power? What would labor do with it? Was it not expected to exercise it?

In response to the railroad workers, Truman announced that the railroads would also be seized. On May 24, 1946, he addressed a joint session of Congress, and said: "This is no longer a dispute between labor and management. It has become a strike against the govern-

*ment of the United States itself. That kind of strike can
never be tolerated." And he said, "I request the Congress
immediately to authorize the president to draft into the
armed forces all workers who are on strike against the
government."*

Garrett continued the story in the October 1946 issue:

From the treachery of the shale on which its foundation is
laid the house of labor had suffered two severe shocks. One
was when the President of the United States proposed to lay
the hand of military compulsion upon the striking coal miners.
Well, that perhaps could happen here, the power of labor
being new and not yet entirely accepted, besides the fact that
it is divided against itself. It could not happen, for example, in
Great Britain, where labor controls the government and the
coal mines have been nationalized. Or could it? On July 24th
last, in the British House of Commons, the Parliamentary
Secretary to the Ministry of Labor, discussing "the future of
labor controls for the coal-mining industry," made the following statement:

"The new provision will be operated with the object of
conserving the labor force of the coal-mining industry. Every
effort will be made by the officers of the two departments concerned to overcome by persuasive means the objections of
men who do not wish to remain in the coal-mining industry
and to induce them to accept suitable openings in it. It is
hoped that it will be necessary to resort to compulsory measures only in very exceptional cases."

Compulsion, it is hoped, only in "exceptional cases." And
in those cases what form would it take? That question was not
discussed, nor was it asked. It could take only one of two
forms. It could be military compulsion, as was proposed here
by the President, or the British Government could say to the
miners, "Dig coal or starve." The British Government has not
yet said it; but Arthur Horner, general secretary of the

National Union of Mineworkers, in a recent speech reported by the London *Times*, said this: "Production needs are so great the time has come to apply the slogan that if a man won't work, neither shall he eat." How ironic to recall that what made it possible to nationalize the coal industry in England was the slogan: "The mines for the miners."

A strange pattern unfolds. The soft-coal mines are still in the hands of the government, operating under a contract signed between the United Mine Workers Union and the Department of the Interior, with the owners looking on. The owners and the union had been unable to agree on terms, and work stopped. That is why the government seized the mines. Then the government signed a contract with the union giving it more than the owners had been willing to offer. The problem now is how to return the mines to the owners in order that the government may get out of the mining business.

The Secretary of the Interior[4] finds that one mine in four is losing money under the Lewis-Government contract. So it may be that on those terms the owners of high-cost mines cannot afford to take their property back. Shall the government keep these mines and run them at a loss, charging it to the taxpayer? Shall the government subsidize them to keep them running and charge the subsidies to the taxpayer? The Secretary of the Interior says that if they cannot make out under this contract they have at least the right to get out of business. But if they go out of business who will support the unemployed miners?

Some will say: "Let the government keep all the mines. Let the industry be nationalized." Against this there is the current history of the British experience. Nationalization of the British coal industry so far has solved nothing.

The high-cost mineowner, like the high-cost wheat producer, lives in the margins of his industry. When times are good and prices are high he comes in; when times are bad and prices fall off he goes out. And so under conditions of free

208

competitive enterprise the law of supply and demand works. Grim as it may be, the high-cost marginal producer is a stabilizer. When prices rise he increases the supply; when the demand lessens and prices for that reason decline he ceases to produce. Unhappily, labor shares his fortunes. But this labor, too, is marginal, because the low-cost producers, paying better wages or providing better conditions and greater stability of employment, get the better and more efficient labor.

Now you may say, "Very well. Let's be really grim about it. Out with the high-cost producer. Let the efficients have it." One answer to that is that you would still have the marginal producer, because efficiency is a relative thing and even among low-cost producers there is variation. The second answer is that if you cast out the high-cost marginal mines you cast out at the same time the high-cost marginal labor, and what will you do with that?

Take wheat. Two-thirds of the farmers now producing wheat might produce all that we need and make a profit at a price which would put the inefficient one-third out of business. Suppose you say: "Instead of supporting the price of wheat with public funds, as we are doing, let's leave wheat production to the efficients." But if you did that, what would happen to agriculture as a whole? What would happen to the inefficients? Should they be pensioned, as a reward for their inefficiency?

Heretofore this problem has worked itself out in the margins of industry and agriculture, just as it does in the margins of a forest. The marginal producer lived a thin life, lost his capital, went away, or somehow got absorbed elsewhere according to his value. But now as it becomes increasingly a government problem it assumes formidable social and political implications, because as a government problem it must be acted upon not as a rash upon the economic body but as a functional disorder. It is not a question of a high-cost coal mine that may go out of business from time to time and be forgotten. It is a question of what to do with one-quarter of the coal mines all at once.

The mines were returned to owners in 1947 on the owners' agreement that the welfare and pension funds set up by the government would be merged into one fund and retained.

Pensions for Capital

From "Comment," *American Affairs,* January 1950

In the act of granting the railroads another increase of passenger rates the Interstate Commerce Commission audibly wondered whether they were going to price themselves out of the market. Later, one member of the commission suggested that if the railroads' passenger revenues continued to fall, Congress might have to consider a federal subsidy to make up the loss. At one of the hearings on Bigness before the Celler Committee[5] this question was raised: What if a corporation got so big that the government, having accepted the responsibility for full employment, could not afford to let it fail? Thus one may note the birth of the idea that the Federal Government may be obliged to provide old age pensions for capital.

That idea was bound to follow from the delusion that by the free application of federal subsidies to any seat of pain we may assure the great blessing of a painless economy. This of course is quackery. There is no such thing as a painless economy; and if you overcome the sensation of pain by anesthetics, how shall the economy know when it is sick or why? The use of pain in a healthy body is to give notice of wrong living. The only way to cure it really is by right living.

Many people have forgotten, if they ever knew, what happened in a free profit and loss system to capital when it ceased to earn a profit. If it could think of no way to get its profit back by improving its tools and methods it was lost—wiped out.

210

But that is all that did happen. The economic mechanism was not hurt at all. Indeed it was generally improved and worked much better when relieved of the weight of old and obsolete capital.

Before there was any Interstate Commerce Commission to say that railroad rates should guarantee a reasonable return on the capital, railroad bankruptcy was very common. Once two-thirds of all the railroad mileage in the country was in receivership. The courts operated the railroads as trustees for the creditors. The trains went on running just the same; wages went on being paid to the employees as before. Receivership certificates with prior lien on all the assets were sold to buy new equipment and new rails. After a while the owners, who were the stockholders, sat down with the creditors, who were the bondholders, and together they worked out a reorganization plan. The capital structure was scaled down. The heavy loss fell on the stockholders, which was only fair, because for the sake of the profit they had taken the owner's risk. Then a new company was formed, new stock was sold, the bankrupt railroad went on the block and was sold to the new company, and that was the end of receivership.

So American railroads were built many times, with new capital taking the place of old, and the cost of transportation fell until it was the lowest in the world. There was pain in it of course, but it was pain that cured itself; and there came to be a hard saying of great wisdom—that the measure of the country's prosperity was the amount of bankruptcy it was willing to stand. This meant only that the faster it sloughed off dead and dying capital the faster it could go forward—provided always that the dynamic principles by which capital endlessly renewed itself were preserved.

The federal seizure of industries, done under Wilson to the railroads and under Truman to the coal mines, ended after 1952. That year Truman seized the steel mills, which were on the verge of a strike. The owners took it all the way to the Supreme Court, and in Youngstown Sheet & Tube v. Sawyer, 343 U.S. 579 (1952), the court said the president could not seize a private industry without authorization from Congress.

CHAPTER EIGHT NOTES:

1 The Civilian Conservation Corps, a New Deal jobs program.

2 John L. Lewis, 1880-1969, was president of the United Mine Workers 1920-1960. In 1935 he broke from the American Federation of Labor and founded the more militant group that became the Congress of Industrial Organizations.

3 The National Labor Relations Act, which assigned workers to unions based on a one-time democratic vote and required management to negotiate with unions in good faith.

4 Julius Krug, who succeeded FDR's acerbic and partisan Harold Ickes.

5 Rep. Emmanuel Celler, D-New York, 1888-1981, served 49 years in the House, much of it as chairman of the Judiciary Committee. The committee to which Garrett refers was the House Subcommittee on Monopoly Power.

Chapter Nine
ORIGINS

The following piece was not written as an essay, but as background in a novel, and is in parts scattered through the novel. Brought together it does make a story. Here is Garrett's vision of laissez faire in practice, from the years just before he was born until he was in his early twenties. His subject is the basic steel industry, which produces metal from ore. Today it is a stockade of old companies concerned with protection from imports, and old unions concerned with job security, medical care and retirement. But steel was once vital and young, and established itself by fighting an industrial battle to replace iron.

The Dawn of Steel

From *The Cinder Buggy,* 1923

The iron man said to his new salesman: "I'll show you the difference between steel and iron."

They went to the mill yard. Laborers were piling up rails that looked all alike except that they varied in length and weight. The iron man led the way straight to an isolated pile and pointed to the name of an English firm embossed on the web of each rail.

"That's a steel rail," he said. "It's imported into this country from England. Now look."

He beckoned. Four men lifted one of those rails and dropped it across a block of pig iron. It snapped with a clean, crisp break in the middle.

"That's steel," he said with a gesture of scorn. "It breaks as you see—like glass. When they unload steel rails for track laying they let them over the side of the car in ropes for fear they will break if they fall on the ground."

The same four men went directly to another pile of rails, carelessly picked up the one nearest to hand, laid it on the ground against a stout iron post and attached to each end of it a chain working to a windlass. As the windlass wound in the chains, the rail began to bend in the middle around the post. The rail bent to the shape of a hairpin, without breaking, without the slightest sound or sign of fracture.

"That is one of our iron rails," the iron man said. "You can't break it. Look at that bend, inside and out."

The bent part was smooth on the outside and a little wrinkled on the inside. There was no break in the fibre.

"Steel is a crime," he said, in a tone of judgment. "The only excuse for it is that it's cheaper than iron. The public doesn't know. Congress doesn't care. It lets these foreign steel rails come in to compete with American iron rails. The gamblers who build railroads are without conscience."

Hitherto iron rails had sold themselves. Now steel rails were coming in and steel rails were being *sold*. The competition was not yet alarming, but it was serious and likely to increase, and the way to meet it was to *sell* iron rails.

The iron salesman went to work. But his sensibility gradually tore away as he discovered the drift of events, which was:

The star of iron was threatened in the first phase of its glory.

The day of steel was breaking.

It was not a brilliant event. It was like a cloudy dawn, unable to make a clean stroke between the light and the dark. Yet everyone had a sense of what was passing in the dimness.

Fate decided the issue. The consequences were such as become fate. They were tremendous, uncontrollable, unimaginable. They changed the face of civilization. Vertical cities, suburbs, subways, industrialism, the rise of a wilderness in two generations to be the paramount nation in the world, victory in the World War—those were consequences.

It is to be explained.

The great Bessemer process, a way of producing steel direct from ore, was successfully evolved in England, and the British began to produce steel, especially rails, in considerable quantities. Americans as usual were procrastinating, digressive, self-obstructing. The Bessemer patents were bought and brought to this country. A Kentucky iron master filed an interference on the ground that although he hadn't developed it in practice he had had that same idea himself, and had had it first, and his contention was sustained. Several years were lost in wrangling over rights. Meanwhile, England entered the American market with steel rails.

When at last the Bessemer process began to be tried in this country the principle of perversity that animates the untamed elements bewitched it. Disappointments were so continuous, so humiliating, so extremely disastrous, that a period was when one would have thought the whole thing much more likely to be abandoned than persevered with. And when at length there was a usable product at all it was a poor and very uncertain product, comparing unfavorably with English steel, and how the English steel rails compared with good American iron rails has been witnessed.

Man is the only animal that whistles in the dark. Being so long in a dogged minority, so much discouraged, so sore in their hope, the protagonists of steel were boastful. They could not boast of their product. It was bad. Nor of their success. It was worse. They had to boast of things which one could believe without proof. The Bessemer steel process, they said, was the enemy of privilege. It was for the many against the few. It would transform and liberate society and cast down all barriers to progress.

They were the radicals, the visionaries, the yes-sayers of their time. Many a sound, conservative, no-saying iron man was seduced by their faith to exchange his money for experience.

And all the time, bad as it was, steel kept coming more and more into use, especially—that is to say, almost exclusively—in the form of rails. And the reason the steel rail kept coming into use was that an amazing human society yet unborn, one that should have shapes, aspects, wants, powers and pastimes then undreamed of, was calling for it—calling especially for the steel rail.

The steel men heard it. That was what kept them in hope. The iron men heard it and were struck with fear.

Why was it calling for steel rails instead of iron rails?—steel rails that broke like clay pipes against iron rails that could be tied in knots? Did it care nothing for its unborn life and limb? It cared only a little for life and limb. Much more it cared about bringing it existence to pass, and that was impossible with iron rails, with anything but steel rails.

It was true of the iron rail that it was unbreakable and therefore safe and superior to the steel rail for all uses of human society in the sixties and seventies of the nineteenth century. That was still the iron age. But human society as it would be in the twentieth century was calling for a rail that would meet the needs of a steel age. This was a society that was going to require a ton of freight to be moved 2,500 miles annually for each man, woman and child in the country. Transportation on that scale of waste and grandeur had never been imagined in the world. Iron rails simply could not stand the strain. They would not break under it. They would be smashed flat. They would wear out almost as fast as they could be spiked down.

It was true of the steel rail, as the iron people said, that it was very breakable, of tricky temper, dangerous to life and limb. Society in 1870 ran much more safely on iron rails. But the unborn society of the steel age was making rail specifications beforehand. It was a society for which a quarter of a million miles of railroad would have to be laid in one generation. That simply could not be done with iron rails. There would not be enough fuel, labor and time by the old wrought iron process to make or replace iron rails on any such scale. Shoeing that society with iron rails would be like shoeing an army with eiderdown slippers.

The iron people of course could make steel in their own way from wrought iron, melted again and carbonized—fine, cutlery steel, very hard and trustworthy—but you could not dream of making rails by the millions of tons from that kind of steel.

The three primary desiderata in the coming society's rail problem were *hardness, cheapness, quantity.*

The new process produced a rail within these three requirements. It was hard because it was steel. It was cheap because the steel was got direct from the ore at an enormous savings in time and fuel. And it could be made in practically unlimited quantities.

The Bessemer method made possible at once an increase of one hundred fold in metallic production. That was miraculous.

The iron age took three thousand years.

The steel age developed in thirty. By 1883 the steel rail superseded the iron rail.

Pittsburgh at this time was not a place prepared. It was a sign, a pregnant smudge, a state of phenomena. The great mother was undergoing a Caesarean operation. An event was bringing itself to pass. The steel age was about to be delivered.

Men performed the office of obstetrics without knowing what they did. They could neither see nor understand it. They struggled blindly, falling down and getting up. Forces possessed them. Their psychic condition was that of men to whom fabulous despair and extravagant expectation were the two ends of one ecstasy. They were hard, shrewd, sentimental, superstitious, romantic in friendship and conscienceless in trade. They named their blast furnaces after their wives and sweethearts, stole each other's secrets, fell out with their partners, and knew no law of business but to lay on what the traffic would bear.

They were always begging money at the banks. When they made money they used it to build more mills and to fill the mills with automatic monsters that grew stranger and more fantastic. Many of these monsters, like things in nature's own history of trial and error, appeared for a short time and because extinct. When they were not making money they were bankrupt. That was about half the time. Then they came to the banks to implore, beg, and wheedle money to meet their payrolls.

The bankers were a tough-minded group. They had to be. Nobody was quite safe. A man with a record of sanity would suddenly lose his balance and cast away the substance of certainty to pursue a vision. The effort to adapt the Bessemer steel process to American conditions was an irresistible road to ruin.

At one time six or eight Bessemer plants had been built in the United States under the English patents at enormous costs and every one had failed. They could produce steel all right, and do it with one melt from the iron ore, which was what they were after. The trouble was that the steel was never twice the same. Its quality and nature varied. The process was treacherous. There were those who said it simply could not be adapted to American ores.

Perhaps it was a puddler who solved the problem—an iron puddler who remarked that pig iron is puddled to make it all the same, and different runs of steel should be mixed along the same principle but on a much larger scale. Men built the first mixer, an enormous, awkward tank or vat resting on rollers that rocked and jigged the fluid, blazing iron, six or eight tons of it, sloshing around. After two or three trials they began to get and continued to get steel that was both good and invariable.

And that was Eureka!

They tried the steel in every possible way and it was all that steel should be and is. They fed it to the fastidious German wire-drawing machines and they loved it. Never again would it be necessary to import German or English steel to make wire—and steel wire was indispensable to the steel age. There were bridges to be cast in the air like cobwebs, chasms to be spanned, a thousand giants to be snared in their sleep with threads of steel wire, single, double, or twisted by hundreds into cables. There was a new kind of nail, the steel wire nail, to drive out the iron nail.

But the steel age required first of all steel rails. And for the first time there was the certainty of being able to produce American steel rails that would not only outwear iron as iron outwears oak, that not only would be satisfactory when they were good, but rails that would be always the same and always good.

Railway building at that time was the enchanted field of creative speculation. Railways were made in hope, rejoicing and sheer abandon of willful energy. Once they were made they served economic ends, as a navigable waterway will, no matter where or how it goes, but for one that was intelligently planned for the greatest good of the greatest need four or five others derived their existence fantastically from motives of emulation, spite, greed, combat and civic vaingloriousness. When in the course of events all these separate translations of the ungoverned imagination were linked up, the result was that incomprehensible crazy quilt which the great American railway system was and is in a geographical sense. It was more exciting and more profitable to build railways than wagon roads. That is how we came to have the finest railways and the worst highways of any country in the civilized world.

At the dawn of the steel age people said rail building had been overdone. They did not imagine the possibility that the locomotive would double in size. It did. Then it doubled again. It could not have done so without steel rails under its feet, and had it not doubled and doubled again this now would be a German world, for the Germans would have won the World War. Democracy even then was shaping its weapons for Armageddon through men who knew nothing about it. They were free egoists, seeking profit, power, personal success, everyone attending to his own greatness. Never before in the world had the practice of individualism been so reckless, so purely dynamic, so heedless of the Devil's harvest. Yet it happened—it precisely happened—that they forged the right weapons.

It seems sometimes to matter very little what men think. They very often do the right thing for the wrong reasons. It seems to matter even less why they work. All that the great law of becoming requires is that men shall work. They cannot go wrong really. They cannot make wrong things. The pattern is foreordained.

The steel age always knew in advance what it needed. Salesmanship was its very breath. Why? Because when it came suddenly, like a natural event, men found themselves in command of means of producing wealth enormously beyond any scale of human wants previously imaginable. Production attended to itself. It ran utterly wild. There was a chronic excess of producing capacity because the supply of steel had been magically increased one hundred fold.

The dilemma that presented itself was unique. Its name was overproduction. It occurred simultaneously in Great Britain, Germany, France and the United States. They all had the same goods to sell, the very same goods, rising from steel, and they sold them to each other in mad competition. Prices fell steadily for many years, continuously, until goods were preposterously cheap, and always there was a surplus still. Rails fell from $125 to $18 per ton, and the face of two continents was netted with railways. Yet there was a surplus of rails.

Never before in the history of mankind did goods increase faster than wants. It is not likely ever to happen again.

In a way that becomes clear with a little reflection, a surplus of steel caused a surplus of nearly everything else—food to begin with. There was a great surplus of food because steel rails opened suddenly to the world the great lands of the American west. The iron age had foreshortened time and distance. The steel age annihilated them.

It made no difference how far a thing was hauled. Transportation was cheap because steel was cheap. Kansas wheat was sold in Minneapolis, Chicago and in Liverpool. Minneapolis made flour and sent it to New York, Europe and back to Kansas.

The great availability of food released people from agriculture. They went to the industrial centers to make more steel and things rising from steel, so that there were more of such things to sell.

More, more, more of everything.

Sell! Sell! Sell!

That was the voice of the steel age.

Modern cities were made and were no sooner made than torn down and built over again. Chicago grew faster than St. Louis because it had less to tear down. Rivers were moved, mountains were leveled, swamps were lifted up. Nothing was right as God left it.

Men lived in strife by doing. They labored and brought it forth. There was never a moment to think. There has not come that moment yet. What it was toward nobody knows.

Steel was to make men free. They said this who required a slogan. Men are not free. Why should they be? What shall they be free to do? Go to and fro, perhaps. What shall they be free to think? Anything wherein there is refuge from the riddles they invent.

The men who delivered the steel age were not thinkers. They were magicians who monkeyed with the elements until they had conjured forth from the earth a spirit that said, "Serve me!"

Those who directly served it were of two kinds.

First were the men who thought with their hands. They were daring in invention. Mechanical impossibilities intoxicated them. They abhorred a pause in the production process as nature abhors a vacuum.

Next were the men of vision, who worked by inspiration, who had a fantasy of things beyond the feeling of them, and ran ahead.

And since men of both kinds were more available here than in Europe, the steel age walked across the ocean.

When the steel age walked across the ocean from Europe a dilemma was created. The will and mentality were here; the labor was there. Until then labor in American mills had been made up of British, Irish, Welsh, Germans, Swedes and, choicest of all, Buckwheats, meaning young American brawn released from the farm by the advent of man-saving agricultural implements. The steel age widened the gap between brain and muscle. It required a higher kind of imagination at the top and a lower grade of labor below. There was no such labor here—at least, nowhere near enough. Hence an inpouring of Hungarians, Slavs, Polacks.

222

Nobody thought of the consequences. Nobody thought at all. The labor was needed. There was no effort to Americanize or assimilate it. There wasn't time. It had to be fed raw to the howling new genie. It lived wretchedly in sore clusters from which Americans averted their eyes. Where it came from life was wretched, even worse, perhaps; but here were contrasts, no gendarmes quelling freedom of dissent, and a new weapon, which was the strike. These men, bred with sullen anger in their blood, melancholy and neglected in a strange land, having no bond with the light, were easily moved to unite against the work bosses who symbolized tyranny anew. Their impulse to violence was built upon by labor leaders, and the steel industry became a battle ground. Strikes were frequent, bloody and futile, save for their educational value, which was hard to see then and is not at all clear yet.

This was all in the way of business—big business. We imported labor and exported steel. We flung Slavs into our racial melting pot and sold rails and bridges in Austria-Hungary. One can easily imagine an invisible force to have been at work, a blind force, perhaps. The centers of power were shifting in the world. Greatness was achieved. The rest is hidden.

"No government believes in laissez faire," Garrett wrote to Rose Wilder Lane. "Why? Because it is a limitation upon government; government by nature has an impulse to touch everything."

Here Garrett relates the story of laissez faire to the freedom of religion.

Laissez Faire

"Laissez Faire," *American Affairs,* January 1949

In Amsterdam, Protestant Christianity, represented by the World Council of Churches, reclaimed an authority that was surrendered at the beginning of the Industrial Revolution

200 years ago—an authority, namely, to impose moral sanctions upon business. In its "Report on the Church and the Disorders of Society," the council said:

> *The Christian Church should reject the ideologies of both communism and capitalism, and should seek to draw men away from the false assumption that these are the only alternatives. Each has made promises which it could not redeem.*

That was the first draft. The American delegate moved to insert in one place before capitalism the words laissez faire. With that amendment the report was adopted, and now reads:

"The Christian Church should reject the ideologies of both communism and laissez faire capitalism."

The shivering ghost that now inhabits the words laissez faire was once an unconquerable fighting spirit. It did not belong to capitalism. It belonged to liberty; and to this day its association with capitalism is valid only insofar as capitalism represents liberty.

When the great struggle for individual liberty began in Europe the one interest that controlled the life of the mind was religion. What men wanted most of all was freedom to worship God in their own way, freedom to believe or disbelieve; and for that they went to death at the stake intoning their hymns of heresy. The religious wars were terrible. They lasted until the lust of fanaticism was sated. Then reason rebelled and there was peace, founded on the principle of laissez faire in religion. That is not what anyone called it, because the words had not yet been invented; but that is what it was. Thereafter, so far as religion was concerned, the individual was to be let alone.

Great transactions of the human spirit have momentum, displacement and direction, but no sharp edges; there is no sudden passage from one time to another. Long after the principle of laissez faire had been accepted in Europe, religious

224

tyranny continued. Men were free to join any church they liked, but if they chose, for example, to be Calvinists, they found themselves enthralled again by a discipline that claimed jurisdiction not only over their souls but over their everyday life and all their economic behavior.

The next phase of the great European struggle for liberty, therefore, was aimed at freedom of enterprise. To say that religious radicalism was followed by economic radicalism is merely to make a statement of chronological fact. How were the two things related? Were they but two aspects of one thing? In the preface to *Religion and the Rise of Capitalism*, R.H. Tawney says:

> *The existence of a connection between economic radicalism and religious radicalism was to those who saw both at first-hand something not far from a platitude. Until some reason is produced for rejecting their testimony, it had better be assumed that they knew what they were talking about.*[1]

But there was, in any case, this difference—that whereas religious radicalism scandalized only the ecclestiastical monopoly that was overthrown, economic radicalism scandalized even itself. This was so because the European mind was deeply religious still. It had been easier to die for a heresy about the Sacrament than to get rid of a sense of guilt in profit. The universal habit of mind was biblical. People whose fathers and grandfathers had been tortured, burned at the stake and buried alive for the office of reading Scripture for themselves might be expected, when they did read it, to construe it literally and in a grim manner. They did. Bunyan's *Pilgrim's Progress*[2] was the authentic account of what happened to the righteous spirit in its passage through this world to the next. The poor were friends of God. They knew for sure they would not meet the rich man in the Kingdom of Heaven. Avarice was a deadly sin. Pursuit of gain was the way to damnation.

Money changers, speculators and traders had always about them that certain odor that came from supping with Satan. To buy cheap and sell dear was extortion. Land was the only honorable form of wealth. Business was the ignoble part of the social anatomy.

But the world had something to say for itself, and the world, too, had something to believe. Somehow, for the first time in the history of human thought, the idea of progress had appeared. It was the Age of Discovery. Knowledge was increasing; and this was not revealed knowledge of things hereafter, but knowledge of things here and now. After all, since everybody had to pass through this world whether he liked it or not, why shouldn't man improve his environment by the practical application of knowledge? Although no one understood them clearly, although there was no such word as economics, great economic changes were taking place, and the realities were uncontrollable.

The religious mind stood in a bad dilemma. It could sense the oncoming world, almost as if it had a premonition of the modern era, and yet it had no way of meeting it and was in fact forbidden by the Bible to meet it at all. Thus it became involved in extreme contradictions. For example, to lend money at interest was unchristian. For money to earn money was usury, and usury was sin. Yet as the necessities of trade increased, the economic function of the moneylender was one that somehow had to be performed, with the result that the Jews were brought in to do for Christians what Christians were morally unable to do for themselves. That is one of the reasons why the Jews became the great moneylenders of Europe.

The question was: Could Bunyan's hero Christian become an economic man and at the same time save his soul? The Dutch were the first to say positively yes, and this was significant, because the Dutch had paid more for religious liberty than any other people. They had carried their struggle for it to a plane of appalling heroism. Sooner than yield they were willing to accept total doom. Their resistance so infuriated the Holy Office of the Inquisition that on February 16, 1568, all the inhabitants of the Netherlands were sentenced to death as heretics and Bible readers, except only a few persons especially named in the edict. In Motley's classic, *The Rise of the Dutch Republic*, one may read that—

> *Men in the highest positions were daily and hourly dragged to the stake... To avoid the disturbance created in the streets by the frequent harangues and exhortations addressed to the bystanders by the victims on their way to the scaffold a new gag was invented. The tongue of each prisoner was screwed into an iron ring and then seared with a hot iron. The swelling and inflammation which were the immediate result prevented the tongue from slipping through the ring and of course effectually precluded all possibility of speech.*[3]

If the spirit of laissez faire had been less than immortal it could never have passed through that valley of death. What emerged was the Dutch Republic, founded upon the ashes of its martyrs, dedicated to liberty of conscience, holding aloft a light to the world.

Then an amazing thing happened. The prosperity of Holland became the wonder and envy of Europe. In the trade of the world it advanced to first place, and took what Tawney calls the role of economic schoolmaster to seventeenth century Europe.

The power of individualism now for the first time was released to perform its examples. The result was that tolerance and trade flourished together.

The English came to it slowly and roundabout. Calvinism as they had got it from Geneva was a severe and rigid doctrine. It perceived very clearly that the three aspects of man were spiritual, political and economic; but since in two of these aspects he was wicked, or much tempted to be, the church was obliged not only to mind his soul but to impose severe discipline upon his political and economic activities. Its regulation of business was medieval and precise; it made ethical and social laws to govern such matters as the use of capital, usury, the just price, profits, the profit motive itself, wages, labor relations, contracts and trade agreements.

It remained for the Puritans of England to make the great rational construction of this doctrine. They could not understand why God should not admire success in work. Was not the universe His work? Why not suppose that the plan of its just order required His children to work and to succeed? If in money making there were spiritual hazards, then all the more reason for keeping it straight with God. The way to do that was to put God in the shop. Where else could one be so sure of His presence and blessing? In the Puritan doctrine the word "calling" was one of special meaning. "God doth call every man and woman to serve in some peculiar employment, both for their own and for the common good." There was a spiritual calling and a temporal calling. The Christian's duty was to take part in the practical affairs of the world, and to succeed could only be a sign that God witnessed his work and was pleased with it. If riches were added to him, that, too, would be to the glory of God. In any case he would never be idle rich. Whether riches were good or bad was a question to be settled between the rich man and God; but idleness, thriftlessness and profligacy were positive evils.

So it was that in the Puritan creed religious liberty and economic freedom were reconciled. The church would let business alone and trust God in the shop to keep it from evil.

The next struggle was to get business free from the restrictions imposed upon it by government, not in the name of morals, but in the name of policy.

228

When that stormy cape had been rounded the victory of laissez faire was complete, and the way was open for that great outburst of European energy which brought on the Industrial Revolution, led by England.

For all its complications, the essential meaning of the triumph of Puritanism in England was a seizure of power. Political and economic power passed from the hands of the hereditary ruling class to the middle class. Tawney says:

> *Puritanism was the schoolmaster of the English middle classes. It heightened their virtues, sanctified, without eradicating, their convenient vices, and gave them an inexpungable assurance that behind virtues and vices alike stood the majestic and inexorable laws of an omnipotent Providence, without whose foreknowledge not a hammer could beat upon the forge, not a figure could be added to the ledger.*
>
> *The medieval epoch was finished. Individualism was exalted to a way of life. The foundations of modern capitalism were laid. The powers of government were limited. Free enterprise began. In pursuit of his economic ends, on his way to transform the world, European man was released from the restraints and sanctions imposed upon him both by the ecclesiastical tyranny and a vast bureaucratic system of administrative law. Looking at it later when most of the consequences were already clear, Montesquieu said, "the English had progressed furthest of all people in three important things—piety, commerce and freedom."*

That would have been about 1750. For more than 200 years the spirit of laissez faire had been acting irresistibly, and yet that name for it was not known. The words had been used by the Physiocrats in 1736 in France, but hardly anywhere else; nor were they familiar to anybody in England when sixty years later, in 1810, a Commission in the House of Commons said:

> *No interference of the legislature with the freedom of trade and with the perfect liberty of each individual to dispose of his time or of his labor in the way or on the terms which he may judge most conducive to his own interest, can take place without violating general principles of the first importance to the prosperity and happiness of the community.*

In those words government, the British government at least, renounced the right to touch business at all. No more forthright statement of the doctrine of laissez faire has perhaps ever been written. Mark, however, that the words do not appear in that statement. They were of French origin, written at first *laissez nous faire*, meaning "let us alone," and then *laissez faire*, meaning, "let it be." They expressed a philosophic idea. The idea was that the movements of society were spontaneous, and that if you let them alone the results in the end would be better for society as a whole—the idea, that is, of a natural order in which there is implicit harmony between public and private interest.

The point is that the spirit of laissez faire had already brought into the world religious liberty and freedom of enterprise, and that the foundations of what may now be called laissez faire capitalism had already been laid before the words were familiar.

Most people would probably say that the bible of laissez faire capitalism was written by Adam Smith. His *Wealth of Nations* appeared in 1776. Since some French economists had been using the term for forty years, Adam Smith must have heard it, and yet in the index to *The Wealth of Nations* (Canaan Edition), you will find no reference to it. Then people say, "Yes, but it is implicit," and ask you to remember the famous passage about the invisible hand:

If each individual, therefore, endeavors as much as he can both to employ his capital and domestic industry and so to direct that industry so that its products may be of the greatest of value; each individual necessarily labors to render the annual revenue of society as great as he can. He generally, indeed, neither intends to promote the public interest or knows how much he is promoting it. . .he intends only his own gain, and he is in this, as in many other cases, led by an invisible hand to promote an end which was not part of his intention. Nor is it always the worse for society that it was not a part of it. By pursuing his own interest he frequently promotes that of society more effectually than when he really intends to promote it.

You may take that to express the doctrine of economic laissez faire. But the true meaning goes far beyond economics and belongs to the philosophy of individualism, founded upon the faith that man's spontaneous works will be more than his reason can explain. Adam Smith did not invent that philosophy, nor in his exposition of it did he surpass others who wrote before him, notably Adam Ferguson, who said: "Nations stumble upon establishments which are indeed the result of human action but not the result of human design."[4]

Poetically, the same thought was expressed in Mandeville's *Fable of the Bees*.[5] More than a century before Adam Smith's time, John Moore was saying in England:

It is an undeniable maxim that everyone by the light of nature and reason will do that which makes for his greatest advantage... The advancement of private persons will be the advantage of the public.

Twenty years after *The Wealth of Nations* appeared, Edmund Burke, another great exponent of individualism, was referring to "the benign and wise disposer of all things who obliges men, whether they will or not, in pursuing their own selfish interests, to connect the general good with their own individual success."[6]

He need not have got that from Adam Smith.

There is no bible of laissez faire capitalism. *The Wealth of Nations* is the finest description ever written of how men will behave in a free economy and what the consequences of that behavior will be, together with the axioms that necessarily follow. But laissez faire by that time was ascendant, its principles were known and its works were observable.

It is confusing to speak—as the World Council of Churches does—of the ideology of capitalism. In the sense that there is a Communist ideology there is no capitalist ideology and never was. Communist ideology begins with the idea of a designed society, conceived by reason alone, directed by master minds, with nothing left either to God or the spontaneity of the human spirit. The philosophy of individualism, on the other hand, supposes that man's free and spontaneous activities create a natural design.

Capitalism was not designed. It came not from thinking but from doing. In the beginning and for a long time it had no more theory about itself than a tree; like a tree it grew, and its only laws were remembered experience. When the writers of political economy began to provide it with a theory they had first of all to study it to find out how it worked. Very few capitalists were ever economists, and it was not until a few years ago that professional economists had anything to do with business actually. They could only write about it, and from that writing about it came what Carlyle called the "dismal science," meaning the science of economics.[7] Many capitalists were innocent of its existence. What could theorists tell them about what they were doing every day?

For this attitude of the capitalist toward economic science one may find an interesting analogy in the world of industry. The men who created the motor car industry were not scientists, nor would they have known in any case what a scientist was for. They were inventors and superb mechanics. They found out what gasoline would do by exploding it in tin cans and sometimes blowing themselves up with it; then they put it to work in the poppet-valve internal combustion engine. All the rest was mechanics. The American motor car industry was already the marvel of the world before the scientists touched it. Then it began to want to know why as well as how; and now it has the finest and best research laboratories in the world, where scientists explore the molecules of matter and the nature of gases and the behavior of materials under all conditions. The motor car, of course, has been greatly improved; but it could not have been created that way in the first place.

In the same manner it has happened only in our time that the professional economist has entered the premises of business. Now every important bank and every large corporation has its staff of economic advisers. Business, no doubt, is thereby improved, even ethically and socially, and certainly it has many new ideas about itself, but capitalism was already there and had been for a very long time.[8]

Secondly, it is confusing to say—as the World Council of Churches does—that capitalism has "made promises which it could not redeem." It is true, of course, that certain promises are implicit in capitalism, but only for those who have the imagination to deduce them and the fortitude to pay the price for economic laissez faire. In the sense that communism and socialism have made promises, capitalism has never made any. Who could have made them? You might as well say liberty had made promises.

Capitalism had neither a Marx nor a prophet. Adam Smith had no vision of things unseen nor any plan for a perfect society. He wrote of things that had happened and were happening, and of the probable consequences if these things instead of others continued to happen. His conviction that the good of society was best served by the utmost economic freedom for the individual, and his argument for it based upon data and observations, became what we may call the classic doctrine of laissez faire.

But always the writers of political economy were divided on it. Those who defended it were called liberals, because liberalism at that time stood for the championship of both religious and economic liberty, and words meant what they said. Those who attacked laissez faire denounced liberal absolutism on social and ethical grounds and their argument became the doctrine of what now is socialism. The meaning of words has changed. The defenders of laissez faire now are called reactionaries; and the socialists who denounce it call themselves liberals; but no matter what happen to be the words, the line of division has never changed.

On one side are those who believe that control of the economic life by government is bad; when it is benign and may seem to be immediately beneficial, it is all the worse, for that makes people dependent and leads to the omnipotent state, which will tempt them to exchange liberty for security. These are the individualists and that word has not changed. They believe in a free economy, free markets, free prices, and in competition as the only trustworthy principle of regulation.

On the other side are those who uphold the doctrine of what we now call the welfare state, which means that government shall plan and control the economy for the common good, limit the right of the individual to do what he likes with his property, and in extreme cases abolish private property, all to the end that wealth shall be distributed according to a program of social justice.

It is a profound fact that these two fundamental positions are the same now as they were 150 years ago, although during this century and a half, with laissez faire capitalism ascendant, the economic environment in which we live has changed more than in any like period of time before since the beginning of civilization. In its indictment of capitalism, the World Council

234

of Churches repeats Sismondi, who at about the end of the eighteenth century led the attack on laissez faire and developed the doctrine of state socialism. The World Council of Churches does admit that the development of capitalism has not been alike in all countries and that the early exploitation of labor has been in a considerable measure corrected by "the influence of trade unions, social legislation and responsible management," but from there goes on to say:

> But (1) capitalism tends to subordinate what should be the primary task of any economy—the meeting of human needs—to the economic advantages of those who have most power over the institutions.
>
> (2) It tends to lead to serious inequalities.
>
> (3) It has developed a practical form of materialism in Western nations in spite of their Christian background, for it has placed the greatest emphasis upon success in money making.
>
> (4) It has also kept the people of capitalist countries subject to a kind of fate which has taken the form of such social catastrophes as mass unemployment.

Nearly 150 years ago Sismondi and his friends, evaluating the theory of state socialism, were attacking laissez faire on the same four points, namely that the fancied harmony between private and public interest did not exist, wherefore liberty to pursue his own economic advantage would leave human needs in the lurch; that it would lead to serious inequalities in the distribution of wealth; that it elevated materialism and success; and that it involved society in such social catastrophes as mass unemployment.

And all of this was before steamships, railroads, electricity, gasoline, motor cars, automatic machines, or mass production—even before there was such a thing in the world as a piece of farm machinery.

At that time all economic and political thought in Europe was basically pessimistic. Nobody could imagine that in the next few generations, under laissez faire capitalism, consumable wealth would be so prodigiously multiplied that the luxuries of the rich in one generation would become the necessary satisfactions of the poor in the next, and that from time to time surplus—a strange word for an incredible thing—would be the superficial cause of economic depression and unemployment. There had never been surplus before. There had never been too much of anything. Poverty was thought to be permanent and irreducible.

The idea that poverty could be abolished did not arise in Europe. That was an American idea. And it could arise here, not because this country was rich in natural resources, but because here the conditions of laissez faire capitalism were more nearly realized than anywhere else in the world. Under stress of unlimited and uncontrolled competition we made the discovery that broke Europe's "iron law of wages"—the law, namely, that since wages were paid out of the profits of capital, the wage fund was limited by the capital fund, and the capital fund was something that could be increased only in a slow and painful manner by limiting consumption.

We discovered that wages were paid not out of profits. They were paid out of production. Therefore, wages and profits could rise together, if only you increased production. Moreover, production itself created capital, as in the Ford example—the example of a company that began with $28,000 in cash and at the end of forty-five years employed in its work $1 billion of capital, all its own and all created out of production. And this was done by making the motor car so cheap that almost nobody was too poor to be able to possess and enjoy it.

After this discovery that wages were paid out of production, came mass production, and with mass production came the further discovery that the indispensable unit in the scheme of a free competitive economy was the consumer, for if people as consumers could not increasingly buy the products of their own labor the whole scheme would fall.

Those who speak of capitalism as if it were in itself a kind of universal order, with hierarchy, creed and orthodoxy, are either unable to make distinctions or find that distinctions inconvenience their argument. Capitalism takes its character from the soil and climate in which it grows. American capitalism is so unlike European capitalism that the two could hardly be transplanted. Why has American capitalism been so much more productive than capitalism anywhere else? The seed was European. The sapling was not. Why did this one tree grow to a size and fruitfulness so prodigious? There was here neither skill nor knowledge not possessed also by the people of Europe. Yet after five generations, with less than one-tenth of the earth's land area and less than one fifteenth its total population, we have now in our hands one half of the industrial power of the whole world. Europe's star did not fall. That is not what happened. The American star dimmed it out. What made that difference?

The difference was that here the magic of liberty was acting as it never had acted anywhere before.

Until the Declaration of Independence, said Lord Acton, the history of freedom would have been "a history of the thing that was not." Liberty came forth from Pennsylvania.

American capitalism not only has been the most successful in the world; it is the one great citadel of economic freedom surviving, and now carries the burden of defending Christian civilization against the Eastern enemy. From this it follows that when you compare capitalism with communism the comparison is in fact between American capitalism, with its Puritan tradition, and Russian communism, which is uncompromisingly materialistic and atheistic. It is all the more astonishing, therefore, that the World Council of Churches finds the aspirations of communism the more attractive. And going further than that, it blames capitalism for the rise of communism, saying:

> *Christians should ask why communism in its modern totalitarian form makes so strong an appeal to great masses of people in many parts of the world. They should recognize the work of God in the revolt of multitudes against injustice that gives communism much of its strength.*
>
> *Christians should realize that for many, especially for many young men and women, communism seems to stand for a vision of human equality and universal brotherhood for which they were prepared by Christian influences. Christians who are beneficiaries of capitalism should try to see the world as it appears to many who know themselves excluded from its privileges and who see in communism a means of deliverance from poverty and insecurity.*
>
> *Communist ideology puts the emphasis upon economic justice and promises that freedom will come automatically after the completion of the revolution. Capitalism puts the emphasis upon freedom and promises that justice will follow as a byproduct of free enterprise. That too is an ideology which has been proved false.*

If one must "reject the ideologies of both communism and capitalism" on the ground that they have disappointed the spirit of man it would seem only fair to say alas! to that—no system on earth having yet failed to disappoint the spirit of man—and then go on to compare their works. Are works nothing? Which has done more to advance the material well-being of people, capitalism or communism? Capitalism has a record. Capitalism abolished famine in the world for the first time in the history of the human race. Russian communism brought it back. Capitalism created conditions under which slavery became uneconomic and, for that reason if no other, slavery was abolished. Communism brings it back. Under capitalism, organized labor received political power. Has labor any political power in Russia? American capitalism has had economic reverses, called depressions. In the last and worst depression here the unemployed were better fed, better housed and better clothed than the fully employed in Russia.

Concerning the works of capitalism, the World Council of Churches says only that—

> *On the other hand, technical developments have relieved men and women of much drudgery and poverty and are capable of doing more. There is a limit to what they can do in this direction. Large parts of the world, however, are far from that limit. Justice demands that the inhabitants of Asia and Africa, for instance, should have the benefits of more machine production. They may learn to avoid the mechanization of life and the other dangers of an unbalanced economy which impair the social health of the older industrial peoples.*

Not to argue the meaning of the word justice, let it be supposed that justice demands more machines for the inhabitants of Asia and Africa. Justice may demand them, but who will provide them? To whom would the inhabitants of Asia and Africa look for machines? To the Communists, who, says the World Council of Churches, put first emphasis on justice, or to the capitalist country which it says puts emphasis on freedom?

And as for what justice means in the common mind of the word, imagine what would happen if there should go forth by radio to all the corners of the earth a message such as this: "By miraculous dispensation people everywhere who want political justice and economic opportunity are now free to choose their country." Whose gates would be overwhelmed—those of communist Russia or those of capitalist America?

The World Council of Churches says: "Two chief factors contribute to the crisis of our age. One of these is vast concentrations of power—which under capitalism are mainly economic and under communism both economic and political."

Concentration of power, wherein it is evil, is a very old evil, peculiar to no political or social system that was ever devised. But if you can choose, which will you have—concentration of power that is economic only or that is both economic and political?

It will be the task of the Christian church, says the World Council of Churches, "to draw men away from the false assumption that capitalism and communism are the only alternatives."

What else there may be it does not say. It is evident, however, from the text—and in fact it was asserted by the British delegates—that what the authors had in mind was the social revolution in England, where laissez faire has been buried with remorseful hymns to liberty. The idea is that in something called democratic socialism there is a workable compromise between American free enterprise and the bondage that is called communism in Russia.

Of this British compromise, Mr. Herbert Morrison, who was one of its architects, has said: "We may find in planning—in fact we already have—that the cost of liberty will be the sacrifice of certain personal freedoms."[9]

How does one buy liberty with freedom? That is not explained. "Freedom," says Crabb, with fine distinction, "is personal and private. Liberty is publick. A slave obtains his freedom. A captive obtains his liberty."[10]

Moreover, even this liberty which the British would buy with personal freedom would have fallen by this time, or have gone utterly bankrupt, but for the aid that it had no right to expect from a country that owes its power and wealth to laissez faire capitalism.

The two ancient enemies of laissez faire were the state and the church. Laissez faire represented the principle of radicalism in both religion and economics. Radicalism was the sword of liberty. Neither the state nor the church has ever loved liberty. Now what was conservative is radical, and laissez faire, which was radical, is reactionary. The wheel has gone all the way around.

\

CHAPTER NINE NOTES:

1 Richard Henry Tawney, 1880-1962, was an English socialist historian. In Religion and the Rise of Capitalism (1926) he argued that Lutheranism and Calvinism adapted to capitalism, opposing Max Weber's view that they had helped create capitalism.

2 *The Pilgrim's Progress* was a popular allegory of a man named Christian in search of salvation. John Bunyan, 1628-1688, wrote it largely while in prison as a religious dissenter.

3 John Lothrup Motley's *Rise of the Dutch Republic*: A History was a multi-volume work published in 1855 and in many editions thereafter, into the 20th century.

4 Adam Ferguson, 1723-1816, wrote, "Civilization is the result of human action, but not the execution of any human design." He was a teacher of Adam Smith.

5 Bernard de Mandeville, 1670-1733, a Dutch physician who emigrated to England at 29, published *Fable of the Bees* in 1714. Its key idea was that private vices were "publick benefits"—an idea that influenced Adam Smith.

6 Edmund Burke, 1729-1797, British parliamentarian, was a defender of the American colonists before the Revolution, but a critic of the revolution in France.

7 Thomas Carlyle, 1795-1891, Scottish essayist and Tory, thought industrial civilization in general to be dismal. He praised feudal society and opposed democracy.

8 Banks and manufacturers dumped their economists in the 1980s and 1990s. By the end of the century, most economists worked in academia or government.

9 Herbert Morrison, 1888-1965, deputy prime minister in the Labour government of 1945-1951, wrote Labour's program for nationalizing British industry.

10 George Crabb, 1778-1851, author of *Crabb's English Synonyms* (1816) and *The History of English Law* (1829).

Index

A

Acton, Lord Emerich 237
Adams, Alva 28, 32
Agricultural Adjustment Act (AAA) 52-52,
  55, 85-94, 109, 110
  unconstitutional (U.S. v. Butler) 94
Agriculture, see Farming
Agriculture, Department of 83
American Debt Commission 139
American Federation of Labor 41-42
American Story, The 131
Atlas Shrugged xviii
Austria 170
Automobile industry 38, 232-233, 236

B

Baldwin, Stanley 139, 162
Baltimore & Ohio Railroad 200
Bank of England 148-151, 156
Banks and banking 6, 15, 37, 107, 116, 147-
  153, 169, 218
  a burglar's view 169-170
Barter 118
Belgium 146, 171
Belloc, Hilaire 8, 32, 69, 71
Bérenger, Henri M. 157
Best, Gary Dean 120
Bible, references to 2, 132, 162, 175, 225-227
Bismarck, Otto von 166
Bonds, see Treasury
Britain, 33, 39, 40, 46, 71, 79, 112, 147, 172,
  175, 221
  coal mines 207-208
  credit 150
  debts 133-134, 139-141, 146, 156
  government 115-116, 149, 150, 160, 162
  labor 207
  puritans in 228-229
  trade of 178
  treasury of 149-151
British Debt Commission 139
Brookings Institution 59
Brooklyn Academy of Music 105
Bunyan, John 225, 226, 242
Bureau of Labor Statistics 74
Burke, Edmund 231, 242

C

Calvinism 225, 227, 242

Capitalism xi, xii, xx-xxi, 224
  American vs. European 237
  capital losses and 210-211
  Christianity and 238-239
  criticisms of 235
  distribution of wealth and 235
  economists and 232-233, 242
  ideology of 232-233
  liberty and 237
  organic origins of 232, 237
  stability and xvii
  wages and 236
  war recovery and 159-161
Carlyle, Thomas 232, 242
Capper, Arthur 139, 162
Caxton Printers xi
Celler, Emmanuel 210, 212
Chamberlain, Neville 178, 187
Chambers of Commerce
  Los Angeles 99
  Philippines 123
  United States 133, 164
Christian church 223, 224
  capitalism and 238-239
Cinder Buggy, The xi, xxi
Civilian Conservation Corps 27, 110, 200
Coal mines, U.S. 205-207
  British 207-208
Commerce, Department of 136
Commodity Credit Corp. 100
Communism 224, 232, 237-239
Community Service 11-12
Conference Board, The, see National
  Industrial Conference Board
Congressional Record 56
Connery, William 16, 32
Conscription,
military xix
labor 207
Constitution, U.S. 30, 46, 69
Coolidge, Calvin xii, xvi, 162
Cotton Stabilization Corp. 84
Crabb, George 240, 242
Crammond, Edgar 134
Credit, public see Public credit
Crisis and Leviathan xx
Crissinger, D. R. 134

243

Cummings, Homer 44
Czechoslovakia 169, 171

D

Daily Herald (U.K.) 150
Davis, Dwight 122, 162
Defend America First xi, xix
Defense Plant Corp. 31
Defense Supplies Corp. 31
Defoe, Daniel 39-40
Democracy 46, 153, 220
Democratic Party xvi, 104, 106, 110, 111
  platform of 1932 106, 109
Depression, Great xv-xvi, xx, 6, 9, 38, 42-43
Des Moines Bureau of Municipal Research
  17-18
Detroit Bureau of Governmental Research 18
Dewey, George 121
Dread of Responsibility, The 20
Dutch Republic 226-227

E

Economy, planned 37, 42, 80, 184
England, see Britain
Estate tax, see Taxes
Export-Import Bank 28

F

Fable of the Bees 231, 242
Faguet, Emile 20
Fair Labor Standards Act 68, 69, 74
Farm Security Administration 72
Farmers Home Corp. 51
Farmers National Grain Corp. 84
Farming and farmers xii-xiii, 1-4, 52-54, 75-
  102, 139-140
  boom of early 1900s 79
  deflation of land post-WWI 77
  foreclosures 82
  freedom of 85-90, 94
  Garrett's farm 101-102
  government backing for 79-80, 100-101
  irrigation and reclamation 95-96
  land ownership in 89
  loans and debt of 82-83, 112
  poor farmers, poor land 88, 93, 97-98
  resettlement program 90-98
  subsistence 88
  taxes on 76-78
Federal Farm Board 82-84
Federal Insurance Contributions Act (FICA)
  67
Federal Reserve 38, 39, 108, 114, 116, 146,
  149
Federal Trade Commission 60
Ferguson, Adam 231, 242
Finance, international and politics 155-157
Florida Ship Canal 28, 32

Ford Motor Co. 236
Four Freedoms 72
Fourier, Charles 33, 37, 74
France, 33, 71, 115, 169, 170, 221, 229
  World War I debts 133-134, 144-147, 157
Franco-Prussian War 166
Funk, Walther 116, 120

G

Germany, 132, 147, 153, 169, 170, 173, 220,
  221
  access to raw materials 170-171, 176-177
  boycott for Jews 172
  debts of 136, 139, 144-156
  gold and 116-117
  inflation in 136-137
  reparations 138, 147
  trade of 178
Gipson, Scott xi
Glass, Carter xvi, 104-105, 111, 112, 120
Glass-Steagall Act 120
Gold
  ancient history and 118
  bullion holdings 112, 114-116, 170
  clauses in bonds 106, 109, 113
  call-in by FDR 107
  certificates 107, 114, 120
  dollar value of 109, 115
  export ban 108
  financial power and 155
  monetary standard xvi, 103-114, 110, 112,
  117
  international payments and 148
  wealth distinguished from 170
Gompers, Samuel 68
Government 20-27, 38
  controls on economy xix-xx
  cost of 8-11
  executive power 30-31, 57
  freedom and 8, 31
  ownership of industry 15
  waste in 13- 14
Graccus, Tiberius and Gaius 62, 74
Grand Coulee Dam 97

H

Harding, Warren 138, 162
Higgs, Robert xx
Hitler, Adolf xix, 174, 179
Hoover, Herbert xvi, 6, 27, 28, 44, 104, 120,
  146, 147, 157, 162
  debt holiday plans of 146-148, 156
Horner, Arthur 207
Housing, public, see Public housing
Hull, Cordell (Secretary of State) 174, 187

I

Ickes, Harold 212

INDEX

In Days to Come 173
Income tax, see Taxes
Individualism 20, 227, 229, 231
Industrial revolution 33-34, 36, 223, 229
Inequality of wealth, see Wealth
Interior, Dept. of 208
International trade, see Trade
Interstate Commerce Commission 60, 189-190, 199, 210-211
Isolationism 138
Italy, WWI debts of 134, 146

J
Japan 162
  trade of 178
Jefferson, Thomas ix, 31
Jews 172, 187, 226
Johnson, Lyndon 120
Jones Act xiii
Jones, Jesse xvii, 27-31

K
Keynes, John Maynard xviii
Krock, Arthur 27
Krug, Julius (Interior Secretary) 208, 212

L
Labor and labor unions
  business unionism 40-42
  eight-hour day and 36-37
  exempt and nonexempt 68-71
  laws for 68-72
  marginal labor 208-210
  mine seizures and xx, 205-206
  railroads and xx, 190-191, 193-194, 200, 204
  state ownership and xx, 205-208
Labour Party (U.K.) 149-150, 156, 242
Laissez-faire xx-xxi, 224, 227-234, 236, 240
  definition of 230
  liberty and 224
Lane, Rose Wilder x, 223
Lewis, John L. 206, 208, 212
Liberals and liberalism 234
Liberty bonds, see Treasury
Lincoln, Abraham 71-72
Lippmann, Walter xvii
Little House on the Prairie x
London Bankers' Institute 134
London Times 208
Lutheranism 242

M
Macaulay, Thomas 46, 74
MacDonald, Ramsay 150, 162
Mandeville, Bernard de 231, 242
Marshall Plan, xiv, 159-161
Marx, Karl xxi, 233
McGraw-Hill Publications 164

Mellon, Andrew (Treasury Secretary) 13, 14, 21, 32, 156, 157, 162
Mencken, Henry xvii
Mills, Ogden 104, 120
Montesquieu, Baron de 229
Moore, John 231
Morgan, J.P. & Co. 138
Morrison, Herbert 240, 242
Motley, John Lothrup 227, 242
Mussolini, Benito 163

N
National Association of Manufacturers 164
National Industrial Conference Board xix, 10
National Labor Relations Act 67-68, 206, 212
National Mediation Board 192, 193
National Railroad Adjustment Board 192-203
National Recovery Administration (Blue Eagle), 55, 69, 74, 87
  NRA case (Schechter Poultry v. U.S.) 53, 57
National Union of Mineworkers (U.K.) 207
Nationalism xiii, xv
Netherlands, see Dutch Republic
New Frontiers 89
New Jersey League of Municipalities 17
New York City Bar Association 13
New York Post x
New York Stock Exchange xvi
New York Sun x
New York Times x, 27, 150, 187
New York Times Annalist x
New York Tribune xi, 137
News media, see Roosevelt, Press and
Oneida colony 74

P
Passamaquoddy project 28, 32
Pensions (social insurance) 16, 17, 62, 72
People's Pottage, The x, xi, xvii
Personal responsibility 20-21
Philippines xii, xiv, 121-132, 162
  independence 128-131
Physiocrats 229
Pilgrim's Progress 225, 242
Planned economy, see Economy, planned
Pope County, Ill. 91-93
Poland 170, 171
Potato Control Act 87
Poverty and the poor x, xviii, 71, 225, 236
Presidency, see Executive power
Press, see Roosevelt, Press and
Pride, Prejudice and Politics 120
Production Credit Corp. 100
Propaganda 135, 137, 138, 153, 178
Public credit and debt 4-6, 15, 19-20, 30, 55, 83, 104, 145, 148-149

Public housing 72
Public Works Administration 27, 110

R

Radicals 14-15
Railroads xx, 15, 34, 189-205
  bankruptcy 7, 211
  rule book 194-195
  seniority rules 203
Railway Labor Act 189, 192
Rand, Ayn xviii
Rathenau, Walter xix, 172-174, 187
Reclamation, Bureau of 95-97
Reconstruction Finance Corp. xvii, 6, 9, 27-
  31, 83, 110
Redistribution of wealth, see Wealth, redistri-
  bution
Religion, freedom of 223-227
Religion and the Rise of Capitalism 225, 242
Republican Party 104
Resettlement Administration 90
Resettlement, see Farmers and Farming
Revue des Deux Mondes 157
Rise of the Dutch Republic 227, 242
Robinson, Joe 133, 162
Rock Island Railroad 200
Roman empire 39, 62, 74, 166
Roosevelt, Franklin 25-27, 32, 44, 56, 74, 97,
  105-108, 111, 112, 120, 162, 179
  and the press 25-27, 56
  and war 164
Roosevelt, Nicholas 126-127

S

Salvos Against the New Deal xi, xxi
Satan's Bushel xii, xxi, 1
Say, Jean-Baptiste 74
Self-reliance x, 1-4.
Servile State, The 8
Shakespeare, William 162
Silver certificates 110, 114, 120
Sismondi, Jean-Charles 33, 36, 74, 235
Slavery 168
Smith, Adam xx, 230-233, 242
Smoot-Hawley tariff xiv
Social insurance See Pensions
Social justice 45
Social Security xviii, 16, 33, 62-68, 74
  trust fund xxi-xxii, 66-67
Social work 16-19
Socialists and socialism 149, 150, 160, 187,
  234, 235, 240
Spanish American War 121, 128
Steel industry xxi, 213-223
  Bessemer process 215-217
  immigration and 222-223
  labor and 222-223

rails 213-214, 219-221
seizure case (Youngstown Sheet & Tube)
  212
Stimson, Henry 156, 157, 162
Supreme Court, U.S. 57
Surplus Commodities Corp. 98, 100

T

Taft, Robert A. 28, 32
Taft, William Howard 162
Tawney, R.H. 225, 227, 229, 242
Taxes and taxation, xix, 5, 12-13, 19, 139-140
  on cigarettes 21
  on estates 21, 44, 58, 62
  on farm land 77
  on gasoline 21
  on incomes 14, 21, 44-45, 54-62
Tennessee Valley Authority 72
Thomas Amendment 109
Thomas, Elmer 120
Trade, international xii, xiv, 118, 133, 138-
  143, 173
  and access to raw materials 176-177
  and capital outflows 142
  and conquest 172, 187
  and isolation 142-143
  and loans 143, 158-160
  and machine industry 176
  and mercantilism 175
Townsend Plan x
Treasury, U.S. and Treasury bonds 27, 56,
  57, 74, 81, 104-110, 113, 114, 120, 139,
  144-146, 153-155
  Liberty bonds 139, 144, 152, 154
Treaty of Rapallo 187
Truman, Harry 183, 205-207

U

Unemployment 6,8, 39-40
  relief of 39, 64, 151
Unions see Labor unions
United Mine Workers 208
United States Notes 120
Upson, Lent 18

V

Versailles, Treaty of 162

W

Wage-Hour Administration 70
Wall Street Journal x
Wallace, Henry A. (Agriculture Secretary)
  27, 31, 85, 89, 102
War, see also World War I & II
  American business and 164-166
  controls xix-xx, 165, 182-186
  economic gain and xix, 163, 166-167
  free economy and 185-186
  hoarding and 181

machine industry and 168-169
presidential powers and 31
price system and 180-182
raw materials and 177
taxes for xix, 182
War Finance Corp. 9
War Labor Disputes Act 205
Warren, George 115, 120
Washington, D.C. 22-25
Washington, George. farewell address 157
Washington Naval Conference 138, 162
Wealth
distinguished from money 113
distribution under capitalism 235
conquest and 172
fear of New Deal 55
inequality of 44-49, 58-60
national, vs. national debts 154
redistribution of 35, 48-54, 61
Wealth of Nations 230-233

Weber, Max 242
Welfare Council of New York City 19, 25
Welfare state 72
Wilhelm II, Kaiser 173
Wilson, Woodrow xix, 104, 120, 157, 182,
184, 211
Wood, Leonard 124, 162
Woodin, William (Treasury Secretary) 107-
108, 111, 120
Works Progress Administration (WPA) 27
World Council of Churches 223, 232-240
World War I xx, 10, 139-140, 152-154, 172-
173, 215, 220
controls xix-xx, 182, 184, 187
debts, see Germany, Britain, France, Italy,
Belgium
World War II xiii, xiv, xix, xx, 114-116, 132

Other thought-provoking
titles from
CAXTON PRESS:

ANTHEM
by Ayn Rand
ISBN 0-87004-124-x
Hardcover $12.95

WHAT SOCIAL CLASSES OWE EACH OTHER
by William Graham Sumner
ISBN 0-87004-165-5
Paperback $6.95

THE ART OF CONTRARY THINKING
by Humphrey B. Neill
ISBN 0-87004-110-x
$17.95

SALVOS AGAINST THE NEW DEAL
by Garet Garrett
ISBN 0-87004-425-7
Paperback $12.95

DEFEND AMERICA FIRST
by Garet Garrett
ISBN 0-87004-433-8
Paperback $13.95

EX AMERICA
by Garet Garrett
ISBN 0-87004-442-7
Hardcover $16.95

CAXTON PRESS

312 Main Street
Caldwell, Idaho 836705

www.caxtonpress.com